Forensic Focus 28

Sexual Offending and Mental Health
Multidisciplinary Management
in the Community

*Edited by Julia Houston
and Sarah Galloway*

Foreword by Dawn Fisher

Jessica Kingsley Publishers
London and Philadelphia

First published in 2008
by Jessica Kingsley Publishers
116 Pentonville Road
London N1 9JB, UK

and

400 Market Street, Suite 400
Philadelphia, PA 19106, USA

www.jkp.com

Library of Congress Cataloging in Publication Data

Sexual offending and mental health : multidisciplinary management in the community / edited by Julia Houston and Sarah Galloway.
    p. cm. -- (Forensic focus 28)
    Includes index.
    ISBN 978-1-84310-550-3 (pb : alk. paper) 1. Sex offenders--Psychology. 2. Sex offenders--Mental health. 3. Sex crimes--Psychological aspects. I. Houston, Julia. II. Galloway, Sarah.
    RC560.S47S498 2008
    362.196'8583--dc22
                            2007043990

British Library Cataloguing in Publication Data
A CIP catalogue record for this book is available from the British Library

ISBN 978 1 84310 550 3

Printed and bound in Great Britain by
Athenaeum Press Ltd, Gateshead, Tyne and Wear

Sexual Offending
and Mental Health

Forensic Focus Series

This series, edited by Gwen Adshead, takes the field of Forensic Psychotherapy as its focal point, offering a forum for the presentation of theoretical and clinical issues. It embraces such influential neighbouring disciplines as language, law, literature, criminology, ethics and philosophy, as well as psychiatry and psychology, its established progenitors. Gwen Adshead is Consultant Forensic Psychotherapist and Lecturer in Forensic Psychotherapy at Broadmoor Hospital.

other books in the series

Working Therapeutically with Women in Secure Mental Health Settings
Edited by Nikki Jeffcote and Tessa Watson
978 1 84310 218 2
Forensic Focus 27

Boys Who Have Abused
Psychoanalytic Psychotherapy with Victim/Perpetrators of Sexual Abuse
John Woods
Foreword by Arnon Bentovim with a contribution from Anne Alvarez
ISBN 978 1 84310 093 5
Forensic Focus 24

Working with Sex Offenders in Prisons and through Release to the Community
A Handbook
Alec Spencer
Foreword by William L. Marshall
ISBN 978 1 85302 767 3
Forensic Focus 15

of related interest

Managing Men Who Sexually Abuse
David Briggs and Roger Kennington
ISBN 978 1 85302 807 6

Managing Sex Offender Risk
Edited by Hazel Kemshall and Gill McIvor
ISBN 978 1 84310 197 0
Research Highlights in Social Work 46

Counselling Adult Survivors of Child Sexual Abuse
3rd edition
Christiane Sanderson
ISBN 978 1 84310 335 6

To Mike, Conor and Kate,
the most important people in my life
Julia Houston

In loving memory of Ryan Conway
and
To Mat, Morgan, Cari and Chloe,
I am eternally grateful for your love and support
Sarah Galloway

Acknowledgements

Much of this book originates from the work of the Sex Offender Service (SOS), part of the Forensic Mental Health Services at South West London and St Georges Mental Health Trust. Many different professionals have contributed to its development as a service since 1993, and we would like to thank them for their part in this, and ultimately the publication of this book. Over the years we have been fortunate to work with psychologists, psychiatrists, nurses and social workers, as well as probation and police officers from whom we have learnt a great deal, and who have enhanced our ability to work in a multidisciplinary and multi-agency way. We are also very grateful for the hard work of a number of psychology students over the years, who have assisted greatly with data collection and analysis. The most important person in our service, however, is our team secretary, Myrtle Aziz, who keeps us organised and without whom the SOS would be much less efficient.

We would also like to thank the editing team at Jessica Kingsley Publishers for their patience with the inevitable delays.

Finally, we would both very much like to thank our families, who have put up with our 'absence', while the book was written.

Contents

Foreword   9

Introduction   13

Part I: Theoretical Perspectives

1. An Overview of Sexual Offending   27
   Julia Houston, Shaftesbury Clinic, London, UK

2. Risk Assessment   45
   Jackie Craissati, Oxleas NHS Foundation Trust, London, UK

3. Mental Disorder and Sexual Offending   68
   Andrew M. Aboud, Queensland Forensic Mental Health Services, London, UK

4. Sexual Offending: Ethnicity, Culture and Diversity Issues in Assessment and Management   90
   Olumuyuiwa J. Olumoroti, Croydon, UK and Shaftesbury Clinic, London, UK

5. The Law and Sex Offending   109
   Sarah Galloway and Sandra MacPhail, Shaftesbury Clinic, London, UK

Part II: Clinical Practice Issues

6. A Sex Offender Service within a Mental Health Setting   131
   Julia Houston, Shaftesbury Clinic, London, UK and Malcolm Scoales, St George's Hospital, University of London, UK

7.   Clinical Assessment and Formulation   152
     *Tim Green, Shaftesbury Clinic, London, UK and St George's
     Mental Health Trust*

8.   Treatment, Relapse Prevention and Building
     'Good Lives'   174
     *Tim Green, Shaftesbury Clinic, London, UK and St George's
     Mental Health Trust*

9.   The Impact of Personality Disorder on Working
     with Sexual Offenders   195
     *Sharon Prince, Leeds Personality Disorder Clinical Network,
     Leeds, UK*

10. Multi-agency or Multidisciplinary Working with
     Sexual Offenders   212
     *Sarah Galloway and Adina Seupersad, Shaftesbury Clinic,
     London, UK*

11. Non-abusing Parents and their Role in Risk
     Management   229
     *Sarah Galloway and Natalie Hogg, Shaftesbury Clinic, London,
     UK*

12. Systemic Interventions with Sexual Offending   248
     *Alison Beck, South West London and St George's Mental Health
     Trust, London, UK*

13. The Impact on Professionals of Working with
     Sex Offenders   263
     *Sharon K. C. Leicht, West London Mental Health NHS Trust,
     London, UK*

     LIST OF CONTRIBUTORS   280
     SUBJECT INDEX   282
     AUTHOR INDEX   286

Foreword

Individuals who display inappropriate sexual behaviour are an extremely heterogeneous group. They cover a wide age range, with a third of all reported sexual offences being perpetrated by the under-18 age group, both male and female, although males account for the vast majority with females accounting for less than 10 per cent. They can come from any ethnic group, socioeconomic status, intelligence level and educational background. Writing a book on this topic is a vast undertaking, and generally necessitates having to focus on a specific area. This book focuses on the work of the Sex Offender Service (SOS) of the Forensic Mental Health Services based at the Shaftesbury Clinic, Springfield University Hospital, South West London and St George's Mental Health NHS Trust. The SOS is a multidisciplinary team that provides an assessment, treatment and consultancy service primarily for adult males with sexually inappropriate behaviour, many of whom have accompanying mental health problems, bringing them under the umbrella of the Forensic Mental Health Service.

Sexually inappropriate behaviour is a difficult enough problem to address as it is without the added complication of mental health issues. Although there are a significant number of individuals who fall into this category, relatively little has been written and researched on this particular group compared to the vast literature on sex offenders generally. This book will therefore be a welcome contribution to the forensic mental health field.

What distinguishes this book from others on this subject is that not only is there a focus on mental health, but the authors have managed to include a range of topics which are highly relevant but frequently overlooked in the literature. In addition to specific chapters on mental disorder and personality disorder, there are also chapters on ethnicity, culture and diversity issues, multi-agency/disciplinary working, the non-abusing parent, systemic interventions, the law and sexual offending, and the impact on professionals of working with sex offenders. Each of these chapters is an area in its own right and the chapters provide a good introduction to the key issues.

This book has a number of additional strengths. It has been written by a multi-disciplinary group of people who provide a range of perspectives. They are also practitioners and so know the difficulties of applying research and theory to the complex cases they are faced with in clinical practice. Real-life case studies are included throughout the book, which clearly illustrate the points being made and bring the issues to life. A further strength is that the book is written by UK based clinicians and it therefore has a UK perspective, rather than much of the literature which is North American and as such can sometimes have limited utility for UK practitioners. The chapter on the law and sexual offending was particularly helpful in this respect, providing an up-to-date overview of the range of legislation that covers sex offenders and the impact on those professionals working in this area.

The authors also point out that a significant number of their referrals have no convictions for their behaviour, only allegations against them. This provides another layer of complexity for assessment, particularly as there is not the certainty of a conviction and actuarial measures cannot be used as they are based on convicted offenders only. The issues faced when working with unconvicted offenders are discussed throughout the book.

The combination of chapters providing a theoretical overview and those devoted to clinical practice issues, in addition to the inclusion of references for finding out about further resources make this an excellent resource for clinicians . This is particularly the case for those chapters covering areas which many clinicians would have trouble accessing key literature on, and are therefore less familiar with. The chapter on ethnicity and diversity issues, for example, includes a discussion of the factors contributing to sexual behaviour and behaviour offending in different groups, and the attitudes, practices and sanctions for sexually inappropriate behaviour in different cultures. This information is highly relevant in the racially and culturally diverse society of the UK.

The book concludes with a chapter on the impact on professionals of working with sex offenders. Many professionals may be reluctant to admit that their work does impact upon them at some level, and as a result may overlook this area. This reluctance will have an impact on the professionals' capacity to undertake the work, and in turn impact upon the effectiveness of their work. It can also affect their working relationships with colleagues. We have a duty as professionals to consider the impact on ourselves and to self-monitor so that we can provide the best service for our clients. How we work with clients and within our multi-agency and multi-disciplinary systems can have far reaching consequences. Having said that it is important to note that, as discussed in the chapter, the work can also be intensely rewarding. The fact that a group of colleagues from the SOS were able to devote the time and energy needed to write this book suggests that they do find the work rewarding. Their motivation and enthusiasm to produce this book is to be congratulated, and they have produced a valuable resource for forensic mental health clinicians.

Dawn Fisher, MClin. Psych, PhD.,
Consultant Clinical and Forensic Psychologist,
Head of Psychological Services, Llanarth Court Hospital

Introduction

Julia Houston and Sarah Galloway

ORIGINS

The idea for this book was conceived out of a national conference on the multidisciplinary risk management of sex offenders, held by the Sex Offender Service (SOS), part of the Forensic Mental Health Services at the Shaftesbury Clinic, Springfield University Hospital, South West London and St George's Mental Health NHS Trust, in March 2005. The conference was the second of its kind held by the SOS and had a truly multidisciplinary contribution. Many of the chapters 'began' as presentations at the conference, others have been added for a holistic approach.

Being part of a forensic mental health service underpins the mental health focus of the SOS and enables a multidisciplinary approach to the assessment and treatment of sex offenders and those who have behaved in sexually inappropriate ways. The SOS has input from psychology, psychiatry, forensic community psychiatric nursing, trainees and students, and from social work when resources permit. As will be discussed further in Chapter 6, the service has developed and expanded since its introduction in 1993, and it now also provides assessment and treatment for the partners of sex offenders, running a psycho-educative group on an annual basis.

THE EXTENT OF SEXUAL OFFENDING

It is important to recognise that the focus on sexual offending by society is not new, and, as noted by Soothill (1993, 2003), there have been concerns about different aspects of sexual behaviour and offending in each of the decades since the Second World War, depending on what attracts concern at a particular time. This concern has encompassed the visibility of prostitution and the decriminalisation of homosexuality, as well as more recently child abuse within the family (Butler-Sloss 1988) and sentencing of rape cases. Recently, concern has focused on the issue of convicted paedophiles living in the community.

When concern focuses on *convicted* and *known* individuals, it is hard for professionals working in the field not to feel some sense of frustration, as by the very nature of their being convictioned the potential risk posed by these individuals is easier to identify, monitor closely and manage, often by a wide professional network. It is the 'hidden figures': individuals who have never been caught or convicted of sexual offending, who comprise a risk that remains unidentified and unmonitored.

It is widely acknowledged that it is difficult to assess the true extent of sexual offending. Official crime statistics can give an indication of different offence patterns, such as the fact that more females are victims of sexual assault than males (Nicholas, Kershaw and Walker 2007), but these are acknowledged to be grossly under-representative. This knowledge is supported by attempts to assess the prevalence of sexual offending by retrospective studies of the experiences of adults, which have their own inherent limitations. Although now over 20 years old, one of the most reliable UK studies still quoted is that of Baker and Duncan (1985), who found that from a random sample of 2019 adults, 12 per cent of females and eight per cent of males reported unwanted sexual contact before the age of 16 years.

Attempts to assess rates of sexual offending more reliably have been made through the British Crime Surveys (1998, 2000). Face-to-face interviews were carried out with 6944 women, aged 16–59 years, and included details of incidents which had not been reported to the police or recorded by them. This found that 4.9 per cent of women reported being raped since the age of 16 years, with 9.7 per cent experiencing some form of sexual victimisation (Myhill and Allen 2002). Some 0.4 per cent of women said they had been raped in the year preceding the 2000 British Crime Survey, which represents an estimated 61,000 victims, yet only 18 per cent of these rapes had been reported to the police.

There are a number of reasons why sexually inappropriate behaviour or assaults may not lead to a conviction. In order to become an official crime statistic an offence has to be disclosed, reported to the police and recorded; enough evidence has to be found to investigate successfully; and a person charged with the offence, and then a prosecution and conviction must occur. There are many obstacles in this process which need to be overcome in order for an individual to be convicted. A recent study in the UK has found that rape convictions are at an all-time low (Feist *et al.* 2007) with only six per cent of reported rape offences resulting in a conviction in a sample of 676 cases from eight police forces between 2003 and 2004. Most cases were lost between the reporting of the offence and the charge, with 40 per cent of cases not proceeding owing to insufficient evidence. In 35 per cent of cases the victim withdrew her complaint, not wishing to go through with the investigation or court process and wanting to move on. Only 15 per cent of cases were deemed *not* to be a crime by the police, including eight per cent in which an allegation was established to be false. The report (Feist *et al.* 2007) states that improved victim care, better communication and addressing concerns of fear or reprisals, would help to minimise the number of cases which were dropped.

Many men who offend against children in family settings are also never convicted. If an individual denies any inappropriate behaviour and the victim(s) are unwilling to press charges or are unable to be a reliable witness, the police are unable to proceed further. For example, McClurg and Craissati (1999) studied alleged perpetrators of sexual abuse in two London boroughs and found that between zero and eight per cent were convicted as a result of the allegations. A recent report by Stuart and Baines (2004) estimated that fewer than one in 50 sexual offences against children result in a criminal conviction. It is also recognised that there is a great difference between official reconviction rates and unofficial recidivism (i.e. a lapse into previous offence-related sexual behaviour), with research by Falshaw and colleagues (2003) suggesting that recidivism rates were five times the official figure.

Men with mental health problems who offend are also not always convicted, again because the victim(s) may be women known to them who are unwilling to report the offence to the police, or because offending occurs against mental health professionals who are unwilling to press charges. Alternatively, such individuals may be 'diverted' at court with the involvement of a mental health team, and formal charges dropped. This means that many agencies, other than those in the criminal justice system, may be working with men who have assaulted others or behaved in sexually inappropriate ways.

WHAT DO WE KNOW ABOUT SEX OFFENDERS AND THEIR VICTIMS?

The first part of the book focuses on theoretical knowledge of sexual offending and offenders, and covers contributory factors, theories of offending, risk assessment, the relationship between mental disorder and offending and ethnicity, culture and diversity issues. It is worth noting that most research on sexual offenders has been carried out on those who are identified or convicted, or both, and, given the above information about conviction rates, could therefore be seen as biased (Brown 2005). However, one consistent feature to be identified from studies of convicted sex offenders is their heterogeneity, with no differences in demographic variables, such as age, ethnicity, socio-economic status, level of intelligence and education, from the general population (Wolf 1985). In fact, Marshall (1996, p. 322) stated that 'the available research suggests greater similarities than differences between sexual offenders and other people', although, as Brown (2005) rightly points out, this should more accurately be described as 'other men', given that the vast majority of sex offenders are male. Women account for about two per cent of convicted sex offenders, and although this is generally accepted to be an underestimate, the true figure is probably still under 10 per cent (Saradjian and Hanks 1996).

Most victims of sexual offending are known to the offender. Finkelhor (1994) reviewed the data from 19 studies of adults in the USA which investigated their experiences of sexual abuse as children. Between 70 per cent and 90 per cent of the abusers were known to the child. Family members accounted for between one-third and one-half of those who had offended against girls, and 10–20 per cent of those who had offended against boys. In the recent Home Office (2007) study of rape cases reported to the police, stranger rapes accounted for 14 per cent of cases: one-quarter were carried out by acquaintances, and one-fifth by current or ex-partners. When examining unreported cases, the figure for assaults being carried out by a current or ex-partner rises to 56 per cent, with 16 per cent by acquaintances, 10 per cent by other intimates, 11 per cent by 'dates' and eight per cent by strangers (Myhill and Allen 2002).

SEXUAL OFFENDING AND MENTAL HEALTH

In this book we have used the term 'mental health problems' primarily to refer to mental illness and personality disorders. Among general populations of sex offenders, the prevalence of mental illness is low (up to 10%; Butler and Allnutt 2003; Sahota and Chesterman 1998a), although that of personality disorders is higher (30–50%; Ahlmeyer *et al.* 2003; Madsen, Parsons and Grubin 2006). However, professionals working specifically within mental health settings will clearly see higher rates of this 'comorbidity'. The premise of this book is that additional issues need to be considered in relation to assessment, treatment and management when sex offenders also have mental health problems. For example, when working with individuals with personality disorders, it is important to understand the processes being manifested in the interpersonal relationship between the offender and clinician(s) (see, in particular, Chapter 13). For those with mental illness, the relationship between the illness and the offending needs to be determined (see, in particular, Chapter 3).

A common but erroneous assumption by some clinicians is that in those with mental health problems, in particular mental illness, any sexual offending is causally related and the only intervention necessary to reduce further risk is to treat the mental illness. In fact, the relationship is much more complex, as highlighted in the review by Sahota and Chesterman (1998a) of sex offenders with schizophrenia. These authors emphasise the importance of not only appraising the role of symptoms in offending behaviour, but also the contribution of more specific factors associated with sexual offending, such as those contributing to aetiology and risk (see Chapters 1, 2 and 7). Their work suggests four ways in which the relationship between symptoms of schizophrenia and sexual offending may be manifested. First, a sexual assault may arise directly as a result of delusional beliefs. Second, a sexual assault may be related to less specific features of the illness, such as heightened feelings of arousal and irritability or confused thinking. Third, an assault may be related to 'negative' symptoms of the illness, such as social withdrawal, impaired social performance and blunting of emotional responses, and, lastly, a sexual assault may be largely unrelated to the schizophrenic illness and more closely related to underlying personality problems or deviant sexual interests, or both.

A key aspect of the assessment of mentally ill sex offenders is determining the relationship between the illness and the offending, and Craissati (2004) notes that determining the temporal aspect of this can be difficult. In the study by Craissati and Hodes (1992) of 11 mentally ill sex offenders, no evidence of mental illness was found within the prosecution evidence, in particular in the transcript of the police interview. However, when assessed shortly afterwards in prison, the majority were found to be floridly psychotic. These authors suggest that, retrospectively, it is likely that although three offences may have occurred as a response to psychotic symptoms, the majority were committed within the context of deteriorating social behaviour and self-care, heightened feelings of anxiety and depression, and a degree of sexual pre-occupation, likely to be the 'prodromal phase' of the illness. Further to this, Chesterman and Sahota (1998) found that only one out of 12 mentally ill sex offenders gave psychotic symptoms as an explanation or motivation for the offence, with six out of seven who admitted to psychotic symptoms at the time, giving a range of alternative explanations, involving revenge, sexual frustration, anger and arousal. These authors also found similarities between the psychosexual profiles of mentally ill and non-mentally ill sex offenders, and suggest that the presence of mental illness alone may provide only a partial explanation of sexual offending in this client group (Sahota and Chesterman 1998b).

PURPOSE OF THIS BOOK

The purpose of this book is to inform readers about the range of theoretical and legal issues relevant to working with sexual offenders, as well as different aspects of clinical practice with this client group, in particular those with mental illness and personality disorders. Although the chapters often refer to 'offenders', many of the men seen by the SOS are, in fact, unconvicted, and the content is also relevant and applicable to those who have not been through the legal process. Similarly, although the title refers to multi-disciplinary risk management in the community, the book will also be relevant to professionals working in inpatient settings. Where possible, the chapters have drawn upon the latest research and evidence base, which will add to the contribution and growth of published work in this specialist area.

THE SCOPE AND CONTENT OF THIS BOOK

Inevitably, this book cannot cover every aspect concerned with sexual offending, and it will focus primarily on adult, male offenders who have committed contact offences (i.e. touching) against women and children. Although it has a predominantly community focus, as discussed in Chapter 2, sexual offenders are also detained under the Mental Health Act 1983, and many of the frameworks or concepts described throughout the book are also applicable to inpatients. Many of the concepts can also be applied to sexual offenders committing non-contact offences (i.e. indecent exposure, child pornography and internet offences).

This book does not cover sexual offences committed by juveniles or adolescents, although the literature is growing in this area (see Calder 2002; O'Reilly *et al.* 2004). Internet offences are discussed briefly and, again, it is acknowledged that knowledge in this area is also developing rapidly; readers who require more information may wish to refer to Calder (2003) and to Seto and Eke (2005). Similarily, readers who require information about sexual offenders with learning disabilities may seek Lindsay (2002) and Lindsay *et al.* (2002).

Women are discussed in relation to the role they play in protecting children. Female sexual offenders have not been addressed specifically, although some of the chapters will still be relevant (see Chapter 7 on assessment). Readers may wish to refer to further specific references (Denov 2004; Lewis and Stanley 2000; Nathan and Ward 2002; Saradjian and Hanks 1996).

This book is divided into two parts: theoretical perspectives and clinical practice issues. Some of the chapters focus on issues that are pertinent to sexual offending in general so that the reader has an understanding of the context in which they are working, and others are more specifically focused on sex offenders with mental health problems.

Part I: Theoretical Perspectives contains chapters focusing on theories, models and frameworks which underpin clinical practice within the UK. The first two chapters present the theoretical background within which clinical practice is set. Chapter 1 opens the book by providing an overview of contributory factors and theories of sexual offending. Julia Houston outlines the range of theories which have been influential in understanding 'why' men offend and 'how' this occurs, and describes the recent developments in this area. In Chapter 2 Jackie Craissati reviews the literature associated with risk prediction in sex offenders and discusses the static and dynamic risk variables. The chapter equips the reader with a practical guide to risk assessment based on the core tools that are currently available.

Having established the key background information to sexual offending in general, Chapter 3 then focuses on sexual offending and mental disorder. Andrew Aboud provides information about the prevalence of mental illness and personality disorder in known sex offenders and considers the relationship between the range of mental disorders and sexual offending.

Chapter 4 focuses on ethnicity, diversity and cultural issues in sexual offending. Olumuyiwa Olumoroti discusses the influence of ethnicity and culture on sexuality and the reporting of sexual offending, and the significance of ethnicity in informing clinical practice. In the final chapter of Part I, Sarah Galloway and Sandra MacPhail provide an overview of the changes in legislation in England and Wales over the last decade, which sets the legal framework for clinicians working with sex offenders. This chapter also discusses the proposed future directions of legal changes and the effect that disclosure of offences to the wider community may have.

Part II: Clinical Practice Issues contains a number of more clinically oriented chapters, which describe working in a multi-disciplinary and multi-agency way with people with mental health problems who have committed sexual offences. Work with partners is also described. The chapters are supported by case examples which have been carefully combined and anonymised to maintain confidentiality, but aim to illustrate some of the patient groups and clinical issues seen within the SOS.

In Chapter 6 Julia Houston and Malcolm Scoales describe the development and operation of the SOS, including current service provision. Information about demographic and referral data over a five-year period is presented, as well as that from a smaller research sample, which examines some of this in more detail, including mental health and personality functioning. Chapters 7 and 8 focus specifically on formulation-based assessment and treatment. Tim Green provides a guide for clinicians on the important contextual issues to consider in assessment, as well as outlining the process and content of assessment. Chapter 8 follows on from this to first review the current evidence base for the treatment of sex offenders and then consider treatment, relapse prevention and building 'good lives'.

As highlighted earlier, working with sex offenders with personality disorders often raises particular issues for the clinician. In Chapter 9 Sharon Prince describes the range of personality disorders commonly found in those convicted of sexual offences and the ways in which these disorders affect treatment and management. In Chapter 10 Sarah Galloway and Adina Seupersad address issues of multi-agency or multidisciplinary working and give clinical examples of how cases can be managed in the community. They discuss the need for multi-agency management and the challenges professionals often face.

Chapters 11 and 12 focus on the wider systems around the individual offender. In Chapter 11, Sarah Galloway and Natalie Hogg discuss relevant factors in the assessment and treatment of protective partners and describe a psycho-educative group run for women in the community. The case examples illustrate the complexities of working with partners of sex offenders. This theme is continued in Chapter 12, where Alison Beck reviews the literature on systemic work with families of sexual offenders and discusses how this approach can give an additional perspective to this area of work.

Finally, Chapter 13 examines the effect of working with sex offenders on professionals. It is only fairly recent that the personal impact of this work has been acknowledged and researched. Sharon Leicht reviews the research in this area, which has addressed the emotional impact of working with sexual offenders on professionals, together with the coping strategies used to deal with this.

The contributors to this book were chosen for both their breadth of expertise in working within the sexual offending arena and also for their differing clinical perspectives and professional backgrounds. We are very proud and grateful for their diligence and commitment, and ability to create such excellent chapters that are rich in clinical experiences, evidence-based and a contribution to the growing literature.

REFERENCES

Ahlmeyer, S., Kleinsasser, D., Stoner, J. and Retzlaff, P. (2003) 'Psychopathology of incarcerated sex offenders.' *Journal of Personality Disorders 17*, 4, 306–318.

Baker, A. and Duncan, S. (1985) 'Child sexual abuse: a study of prevalence in Great Britain.' *Child Abuse and Neglect 9*, 457–467.

British Crime Survey (1998) Available at www.homeoffice.gov.uk/rds/bcs1.html, accessed on 14 November 2007.

British Crime Survey (2000) Available at www.homeoffice.gov.uk/rds/bcsl.html, accessed on 14 November 2007.

Brown, S. (2005) *Treating Sex Offenders: An Introduction to Sex Offender Treatment Programmes.* Uffculme: Willan Publishing.

Butler, T. and Allnutt, S. (2003) *Mental Illness among New South Wales' Prisoners.* Sydney: NSW Corrections Health Service.

Butler-Sloss, E. (1988) *The Cleveland Report.* London: HMSO.

Calder, M. C. (2002) *Young People Who Sexually Abuse: Building the Evidence Base for Your Practice.* Lyme Regis: Russell House Publishing.

Calder, M. C. (2003) *Child Sexual Abuse and the Internet: Tackling the New Frontier.* Lyme Regis: Russell House Publishing.

Chesterman, P. and Sahota, K. (1998) 'Mentally ill sex offenders in a regional secure unit. I: Psychopathology and motivation.' *Journal of Forensic Psychiatry 9*, 150–160.

Craissati, J. (2004) *Managing High Risk Sex Offenders in the Community: A Psychological Approach.* Hove: Brunner–Routledge.

Craissati, J. and Hodes, P. (1992) 'Mentally ill sex offenders: the experience of a regional secure unit.' *British Journal of Psychiatry 161*, 846–849.

Denov, M. S. (2004) *Perspectives on Female Sex Offending.* London: Ashgate.

Falshaw, L., Friendship, C. and Bates, A. (2003) *Sexual Offenders – Measuring Reconviction, Re-offending and Recidivism.* Home Office Research Development and Statistics Directorate, Findings No. 183. Available at publications.rds@homeoffice.gsi.gov.uk, accessed on 14 November 2007.

Finkelhor, D. (1994) 'Current information on the scope and nature of child sexual abuse.' *Future of Children 4*, 2, 31–53.

Feist, A., Ashen, J., Lawrence, J., McPhee, D. and Wilson, R. (2007) *Investigating and detecting recorded offences of rape.* Home Office Online Report 18/07. Available at www.homeoffice.gov.uk/rds/pdfs07/rdsolr1807.pdf, accessed on 19 March 2008.

Lewis, P. and Stanley, C. R. (2000) 'Women accused of sexual offenses.' *Behavioral Sciences and the Law 18*, 1, 73–81.

Lindsay, W. R. (2002) 'Research and literature on sex offenders with intellectual and developmental disabilities.' *Journal of Intellectual Disability Research 46*, 1, 74–85.

Lindsay, W. R., Smith, A. H. W., Law, J., Quinn, K. *et al.* (2002) 'A treatment service for sex offenders and abusers with intellectual disability: characteristics of referrals and evaluation.' *Journal of Applied Research in Intellectual Disabilities 15*, 166–174.

Madsen, L., Parsons, S. and Grubin, D. (2006) 'The relationship between the five-factor model and DSM personality disorder in a sample of child molesters.' *Personality and Individual Differences 40*, 227–236.

Marshall, W. L. (1996) 'The sexual offender: monster, victim or everyman?' *Sexual Abuse: A Journal of Research and Treatment 8*, 4, 317–335.

McClurg, G. and Craissati, J. (1999) 'A descriptive study of alleged sexual abusers known to social services.' *Journal of Sexual Aggression 4*, 1, 22–30.

Myhill, A. and Allen, J. (2002) *Rape and Sexual Assault on Women: Findings from the British Crime Survey.* Home Office Research Development and Statistics Directorate, Findings Number 159. Available at publications.rds@homeoffice.gsi.gov.uk, accessed 14 November 2007.

Nathan, P. and Ward, T. (2002) 'Female sex offenders: clinical and demographic features.' *Journal of Sexual Aggression 8*, 1, 5–21.

Nicholas, S., Kershaw, C. and Walker, A. (2007) *Crime in England and Wales 2006/7.* Available at www.homeoffice.gov.uk/rds/crimeew0607.html, accessed on 2 February 2008.

O'Reilly, G., Marshall, W., Carr, A. and Beckett, R. C. (2004) *The Handbook of Clinical Intervention with Young People who Sexually Abuse.* Hove: Brunner–Routledge.

Sahota, K. and Chesterman, P. (1998a) 'Sexual offending in the context of mental illness.' *Journal of Forensic Psychiatry 9*, 267–280.

Sahota, K. and Chesterman, P. (1998b) 'Mentally ill sex offenders in a regional secure unit. II: cognitions, perceptions and fantasies.' *Journal of Forensic Psychiatry 9*, 1, 161–172.

Saradjian, J. and Hanks, H. (1996) *Women who Sexually Abuse their Children: From Research to Practice.* Chichester: Wiley.

Seto, M. and Eke, A. (2005) 'The criminal histories and later offending of child pornography offenders.' *Sexual Abuse: A journal of Research and Treatment 17*, 201–210.

Soothill, K. (1993) 'The serial killer industry.' *Journal of Forensic Psychiatry 4*, 2, 341–354.

Soothill, K. (2003) 'Serious sexual assault: using history and statistics.' In: A. Matravers (ed.) *Sex Offenders in the Community: Managing and Reducing Risks.* Uffculme: Willan Publishing.

Stuart, M. and Baines, C. (2004) *Progress on Safeguards for Children Living Away from Home: A Review of Action Since the People Like Us Report.* Available from York Publishing Services, 64 Horefield Road, Layerthrope, York YO31 7ZQ.

Wolf, S. C. (1985) 'A multi-factor model of deviant sexuality.' *Victimology: An International Journal 10*, 359–374.

Part I:

Theoretical Perspectives

An Overview of Sexual Offending

Julia Houston

INTRODUCTION

This opening chapter provides an overview of contributing factors and theoretical models of sexual offending. In order to understand how mental health problems may affect sexually inappropriate behaviour, it is first necessary to be aware of the range of other factors involved. The chapter starts by considering what is known about the range of factors that are potentially contributory to sexual offending. This covers biological vulnerabilities and predispositions, childhood and developmental experiences, sexual development and learning, interpersonal functioning, and underlying beliefs. Current influential theories are then outlined, including aetiological theories of *why* men offend against children and adults, and theories to account for *how* this occurs.

CONTRIBUTORS TO SEXUAL OFFENDING

Individuals who sexually offend are a widely heterogeneous group and it would be presumptuous to assume that the factors outlined below are relevant for every individual. However, these are the key areas that have been studied in populations of men who have sexually offended, and which have been drawn together to develop aetiological models. It is important for clinicians working with offenders with mental health problems to be aware of these factors in order to consider which of them may also be relevant.

Predispositional and biological vulnerabilities

Early theories of sexual offending attempted to explain this by one predominant factor. One such theory was Goodman's (1987) biological theory, which emphasised the role of genetic and hormonal factors. The limitations of such 'single-factor' theories led to the development of more complex multivariate theories, such as Marshall and Barbaree's (1990) integrated theory of sexual offending. However, hormonal factors were still viewed as playing a key role. One aspect of this theory is that a critical developmental task for adolescent males involves learning to distinguish between aggressive and sexual impulses, as this has consequences for their ability to control aggressive tendencies during sexual experiences. The authors argue that both types of impulse originate from the same brain structures. Differences in hormonal functioning will make this task more difficult, particularly for vulnerable individuals who have had adverse early developmental experiences.

The role of biological factors was not predominantly considered throughout the 1990s, as other contributors to sexual offending gained more prominence. However, recently Smallbone (2006) has proposed an 'attachment–theoretical revision' of Marshall and Barbaree's (1990) integrated theory, in which he argues that the focus on biological influences should be expanded, and it is becoming acknowledged that genetic and environmental factors which cause psychopathology need to be considered relevant in relation to sexual offending (Ward, Polaschek and Beech 2006a, pp. 331–340).

Childhood and developmental experiences

It is well-recognised that negative childhood and developmental experiences can have an important contributory role in the development of later sexual offending, in particular those experiences which affect the development of secure attachments. Many studies have found that the family backgrounds of sexual offenders are characterised by high levels of disruption, neglect and violence (Craissati, McClurg and Browne 2002) and by high rates of childhood disturbances (Craissati and McClurg 1996). Prentky *et al.* (1989) also found that caregiver inconsistency and sexual deviation and abuse in the family were both related to severity of sexual aggression in convicted rapists.

One specific area of focus has been offenders' own experiences of sexual and physical victimisation. With regard to physical abuse, rapists have been found to have experienced more physical violence in their families than other types of sex offenders (Marshall *et al.* 1991) and non-sex offenders (Leonard 1993), although high rates (40%) have also been reported among convicted child abusers (Craisatti and McClurg 1996).

There is a wide variation in rates of reported sexual abuse across studies, although a consistent finding is that the rates are higher than for non-sex offenders and non-offenders. In studies of men who have offended against children, rates of victimisation have been reported between 44 per cent and 51 per cent (Craisatti and McClurg 1996; Craissati *et al.* 2002; Scoales and Houston 2006). Carter *et al.* (1987) found that 23 per cent of detained rapists had been victims of sexual abuse themselves. However, although it may be an important contributor for some individuals, clearly sexual victimisation is neither always necessary nor sufficient for future perpetration of sexual offending.

Sexual development and learning

Another important area of research with regard to sexual development and learning has been whether or not men who sexually offend are more aroused by sexually deviant images, than men who do not offend. A meta-analysis of studies using the penile plethysmograph (PPG) suggested that convicted rapists tend to show different sexual preferences to non-offenders, and responded more to rape cues than non-sex offenders (Lalumiere and Quinsey 1994). Differences have also been found between men who offend against children within a family setting and non-offenders (Marshall, Barbaree and Christopher 1986). Although about 18–19 per cent of both these groups showed some level of sexual arousal to pre-pubescent children, the former group showed lower levels of arousal to adult females. When considering arousal to images of children post-puberty, the rates increased. Thirty-two per cent of non-offending men were aroused by this age group compared to 52 per cent of the intra-familial offenders and 70 per cent of extra-familial offenders. Clearly, being sexually aroused by children is, in itself, not sufficient to explain sexual offending. Similarly, although in some individuals the presence of deviant sexual fantasies are a significant contributor to their offending, the presence of coercive sexual fantasies *per se* are not sufficient to define a rapist population and are commonly reported by non-offending males (Leitenberg and Henning 1995).

Interpersonal functioning

There is a clear link between childhood experiences and the development of adult attachment styles, and the ability of men who offend sexually to establish and maintain intimate relationships with adults has been studied extensively. Marshall (1989) first observed that there was a link between intimacy deficits and sexual offending and developed this further into one of the most influential earlier theories, the 'integrated' theory of sexual offending (Marshall and Barbaree 1990). Marshall (1989) suggested that men who offend sexually against children are likely to have high levels of 'emotional loneliness', difficulties in developing or maintaining close intimate relationships with adults and insecure attachment styles. This has been supported by subsequent research (Fisher, Beech and Browne 1999). Men who have offended against children tend to be characterised more by an anxious, pre-occupied and fearful style of attachment (Hudson and Ward 1997). Convicted rapists have also been found to have intimacy deficits and a limited capacity to form attachments (Seidman *et al.* 1994). They have a greater tendency than both non-offenders and those who have offended against children to have a 'dismissive' style of attachment towards women, in other words to be sceptical of the value of close relationships and blame others for their lack of intimacy.

Underlying beliefs and cognitive factors

Much research has examined the underlying beliefs held by sex offenders, and the ways in which these contribute to the development and maintenance of offending. Over the past 20 years the concept of 'cognitive distortions' has been extremely influential, defined by Abel *et al.* (1989, p.137) as 'justifications, perceptions and judgements used by the sex offender to justify his child molestation behaviour'. An example would be something like 'just touching isn't doing any harm'. Identifying and challenging cognitive distortions has been a key part of treatment with offenders against both children and adults. The most recent work in this area has moved on to examine deeper-held beliefs about children and adults. These are more akin to the notion of schemas in cognitive psychology (Young 1990), and have been described by Ward and Keenan (1999) and Polaschek and Ward (2002) as 'implicit theories'.

Ward and Keenan (1999) analysed information from existing questionnaires about cognitive distortions. They proposed that men who offend against children hold implicit theories about the nature of the world which underlie the distorted beliefs used to justify their offending. These are:

- *Children as sexual beings*: children are inherently sexual and possess the capacity to make decisions about sexual activity.

- *Nature of harm*: there are degrees of harm and sexual activity is unlikely to be harmful unless there is physical injury.

- *Entitlement*: superior individuals (such as adults) have the right to assert their needs above others (such as children).

- *Dangerous world*: other people are likely to behave in an abusive and rejecting manner towards the offender. This can include either both children and adults (in which case children need to be dominated and controlled) or just adults, and children therefore represent a 'safe haven'.

- *Uncontrollable world*: events just happen and individuals can do little to control emotions, events or sexual feelings.

Similar work was carried out for rapists (Polaschek and Ward 2002) and the implicit theories proposed are as follows.

- *Women are unknowable*: women are fundamentally different from men and therefore cannot be understood. Encounters with women will therefore be adversarial and women will be deceptive about what they really want.

- *Women are sex objects*: women are constantly sexually receptive to men's needs but not always conscious of this. Their body language is more important than what they say and women cannot be hurt by sexual activity unless they are physically harmed.

- *Male sex drive is uncontrollable*: men's sexual energy can build up to dangerous levels if women do not provide them with sexual opportunities, and once aroused it is difficult not to progress to orgasm.

- *Entitlement*: needs (which include sexual needs) should be met on demand and men should be able to have sex when they want to.

- *Dangerous world*: again, the world is a hostile and threatening place and people need to be on their guard, but there is no safe haven.

Preliminary studies have found supportive evidence for the presence of implicit theories in interview-based research with offenders (Beech and Ward 2004).

THEORIES OF SEXUAL OFFENDING

An extensive review of theories of sexual offending is beyond the scope of this chapter. This can be found in Ward *et al.* (2006a), where theories are comprehensively critically evaluated and their application to clinical practice discussed. Ward *et al.* (2006a, p. 15) note that 'Theories are indispensible resources for clinical work with sexual offenders'. Theories should direct the clinician towards areas for assessment, assist with formulation and identify areas for treatment and risk management. Below are outlined the predominant theories which have been, or are currently, influential in this respect. It is perhaps a reflection of the complexity of sexual offending that most theories have been developed to account for one type of offender, or one aspect of the process.

Theories of sexual offending against children

Finkelhor's four preconditions model

Finkelhor's (1984) model of sexual offending against children (see also Ward *et al.* 2006a, pp. 19–31) was one of the first to take into account its complexity, and tried to account for both the factors that contributed to motivation for sexual offending as well as the process by which it occurred. It is now acknowledged that one of the major limitations of this model is that it is only applicable to certain types of offenders – those who are aware that their offending is wrong, and therefore for whom the process of offending involves overcoming inhibitions. It does not describe those men who have harmful goals, who deliberately set out to abuse a child. However, the model has been extremely influential in clinical practice in the UK, in particular in providing a framework for which many offenders can gain insight into the way their offending occurred. It is therefore described in some detail.

Finkelhor (1984) suggests that there are four factors which are complementary in accounting for the motivation to sexually offend against a child, and these make up the first of his preconditions.

MOTIVATION

- *Emotional congruence:* this describes the way in which children have a special meaning for many men who abuse children. For such individuals their emotional needs are met by children, who are viewed as safe and accepting, in contrast to adults.

- *Sexual arousal:* although the developmental cause may not be clear, some individuals acquire entrenched deviant sexual interests. For other offenders however, sexual arousal to a child may be more temporary and situational.

- *Blockage:* this describes the way in which some offenders are 'blocked' in their ability to meet their sexual and emotional needs in adult relationships. This could either be a developmental, persistent blockage (such as fear of intimacy) or situational and temporary (e.g. breakdown in an adult relationship). However, a situational blockage would not in itself be enough to lead to sexual offending without some pre-existing sexual interest.

- *Overcoming inhibitions:* the above motivational factors therefore make up the first precondition for sexual offending against a child to occur. However, these are unlikely on their own to lead to actual offending behaviour, as further inhibitions need to be overcome. Finkelhor's subsequent preconditions describes the way this occurs.

OVERCOMING INTERNAL INHIBITIONS

Many men who sexually offend against children know at some level that their behaviour is wrong and therefore need to overcome their internal inhibitions. Finkelhor (1984) suggests that an individual's capacity for control may be diminished in a number of ways. These could involve internal psychological factors, such as using alcohol or drugs as a disinhibitor, or by or failure of the 'incest inhibition mechanism' (i.e. a stepfather not having the usual inhibitions against sexual contact with children). Disinhibiting factors can be temporary or enduring (e.g. distorted beliefs, 'he or she doesn't mind'). Fisher (1994) noted that men are also likely to use distorted beliefs to blame the disinhibitor for the offending, rather than acknowledging that this allowed them to offend. Finkelhor (1984) also suggested that external factors contribute to the overcoming of inhibitions, and a current example of this is the wide availability of child pornography on the internet (Ward *et al.* 2006a). Such socio-cultural factors may undermine individuals' attempts to control their behaviour and reinforce their cognitive distortions.

OVERCOMING EXTERNAL INHIBITIONS

Once an individual has acquired the motivation to sexually offend against a child and overcome their internal inhibitions, the next step is to overcome external obstacles and create an opportunity to offend. Many offenders go to great lengths to set up situations where they can offend, for example by befriending vulnerable women and children and encouraging the development of trust. This is often described as 'grooming'. In other situations the opportunity to offend may occur more unexpectedly. Conditions that make it easier for an offender to overcome normal external inhibitions (i.e. parental supervision) include a mother who is absent, ill or emotionally distant, a socially isolated family or poor familial supervision of a child.

OVERCOMING THE RESISTANCE OF THE CHILD

The final step is for the offender to overcome any resistance from the child. This may be done in a number of ways, from gradually developing a friendship with the child and offering gifts, or using bribes, overt threats and violence. Often offenders desensitise children to sex by exposing them to pornography or present their behaviour under the guise of sex education. Children who are emotionally insecure or have previously been abused are particularly vulnerable and may be deliberately targeted by offenders.

There are undoubtedly many limitations with the Finkelhor (1984) model. From a theoretical viewpoint, Ward *et al.* (2006a) note that the model draws on such a range of psychological theories that it lacks internal coherence and does not really explain how developmental factors contribute to the onset of offending, nor why emotional congruence and blockage are necessarily manifested in a sexual way. There is overlap between the key concepts of developmental blockage and emotional congruence. However, a key limitation is that it assumes that all men who offend against children do so because of a breakdown in their ability for self-control and self-regulation, and need to overcome personal inhibitions. It does not therefore account for the men who have no conflict about sexually offending against children and no inhibitions to overcome. Such individuals have clear 'approach goals' (Ward and Hudson 1998), and their problem lies in their choice of harmful goals rather than their inability for self-control. Nonetheless, despite the above theoretical limitations, Ward *et al.* (2006a) acknowledge that Finkelhor's (1984) preconditions model is useful in clinical practice in helping individuals to understand that their offending did not 'just happen', and to identify the processes which preceded this. Areas for intervention, change and monitoring may then be identified.

Wolf's multi-factor model

Wolf (1985) proposed that experience of, or exposure to, early childhood adversity (such as physical, sexual or emotional abuse or neglect) led to the development of a personality type in which the individual is vulnerable to developing deviant sexual interests. Such individuals are likely to have low self-esteem and a negative self-image, which then leads to an expectation of rejection by others and withdrawal from social contact. Sexual fantasies and masturbation become a way of compensating for a feeling of deprivation and powerlessness, and when those fantasies involve deviant imagery, such as children, they become further reinforced. Wolf (1985) argued that these processes operate in a cyclical way, in which after fantasy a process of grooming a potential victim occurs, accompanied by cognitive distortions to justify the behaviour. Individuals who show this pattern of offending are likely to feel guilty, but alleviate these feelings by further rationalisation and minimisation. However, at some level, they are aware that what they have done is wrong, which may further lower their self-esteem, increasing their vulnerability to start the cycle again.

It is now acknowledged that this model has only limited applicability to a single 'type' of offender, and again, does not account for the range of patterns of offending shown by men who abuse children. However, its focus on how sexual offending can be maintained, and its accessibility to both offenders and professionals, has meant that the model has been extremely influential in treatment programmes in the UK. Certainly for those individuals for whom the model *does* describe their pattern of offending, it can be extremely useful, first in helping them to identify this, and then to guide subsequent interventions and strategies required to break the cycle.

Ward and Siegert's pathways model

The pathways model of child sexual abuse, developed by Ward and Siegert (2002) (see also Ward *et al.* 2006a, pp. 61–77) is the most recent and comprehensive aetiological theory to account for the complexity of contributory factors to sexual offending against children and the heterogeneity of offenders. It was originally constructed by 'theory knitting' the best elements of three previously very influential models (Finkelhor 1984; Marshall and Barbaree 1990; Hall and Hirschmann 1992). The model is detailed and complex and the danger with presenting a summary is that it appears oversimplified. However, with that caveat, the key elements are outlined below, and readers are directed to the references above for a more comprehensive account.

Ward and Siegert (2002) observed that there are four clusters of difficulties frequently found in men who offend against children, namely: difficulties in identifying and controlling emotional states, such as anxiety or anger; intimacy deficits, social isolation and loneliness; offence-supportive beliefs (cognitive distortions); and deviant sexual fantasies and arousal. These correspond to the four key dynamic risk factors identified by Thornton (2002) (see Chapter 2). Vulnerability to these key difficulties will be influenced by biological factors, family environment, social learning and cultural issues. Sexual abuse of children may occur when these varying predispositions interact with situational triggers.

The pathways model suggests that each of the four problem areas and consequent 'implicit theories' (see above) are present to different degrees in men who offend against children. The particular pathway to offending will depend on which cluster provides the primary aetiological mechanism.

PATHWAY 1: MULTIPLE DYSFUNCTIONAL MECHANISMS

This pathway represents individuals who have difficulties in all four of the problem areas, and are likely to be 'pure paedophiles'. They are likely to have been sexually victimised and acquired a 'sexual script' in which an ideal sexual relationship is one between an older person and a child. They are likely to have an implicit theory of children as sexual beings.

PATHWAY 2: DEVIANT SEXUAL SCRIPTS

This pathway represents individuals who may have been sexually victimised as a child and subsequently developed 'sexual scripts' in which sex takes place in an impersonal context and as a purely physical means of release. Such individuals may be likely to confuse sexual cues with those of affection, and offend against children following periods of rejection by adults.

PATHWAY 3: INTIMACY DEFICITS

The third pathway is developed by individuals who have an insecure attachment style and difficulties with the development of intimate relationships. These individuals will be aroused by adults and generally prefer sexual relationships with adults, but treat children as a 'pseudo-partner' in certain situations, for example if there is a deterioration or break-up in an adult relationship.

PATHWAY 4: EMOTIONAL DYSREGULATION

This pathway represents individuals who have enduring problems with emotional regulation. Abuse of a child may be motivated by anger or become associated with a way of managing low mood and self-esteem.

PATHWAY 5: ANTISOCIAL COGNITIONS

The final pathway represents individuals whose sexual offending is just one of a wide range of criminal behaviours. These individuals are unlikely to have enduring deviant arousal to children but hold general antisocial attitudes and disregard all social norms. They are likely to hold implicit theories of entitlement and 'dangerous world', that is, there is often a need to make a 'pre-emptive strike'.

Ward and Siegert (2002) acknowledge that the theory still needs refining in some areas and there is not, as yet, a supportive evidence base. The primary strength and subsequent influence of the model is its acknowledgement that there are multiple pathways to offending, and that therefore a 'one size fits all' approach to treatment is unlikely to be successful (Ward *et al.* 2006a).

Theories of sexual offending against adults

Hall and Hirschmann's Quadripartite model

Hall and Hirschmann's (1991) quadripartite model was originally developed to account for sexual aggression towards women, and was reformulated to account for child sexual abuse (Hall and Hirschmann 1992). These authors propose that there are four key vulnerabilities which contributing towards sexual offending: sexual arousal; cognitions justifying sexual aggression; affective dyscontrol (e.g. anger and hostility); and antisocial personality traits. Although each of these factors will contribute to offending, it is likely that one will be prominent, and an offence may occur when a 'critical threshold' is reached and other situational factors and an opportunity are present. Negative early experiences increase the likelihood of the formation of antisocial attitudes and decrease the probability of adequate socialisation. A key component of the model is whether an individual appraises the benefits of sexual aggression to outweigh the costs. This model also leads to a typology of offenders according to which factor is most prominent, and treatment can then be focused accordingly.

Again, this model has been comprehensively critically evaluated by Ward et al. (2006a, pp. 47–59), who point out the theoretical weaknesses, such as how the main components interact to cause sexual offending. However, these authors also note that the model 'does a marvellous job of identifying the significant clinical phenomena evident in sexual offenders' (Ward et al. 2006a, p. 59). The identification of the four clusters of problems are similar to the four dynamic risk domains later identified by Thornton (2002) (see Chapter 2) and are useful to clinicians in identifying areas of intervention.

Malamuth's confluence model

An important model of understanding sexual aggression towards women, supported by extensive research primarily using college students, has been developed by Malamuth, Heavey and Linz (1993). This starts with the concept of 'rape proclivity', which is defined as 'the likelihood that an individual would commit a rape if they were guaranteed to get away with it'. Research to develop the model has focused on the characteristics of coercive men, and is therefore particularly useful as a framework to begin to conceptualise men who have behaved in sexually aggressive ways towards women but who have not been convicted.

Malamuth and colleagues (1993) suggest that childhood experiences lead to individual differences in six variables which have been shown to predict rape proclivity on self-report measures. These are: sexual arousal to rape; dominance as a motive for sex; hostility towards women; attitudes facilitating aggression towards women; antisocial personality characteristics; and sexual experience. These proclivity factors make up two separate pathways which converge to provide the motivation for sexually aggressive behaviour: sexual promiscuity (a preference for impersonal sex) and hostile masculinity (hostile, dominating and controlling personality traits). An individual is at high risk of committing a sexually aggressive act when these motivational factors combine with disinhibiting factors and the opportunity to behave in a sexually aggressive way.

Developing this model on the basis of research with men who have not been convicted of sexual offences is a unique strength. Although it cannot fully inform individual case formulation, the model can suggest useful areas of assessment and draws attention to areas which may otherwise be neglected in risk management, such as a continuing preference for consenting impersonal sex (Ward *et al.* 2006a, pp. 79–93).

Theories of the offence process

The above models have been primarily developed to understand *why* men sexually offend. The following two models were designed to explain *how* this occurs.

Relapse prevention

The relapse prevention model of sexual offending has been hugely influential in shaping treatment programmes with sexual offenders. Originally, a model developed in the early 1980s, in the field of substance abuse (Marlatt 1985), relapse prevention was adapted by Pithers *et al.* (1983) for the treatment of sexual offending. The models starts from the basis that the individual is trying to abstain from further sexual offending, and is likely to be confident about this process until he reaches a 'high-risk situation'. This can either occur unexpectedly or individuals can put themselves in a HRS by making 'apparently irrelevant decisions'. (These are usually renamed 'seemingly irrelevant decisions' in UK clinical practice.) An example of this would be if a person who had previously assaulted a child told himself that it would be quicker to walk past a school to get home rather than go a longer way. If the individual failed to cope effectively in the high-risk situation he is likely to feel hopeless and discouraged about preventing re-offending and move into the 'lapse' stage. This is a step immediately before re-offending, such as having a deviant sexual fantasy, buying pornography or identifying a potential victim. The individual is then likely to experience the 'abstinence violation effect' (conflict between his behaviour and the image of himself as an abstaining offender, attributed to his own weaknesses that he cannot prevent) and the 'problem of immediate gratification' (PIG) the anticipation of short-term gain which outweighs the long-term consequences ('short-term gain, long-term pain'). Failing to cope effectively with those experiences leads to re-offending.

This model clearly identifies points in a process towards potential re-offending which need to be coped with effectively in order to prevent re-offending. Because of the accessibility of this model for both professionals and offenders and its 'face validity' in terms of applicability to the experiences of many offenders, it has had a wide influence on the content of treatment. However, recently Ward *et al.* (2006a, pp. 213–235) have pointed out the limitations of this model, in particular in terms of its lack of applicability to the diversity of offending patterns shown by individuals whose offending does not fit into this process. Relapse prevention also puts the emphasis very much on what the individual needs to *avoid* in order to stay safe in the future. Research has shown that people are more likely to be successful in achieving *approach* goals (i.e. working towards something positive that they want to achieve) rather than achieving *avoidance* goals (i.e. avoiding behaving in a particular way) (Emmons 1996; Wegner 1994). Ward *et al.* (2006a) have therefore revised the relapse prevention theory to encompass these points, and developed a self-regulation model of offending.

The self-regulation model of offending

In order to account for the diversity of patterns of offending, the self-regulation model is complex, with the authors proposing that the offender goes through nine phases in the process of offending. These are: encountering a life event; having a desire for deviant sex or activity; establishing offence-related goals; selecting a strategy; entering a high-risk situation; experiencing a lapse; committing a sexual offence; evaluating the offence; and having an attitude towards future offending. The individual goes through these phases along one of four different pathways, depending on whether they have avoidant goals (i.e. trying not to offend but failing because of ineffective self-regulation strategies) or approach goals (i.e. having more effective self-regulation strategies but working towards harmful or socially unacceptable goals). The four pathways are described below.

- *Avoidant-passive*: an individual who follows this pathway typically offends when he has failed to cope effectively with stressful life events, and has a desire to 'cope' through deviant sexual activity. He is likely to get into a high-risk situation through covert planning, give in to his desire to offend and feel ashamed afterwards.

- *Avoidant-active*: this pathway starts in the same way as that above, but individuals use inappropriate coping strategies to deal with the desire to offend (such as alcohol), which have the consequence of increasing risk. Attempts to avoid offending are then abandoned, and the offence is followed by feelings of guilt.

- *Approach-automatic*: in this pathway the individual has already developed a template or 'script' for offending as a result of his previous experience or extensive fantasising. When a high-risk situation is encountered opportunistically, this becomes activated and offending occurs with minimal attention. Afterwards the offender experiences positive feelings, but feels negatively towards the victim.

- *Approach-explicit*: this pathway involves conscious planning to offend with a strong desire to obtain sexual gratification from offending. Again subsequent feelings will be positive, with further refinement of offence-related strategies.

Ward *et al.* (2006a) acknowledge that this model still requires further development and validation, although initial studies have demonstrated that both rapists and offenders against children can be allocated to one of the four self-regulation pathways (Bickley and Beech 2002; Yates, Kingston and Hall 2003). With regard to its implications for assessment and treatment, the self-regulation model identifies a wider range of goals and strategies than any of the above models and treatment can therefore be targeted specifically to individual need. To this end, both an assessment and a treatment manual have been published using this model (Ward *et al.* 2004; Ward, Yates and Long 2006b).

SUMMARY AND CONCLUSIONS

Individuals who commit sexual offences clearly make up a widely heterogeneous group, and the contributory factors to, and aetiology of, their behaviour are varied and complex. Information from the research and theories outlined in this chapter underpin approaches to both assessment and treatment, and it is therefore important for forensic mental health professionals to be aware of this. Clearly, a range of biological, developmental, sexual, psychological, interpersonal and cognitive factors may be relevant to the development and maintenance of sexual offending. Understanding why and how an individual sexually offends is crucial in making decisions about treatment and risk management. By being aware of the relevant theoretical background, clinicians are in a more informed position to carry out individualised, formulation-based clinical assessments and treatment, as discussed in Chapters 7 and 8.

REFERENCES

Abel, G., Gore, D., Holland, C., Camp, N., Becker, J. and Rathner, J. (1989) 'The measurement of the cognitive distortions of child molesters.' *Annals of Sex Research 2*, 135–153.

Beech, A. R. and Ward, T. (2004) 'The integration of etiology and risk in sexual offenders: a theoretical framework.' *Aggression and Violent Behavior 10*, 31–63.

Bickley, J. and Beech, A. R. (2002) 'An investigation of the Ward and Hudson pathways model of the sexual offence process with child abusers.' *Journal of Interpersonal Violence 17*, 371–393.

Carter, D. L., Prentky, R. A., Knight, R. A., Vanderveer, P. L. *et al.* (1987) 'Use of pornography in the criminal and developmental histories of sexual offenders.' *Journal of Interpersonal Violence 2*, 196–211.

Craisatti, J. and McClurg, G. (1996) 'The Challenge Project: perpetrators of child sexual abuse in South East London.' *Child Abuse and Neglect 20*, 1067–1077.

Craissati, J., McClurg, G. and Browne, K. (2002) 'Characteristics of perpetrators of child sexual abuse who have been sexually victimized as children.' *Sexual Abuse: A Journal of Research and Treatment 14*, 3, 225–238.

Emmons, R. A. (1996) 'Striving and Feeling: Personal Goals and Subjective Well-being.' In: P. M. Gollwitzer and J. A. Bargh (eds), *The Psychology of Action: Linking Cognition and Motivation to Behavior*. New York, NY: Guilford Press; 313–337.

Finkelhor, D. (1984) *Child Sexual Abuse: New Theory and Research*. New York, NY: Free Press.

Fisher, D. (1994) 'Adult sex offenders: who are they? Why and how do they do it?' In T. Morrison, M. Erooga and R. C. Beckett (eds) *Sexual Offending Against Children: Assessment and Treatment of Male Abusers.* Abingdon: Routledge.

Fisher, D., Beech, A. R. and Browne, K. (1999) 'Comparison of sex offenders to non-sex offenders on selected psychological measures.' *International Journal of Offender Therapy and Comparative Criminology 43,* 473–491.

Goodman, R. E. (1987) 'Genetic and hormonal factors in human sexuality: Evolutionary and developmental perspectives.' In G. D. Wilson (ed.) *Varient Sexuality: Research and Theory.* Baltimore: John Hopkins University.

Hall, G. C. N. and Hirschmann, R. (1991) 'Towards a theory of sexual aggression: a quadripartite model.' *Journal of Consulting and Clinical Psychology 59,* 662–669.

Hall, G. C. N. and Hirschman, R. (1992) 'Sexual aggression against children: a conceptual perspective of etiology.' *Criminal Justice and Behavior 19,* 8–23.

Hudson, S. M. and Ward, T. (1997) 'Attachment, anger and intimacy in sexual offenders.' *Journal of Interpersonal Violence 12,* 13–24.

Lalumiere, M. L. and Quinsey, V. L. (1994) 'The discriminability of rapists from non-rapists using phallometric measures: a meta-analysis.' *Criminal Justice and Behaviour 5,* 435–445.

Leitenberg, H. and Henning, K. (1995) 'Sexual fantasy.' *Psychological Bulletin 117,* 469–496.

Leonard, R. A. (1993) 'The family backgrounds of serial rapists.' *Issues in Criminological and Legal Psychology 19,* 9–18.

Malamuth, N. M., Heavey, C. L. and Linz, D. (1993) 'Predicting Men's Antisocial Behaviour against Women: The Interaction Model of Sexual Aggression.' In G. C. N. Hall, R. Hirschman, J. R. Graham and M. S. Zaragoza (eds) *Sexual Aggression: Issues in Etiology, Assessment and Treatment.* Washington, DC: Taylor and Francis.

Marlett, G. A. (1985) 'Relapse prevention: theoretical rationale and overview of the model.' In G. A. Marlett and J. R. Gordon (eds) *Relapse prevention: Maintenance strategies in the treatment of addictive behaviours.* New York: Guilford Press.

Marshall, W. L. (1989) 'Invited essay: intimacy, loneliness and sexual offenders.' *Behaviour Research and Therapy 27,* 491–503.

Marshall, W. L. and Barbaree, H. E. (1990) 'An Integrated Theory of the Etiology of Sexual Offending.' In W. L. Marshall, D. L. Laws and H. E. Barbaree (eds) *Handbook of Sexual Assaults: Issues, Theories and Treatment of the Offender.* New York, NY: Plenum Press.

Marshall, W. L., Barbaree, H. E. and Christopher, D. (1986) 'Sexual offenders against female children: preferences for age of victim and type of behaviour.' *Canadian Journal of Behavioural Science 18,* 424–439.

Marshall, W. L., Jones, R. J., Ward, T., Johnston, P. W. and Barbaree, H. (1991) 'Treatment outcome with sex offenders.' *Clinical Psychology Review 11,* 465–485.

Pithers, W. D., Marques, J. K., Gibat, C. C. and Marlett, G. A. (1983) 'Relapse prevention with sexual aggressive: a self-control model of treatment and maintenance of change.' In J. G. Greer and I. R. Stuart (eds) *The sexual aggressor: Current perspectives on treatment.* New York: Van Nostrand Reinhold.

Polaschek, D. L. L. and Ward, T. (2002) 'The implicit theories of potential rapists: what our questionnaires tell us.' *Aggression and Violent Behavior 7,* 385–406.

Prentky, R. A., Knight, R. A., Sims-Knight, J. E., Straus, H., Rokous, F. and Cerce, D. (1989) 'Developmental antecedents of sexual aggression.' *Development and Psychopathology 1,* 153–169.

Scoales, M. W. and Houston, J. (2006) *A Descriptive Study of Personality Disorder Traits and Offence-related Factors in an Outpatient Sex Offender Sample.* Internal research report commissioned by the South West London and South East Region Forensic Consortium. Available from the second author.

Seidman, B., Marshall, W. L., Hudson, S. M. and Robertson, P. J. (1994) 'An examination of intimacy and loneliness in sex offenders.' *Journal of Interpersonal Violence 13,* 555–573.

Smallbone, S. W. (2006) 'An Attachment–Theoretical Revision of Marshall and Barbaree's Integrated Theory of the Etiology of Sexual Offending.' In W. L. Marshall, Y. M. Fernandez, L. E. Marshall and G. A. Serran (eds) *Sexual Offender Treatment: Controversial Issues.* Chichester: John Wiley and Sons Ltd.

Thornton, D. (2002) 'Constructing and testing a framework for dynamic risk assessment.' *Sexual Abuse: A Journal of Research and Treatment 14,* 139–154.

Ward, T. and Hudson, S. (1998) 'A model of the relapse process in sexual offenders.' *Journal of Interpersonal Violence 13,* 700–725.

Ward, T. and Keenan, T. (1999) 'Child molesters' implicit theories.' *Journal of Interpersonal Violence 14,* 821–838.

Ward, T. and Siegert, R. J. (2002) 'Toward a comprehensive theory of child sexual abuse: a theory knitting perspective.' *Psychology Crime and Law 9,* 319–351.

Ward, T., Bickley, J., Webster, S. J., Fisher, D., Beech, H. and Eldridge, H. (2004) *The Self-regulation Model of the Offense and Relapse Process. A Manual. Volume I: Assessment.* Victoria, BC: Pacific Psychological Assessment Corporation.

Ward, T., Polaschek, D. L. L. and Beech, A. R. (2006a) *Theories of Sexual Offending.* Chichester: Wiley.

Ward, T., Yates, P. M., and Long, C. A. (2006b) *The Self-regulation Model of the Offense and Relapse Process. A Manual. Volume II: Treatment.* Victoria BC: Pacific Psychological Assessment Corporation.

Wegner, D. M. (1994) 'Ironic processes of mental control.' *Psychological Bulletin 101,* 34–52.

Wolf, F. C. S. (1985) 'A multi-factor model of deviant sexuality.' *Victimology 10,* 359–374.

Yates, P. M., Kingston, D. and Hall, K. (2003) Pathways to Sexual Offending: Validity of Ward and Hudson's (1998) Self-regulation Model and Relationship to Static and Dynamic Risk among Treated Sex Offenders. Paper presented at the 22nd Association for the Treatment of Sexual Abusers Annual Conference, St Louis, MO, October.

Young, J. E. (1990) *Cognitive Therapy for Personality Disorders: A Schema-Focused Approach.* Sarasota, Fla: Professional Resource Exchange, Inc.

Risk Assessment

Jackie Craissati

INTRODUCTION

This chapter aims to review the literature associated with risk prediction in sex offenders, and to equip the reader with practical guidelines for risk assessment based on the core tools that are currently available. Mental illness and personality disorder are sometimes referred to within the criminogenic literature but are not considered in great detail, and these issues will be developed in the subsequent chapter.

Much of the work on risk prediction is based on the goal of accurately identifying the likelihood of a further sexual offence occurring. This should be considered quite separately to the question of victim impact – the likelihood of serious harm occurring – a valid consideration in its own right. There are also quite legitimate public interest or institutional concerns – the harm to a professional or agency should an offence take place while an offender is under their care. Thus, an offender might pose a low risk of re-offending, but should an offence take place, irreparable harm might be caused to that victim. Furthermore, the current public interest in paedophiles and their potential risk to the public raises anxieties for the agency involved – public scrutiny may be disproportionately critical if a child molester re-offends. Mistakes in risk prediction will occur if these three areas of assessment are confused.

RECIDIVISM RATES FOR SEX OFFENDERS

There are numerous inadequacies in the published research literature on sex offenders. Sampling bias, length of follow-up and failure to distinguish between subgroups of sex offender and different types of recidivism are probably the main limitations of the recidivism literature (Furby, Weinrott and Blackshaw 1989). However, over the past 10 years, sufficient data have been accumulated to provide us with a reasonably confident estimate of base rates. The most recent meta-analytic review (Hanson and Morton-Bourgon 2004) summarises the findings: with a combined sample of over 31,000 sex offenders followed up for an average of five to six years, the observed sexual recidivism rate was 13.7 per cent; the violent non-sexual recidivism rate was 14 per cent, the combined sexual and violent recidivism rate was 25 per cent, and the general (any) recidivism rate was 36.9 per cent.

In terms of child molesters, Hanson and Bussiere (1998) found that 12.7 per cent sexually re-offended over a follow-up period of four to five years, whereas the recidivism rate for non-sexual violence was 9.9 per cent. Thornton and Hanson (1996) examined the gender and relationship specificity in sex offenders, and found that 41–45 per cent of men with an index offence against a male child re-offended as compared to 9–19 per cent of men with an index offence against a female child. Alexander (1999) also found a different recidivism rate for incest offenders (12.5%), child molesters with female victims (15.7%) and with male victims (34.1%).

There is a growing literature on internet pornography (child) offenders, although the evidence for recidivism rates is in its infancy. Early studies suggest that both the recidivism rate for further pornography offences and for escalation to contact sexual offences is low. For example, Seto and Eke (2005) found that only one per cent of the child pornography offenders (with no prior history of criminal or contact sexual offences) escalated to contact sex offending, although four per cent of them committed a further pornography offence.

Reported sexual recidivism rates for rapists are variable, and predictor variables have been difficult to establish (Quinsey *et al.* 1995). However, the majority of studies have found that rapists were more likely to re-offend violently than sexually. Hanson and Bussiere (1998) found that 18.9 per cent of 1839 rapists sexually re-offended over an average follow-up period of four to five years, whereas 22.1 per cent re-offended violently.

Mentally ill and personality-disordered sex offenders have rarely been considered in the literature as a typology in their own right. Sahota and

Chesterman (1998) reviewed the published literature on sexual offending in the context of mental illness. These authors identified a number of studies that found that up to 10 per cent of all sex offenders are found to have a mental illness. The remaining majority either have no diagnosis or are labelled as personality-disordered or paraphiliacs. Home Office statistics demonstrate a rise in the number of restricted patients (sectioned under the Mental Health Act) admitted to hospital for sexual offences between 1983 and 1995, from 23 to 105 patients. In terms of high-secure hospital patients, it was estimated that over two-thirds of patients on some wards presented with a sexual element to their offending (Lewis 1991). They were more likely to have adult female or pubescent victims. It is most unusual for mentally ill sex offenders to have child victims (Murray, Briggs and Davies 1992). Thus, although only a small minority of sex offenders are thought to be mentally ill, they comprise a large proportion of the medium- and high-secure hospital populations.

A follow-up study of mentally disordered offenders, detained under the Mental Health Act with restrictions, and subsequently released (Street 1998), found that 14 per cent had been convicted of a sexual offence at the time of the original sentencing; during a follow-up period of at least four years, five per cent were re-convicted of serious offences (including violent and sexual offending), these re-convictions being more likely in cases where there were previous convictions for sexual offences. However, interestingly, 13 per cent of patients reported being victimised during the follow-up period, most commonly involving violent or sexual offences. A subsequent study of conditionally discharged restricted patients (Ly and Howard 2004), discharged from hospital over a five-year period and followed up for two years, found that only two per cent were re-convicted for sexual or violent offences, as compared to an expected percentage of 11 per cent (based on offenders on community orders and released from custody, matched for criminal history and demographic characteristics).

RISK ASSESSMENT: GETTING STARTED

The research evidence is clear: actuarial approaches are nearly always shown to be superior to unstructured clinical judgement. This holds true in different settings (Harris, Rice and Quinsey 1993). Specifically, for sex offenders, Hanson and Bussiere (1998) found that professional judgement to predict sex offence recidivism was only slightly better than chance (average $r = 0.10$). Hanson and Morton-Bourgon (2007) also found that unstructured professional judgements were consistently the least accurate in their meta-analysis, when compared to both actuarial assessments and structured professional judgements.

There is little doubt that professionals – both experienced and inexperienced – can often feel undermined by actuarial approaches to risk assessment. It may seem incredible that such an apparently complex and serious issue as risk assessment could be condensed into a few variables. Experience suggests that some clinicians may simply dismiss the contribution made by actuarial tools, preferring to highlight the statistical limitations to such approaches; others accept the need for an actuarial approach, but then override the findings on the basis that it is not consistent with their clinical judgement. Conversely, clinicians can be paralysed by actuarial findings, passively acquiescing to the inevitable.

Actuarial approaches are derived from large pools of data, statistically manipulated to provide a probability estimate of the likelihood of a particular event (in this case, re-offending – sexual, violent or otherwise) occurring. Structured professional judgement tends to be based on conceptual approaches which may be rooted in empirical evidence to a greater or lesser extent; predetermined items are rated, but the final evaluation is left to professional judgement. Unstructured clinical judgement may or may not be informed by a knowledge of the relevant evidence base: the greater the dissemination and adherence to the current evidence base, the more likely it is that such judgement will approximate to structured approaches.

Actuarially based measures of re-offending risk have become increasingly available in recent years. Many overlap in terms of the important variables incorporated into the measure, but they differ in terms of the populations from which they were derived and in the extent to which they have been validated, and they have established generalisability across settings and countries. As with all psychometric instruments, it is important to bear in mind the basic properties of the scales and the correct scoring procedure; with risk prediction in particular, the reader should take note of the base rate for violence on which the scales were based, whether the validation studies have been reliant on secure hospital populations, incarcerated criminal justice populations or community populations, and whether the scales are reliable in predicting general recidivism or violent recidivism in particular, and over what timescale.

The core dilemma with psychometric tools is the extrapolation from the group risk prediction (as determined by published data on the scales) to the individual risk prediction, as it is well-known that the margin of error for the group is smaller than for the individual; or, as Sir Arthur Conan Doyle said, 'while the individual man is an insoluble puzzle, in the aggregate he becomes a mathematical certainty.' If, for example, we look at the predictive certainty of the Risk Matrix 2000, a low risk estimate of seven per cent likelihood is associated with a 3–14 per cent group confidence interval but a 0–82 per cent individual confidence interval (Hart 2005).

Generally, psychometric measures for sexual and violent offending contain both static (fixed or historical factors) and dynamic (changeable) variables; however, sex offender scales have tended to separate out these two domains. The static items allow us to place an individual in a risk category *relative* to others; the dynamic items allow us to consider whether an individual is likely to fall into the offending cluster of that category, identifies potential treatment needs and provides a basis for measuring change over time.

There is a competent and comprehensive review of risk management tools available from the Risk Management Authority in Scotland (2006) (also available online at www.rmascotland.gov.uk), which contains a summary of all tools currently in use (not just for sexual offenders) in terms of the use of their scores and type of judgement required, applicability and current published validation studies. Hanson and Morton-Bourgon (2007) also provide a comprehensive review of all the main tools, a few of which – those most accurate and accessible – are detailed below.

STATIC MEASURES

Static 99

The Static 99 (Hanson and Thornton 1999, 2000) was developed from three Canadian samples and one UK, from both mental health and criminal justice settings. It is intended for use with adult, male, convicted sex offenders and comprises 10 static/fixed variables that may be derived from file information. An individual's score can range from zero to a maximum of 12. The Static 99 performs well for rapists and child molesters in predicting both sexual and violent recidivism, although other tools are likely to be superior for the latter.

Information about the Static 99 may be obtained from the Public Safety and Emergency Preparedness Canada website (www.gc.ca/publicsafety). This includes advice on scoring, the scale itself, and the sexual and violent re-offending probability estimates. The tool requires a limited amount of file information relating to criminal variables, and may be completed within a few minutes if the information is available.

Risk Matrix 2000

The Risk Matrix 2000 (Thornton *et al.* 2003) has been widely used in the UK. The revised system contains a section – Risk Matrix 2000/S – that is concerned with sexual re-conviction, and a second dimension – Risk Matrix 2000/V – that is designed to predict future non-sexual violent re-conviction by sex offenders. The development and cross-validation of the tool was based on two samples of male sex offenders released from prison in England and Wales, and followed up for between two and 16 years. The scale has subsequently been cross-validated (Craig, Beech and Browne 2006) and performed well in comparison to other risk prediction measures.

The Risk Matrix 2000 is intended for use with adult, male, convicted sex offenders. It has not been validated on child, juvenile or female sex offenders. It comprises three steps, and all the data may be derived from file information: step one consists of three static variables which result in an individual score ranging from zero to six, and an associated risk category. Step two relates to four aggravating factors – if two are present, the risk category is raised one level; if all four are present, the risk category is raised two levels. The final category denotes the risk of sexual reconviction. Step three relates to the prediction of non-sexual violence: it comprises three static variables which result in an individual score ranging from zero to eight, and an associated risk category. This category denotes the risk of future violent reconviction.

Clinical relevance of static variables

So much emphasis over the past few years has been placed on persuading professionals to anchor their clinical judgement with actuarial assessments, there is a danger that we can lose sight of the meaning behind risk factors (Grubin and Wingate 1996). Sex offenders are more than a handful of historical variables; they have complex behavioural and emotional difficulties which, admittedly, the actuarial tools may represent in summarised form.

Age

Strictly speaking, age is a dynamic factor, but since it is not amenable to intervention, it falls best among the fixed factors. The actuarial tools clearly demonstrate the importance of age in determining risk. A recent review of recidivism and age (Hanson 2006) established that it is important to differentiate between types of offender: rapists tended to be younger than child molesters, and their recidivism rate steadily decreased with age; extrafamilial child molesters showed relatively little reduction in recidivism until after the age of 50, whereupon recidivism dropped significantly; incest offenders were older, and the recidivism rate was – as expected – low. Hanson (2002) hypothesised that developmental changes in key variables – sexual drive, self-control/impulsivity and opportunities to offend – underpinned these findings.

Previous sexual charges or convictions

The salience of this variable is, perhaps, obvious; and there is no risk assessment which does not give it key importance. It represents those sex offenders who are prepared to put their urges into practice. It may suggest a compelling drive to offend, or a disregard for personal and social rules. Critics will immediately point out that a large number of sex offenders remain undetected or are only caught for a small proportion of their crimes. This view is based on the assumption – as yet unproven – that convicted sex offenders are no different from their unconvicted counterparts.

Previous convictions

Some caution needs to be applied in considering this variable, not least because it may be of differential importance in rapists as compared to child molesters. Arguably, these two variables are capturing the essence of the dynamic variable, antisocial personality disorder; that is, a propensity for aggressive behaviour, anti-authoritarian attitudes and general criminality, which may be associated with substance misuse problems or a poor employment record.

Violence

The use of excessive force in the index sexual offence is alluded to in Static 99 in terms of an additional index conviction for violence. However, the degree of physical harm inflicted on the victim has not been shown to be reliably related to risk unless there has been clear evidence of an escalation in the degree of violence over time (e.g. with sadistic interests, see MacCullough *et al.* 1983). One of the greatest pitfalls in assessing the likelihood of future offending in rapists is to place too much emphasis on the degree of terror or humiliation experienced by the victim, unless there is clear evidence of sadistic sexual interests. In a similar vein, there is no evidence to suggest that penetration in the offence, or the duration of offending against one particular victim (as in some incestuous offences) is related in any way to future risk.

Victim variables: gender and relationship to perpetrator

All research identifies male victims in child molesters as a key risk variable. It is not clear to what extent this applies to rapists as, historically, convictions of sexual assaults by men on men are extremely rare. The evidence suggests that a male victim is much more likely to represent a fixed and enduring deviant sexual interest; this is particularly the case if the offender also has previous sexual convictions (Hanson and Harris 1998). Clinically, this group of sex offenders may present with more 'perverse' psychosexual functioning, a tendency to relate to their victim as an extension of their internal world (Glasser 1998).

Risk also rises the less close the pre-existing relationship between offender and victim – from relative, to aquaintance, to stranger (Hanson and Harris 2000), and applies to both rapists and child molesters. Clinical judgement may differ as to the explanation for this. It may be 'practical' considerations which apply; that is, offenders who seek victims who are close to them, wish to minimise the chances of apprehension and take pains to seduce the child carefully over time; they may have difficulty in selecting future victims because of these considerations. Clinical experience suggests that intimacy deficits and attachment problems may be more profound in offenders who select stranger victims, and they may be more able to dehumanise their victim, more impervious to victim distress and fear.

A contentious issue, and one that is highly pertinent to risk, is the potential for cross-over in offending, either in terms of victim gender or – as discussed below – offence type. As with other relatively rare characteristics, actuarial tools, based on large sample sizes, do not find gender cross-over to be predictive of risk. Individual studies have found variable results. A recent study of adult male sex offenders with multiple victims found that a quarter of the sample showed cross-over behaviour with respect to one of the three victim variables examined: age, gender and relationship (Cann, Friendship and Gozna 2007), and that *as a group*, these individuals rated as higher risk using Static 99 than those with no cross-over behaviour. However, child molesters who have offence victims of both sexes do not usually pose a greater risk than those with male-only victims (Firestone *et al.* 2000). Approximately 10 per cent of child molesters have victims of both sexes (Grubin 1998). Thornton and Hanson (1996) found that only those child molesters with male child victims (aged <13 years) were at risk for re-offending against females (14%); fewer than three per cent of offenders with female child or adolescent victims re-offended against males; there were almost no rapists who crossed-over gender when re-offending.

Similarly, the question is often raised about the likelihood of cross-over between child molestation and rape. Craissati *et al.* (2002) found that four per cent of their child molesters had previous sexual convictions against adult women; Quinsey *et al.* (1995) found five per cent of their child molesters re-offended against adults, and none of their rapists re-offended against children. Eight per cent of the sample in the study by Cann *et al.* (2007) had offended against children and adults. However, as the research on actuarial tools highlights, those offenders with mixed victim types – child and adult – are more likely to be psychopathic, more like to recidivate at a faster rate, and most likely to sexually re-offend.

Prior non-contact offences

Both static scales rate prior non-contact offences as a significant variable. This issue must be considered quite separately from the question of risk in those offenders who have *only* committed non-contact sex offences. There are probably two main behaviours to consider: indecent exposure or exhibitionism and illegal pornography, including that available on the internet.

INDECENT EXPOSURE

In a study, much criticised for its confused presentation of results and its biased sampling procedure (Craissati 1998; Fisher and Thornton 1993), Abel *et al.* (1988) attempted to assess self-reported sexual behaviours in a specially recruited group of sex offenders. They found that 11 per cent of rapists and between six per cent and 18 per cent of child molesters had a secondary diagnosis of exhibitionism. Bard *et al.* (1987) found that rapists and child molesters had equal rates of prior offences for indecent exposure and voyeurism (30–31%).

Essentially, this is a question of escalation. It is a commonly held belief, among both professionals and the public, that sex offenders escalate their behaviour over time. Clearly, a small proportion of indecent exposers go on to commit contact offences. But within an offence type there is little evidence for escalation; if anything, child molesters are re-convicted for less violent or intrusive offending over time (McClurg and Craissati 1997).

PORNOGRAPHY

Pornography as a clearly identifiable risk factor is usually meant as prior arrests or convictions for the possession of, or intent to supply, illegal pornography. It must be said that pornography, in some ways, is in the eye of the beholder. Child molesters have long been noted to identify apparently harmless films, such as *Oliver Twist*, or children's television as a source of sexual fantasy and stimulation. The same is true of rapists who may feed on mainstream violent imagery or legal 'soft' pornography, to fuel sexually aggressive impulses. The use of explicit child pornography is probably uncommon (Howitt 1995) and Elliott, Browne and Kilcoyne (1995) found that only one-fifth of their sample of child molesters said they knew where to obtain child prostitutes and illegal child pornography.

There is clearer evidence that a proportion of sex offenders – ranging from 16 per cent to 38 per cent in different studies – report pornography played a role in their offending, either as preparation for the offence or part of the act itself. However, only a small proportion of this pornographic material would have been illegal. There is no evidence that use of pornography is related to key aspects of the offending behaviour, such as the number of victims or the degree of violence used. It is worth noting that many sex offenders have been reported as stating that pornography provided a 'safety valve' for antisocial impulses, relieving them of impulses to commit an offence. However, there does not appear to be empirical research to corroborate this assertion.

The more recent literature on internet child pornography offenders has provoked heated clinical debate about the nature of this 'new' group of offenders; although, clearly, a relatively small subgroup comprise child molesters who have re-offended, the majority present with some of the socio-affective features of child molesters but without their pro-offending attitudes (Webb, Craissati and Keen 2007).

Attachment

There are three main variables discussed in the research literature which relate broadly to attachment issues.

NEGATIVE RELATIONSHIP WITH MOTHER

Hanson and Bussiere (1998) found that a negative relationship with mother was the sole developmental history variable related to sexual offence recidivism, but this was not replicated in Hanson and Morton-Bourgon (2004). Smallbone and Dadds (1998) found that sex offenders only differed from property offenders in their maternal attachments, which were less secure; specifically, these authors found intra-familial child molesters to be more likely to regard their mothers as unloving, inconsistent and abusive, whereas rapists were more likely to regard their fathers as uncaring and abusive to them.

SINGLE STATUS OR NEVER HAVING LIVED WITH A LOVER FOR TWO OR MORE YEARS

Being single, of course, may well reflect a primary lack of interest in forming relationships with adults, and would therefore be considered an indicator of deviant sexual interest. However, it may reflect a deficit in an individual's capacity for empathy or marked avoidance of potentially threatening – albeit desirable – adult intimacy. Looked at from the opposite point of view, being married may have a protective effect (Grubin and Wingate 1996): offenders no longer need to seek out partners; or the emotional support of a partner may decrease loneliness or feelings of inadequacy.

SEXUAL ABUSE AS A CHILD

Strictly speaking, sexual abuse as a child has not been shown to be a strong predictor of risk. It is clinically important, and may well have an indirect relationship to recidivism. Sex offenders are more likely than other offenders – and, of course, the general population – to have been sexually abused in childhood (Craissati, McClurg and Browne 2002; Weeks and Widom 1998), and this finding is usually stronger for child molesters than rapists (Bard et al. 1987; Weeks and Widom 1998). Craissati et al. (2002)

found that sexually abused child molesters were significantly more likely to have male victims, to have engaged in sex play with male peers in childhood, to have homosexual contacts in adulthood, to be more honest in reporting offence-related cognitions and sexual preoccupations. In other words, childhood sexual victimisation is likely to make an important contribution to the development of psychosexual disturbance.

Personality disorder: psychopathy

In terms of sex offenders, the prevalence of psychopathy (a score of 30 plus on the *Psychotherapy Checklist – Revised* (PCL-R) (Hare 2003) appears to be relatively high among convicted rapists and those identified as sexually dangerous. Forth and Kroner (1995) found that 26.1 per cent of incarcerated rapists, 18.3 per cent of mixed rapist/child molester offenders and 5.4 per cent of incest offenders were psychopaths. Of those rapists who were serial offenders or killed their victims, 35 per cent were psychopaths. Those sex offenders that crossed over from child to adult victims were nearly all psychopaths and also had the highest Factor 1 scores, indicating a ruthless and callous personality. Rice and Harris (1997) reported that sexual recidivism was strongly predicted by a combination of a high PCL-R score and phallometric evidence of deviant sexual arousal. They postulate that deviant sexual interests are the driving motivation to offend, but the empathy deficits inherent in psychopathy result in a failure to inhibit impulses to act on sexual interests.

DYNAMIC RISK VARIABLES

This area of recent work is reviewed by Craissati and Beech (2003) and Craissati (2004). The approaches tend to rely either on self-report questionnaires (Beech 1998; Thornton 2002) or on practitioner-observed assessments derived from file information and offender interviews (Hanson and Harris 2000). Dynamic risk assessments have been found to significantly enhance risk assessment predictions in sex offenders, independently of static risk assessments, and a combination of the two approaches provides the optimum prediction.

The 'Sex Offender Need Assessment Rating' (SONAR) (Hanson and Harris 2000, 2001), incorporating stable dynamic and acute dynamic factors, provides a standardised method for measuring change in sex offender risk levels over time. It is now known as 'Stable 2000' and 'Acute 2000'. It was developed from the work of Hanson and Harris's (1998) with both child molesters and rapists (excluding incest offenders), in which they identified groups of recidivists and non-recidivists, matched on key static variables, and then interviewed their supervising officers in the community using a structured interview schedule and examined the offenders' files.

Stable 2000 and Acute 2000 are based on six stable dynamic categories (expected to persist for months or years), with the addition of seven acute factors (the 'worry now' features, which may persist for minutes or days). Overall, the scale showed adequate internal consistency and moderate ability to differentiate between recidivists and non-recidivists ($r = 0.43$; receiver operating characteristic (ROC) area of 0.74). The tool is currently being validated on a large Canadian population of sex offenders who are being assessed prospectively and followed up.

Stable 2000 comprises six domains:

1. Significant social influences, that is, the balance of pro-social versus antisocial influences among the offender's family members and social peers.

2. Intimacy deficits, that is, the presence of intimate partners, emotional identification with children, hostility towards women, general social rejection or loneliness, lack of concern for others.

3. Sexual self-regulation, that is, degree of sex drive and preoccupation, sex as coping, deviant sexual interests.

4. Attitudes supportive of sexual assault, that is, sexual entitlement, rape attitudes and child molester attitudes.

5. Co-operation with supervision.

6. General self-regulation, that is, impulsive acts, poor cognitive problem-solving skills, negative emotionality or hostility.

Acute 2000 comprises:

- opportunities for victim access
- emotional collapse
- collapse of social supports
- hostility

- substance abuse
- sexual preoccupations
- rejection of supervision.

The Sexual Violence Risk – 20 (SVR-20) (Boer *et al.* 1997) is a 20-item checklist of risk factors for sexual violence that were identified by a review of the literature on sex offenders. The 20 factors fall into three main categories: psychosocial adjustment; history of sexual offences; and future plans. The actual risk for sexual violence depends on the combination (not just the number) of risk factors present in a specific case. Items may be scored as zero (does not apply), one (applies somewhat) and two (item definitely applies); items may be summed to produce a total score as an actuarial measure. The SVR-20 has been found to have good reliability and has been validated in other sex offender populations. In the review by Hanson and Morton-Bourgon (2007) of the accuracy of risk assessment tools for sex offenders, the SVR-20 was found to be a moderately good predictor of sexual recidivism (although this was based on only a few studies with variable findings).

The Risk for Sexual Violence Protocol (RSVP) (Hart *et al.* 2003) is an evolved version of the SVR-20, and comprises a set of structured professional guidelines. It comprises 22 individual risk factors reflecting five domains:

1. *Sexual violence history*, including chronicity, diversity, escalation, physical and psychological coercion.

2. *Psychological adjustment*, including attitudes that support sexual violence, extreme minimisation, problems with self-awareness, problems with stress or coping, and problems resulting from child abuse.

3. *Mental disorder*, including sexual deviance, psychopathic personality disorder, major mental illness, problems with substance use and violent or suicidal ideation.

4. *Social adjustment*, including problems with intimate relationships, problems with non-intimate relationships, problems with employment and non-sexual criminality.

5. *Manageability*, including problems with planning, problems with treatment and problems with supervision.

The RSVP is intended for use with adult men with a known or suspected history of sexual violence, but may also be used – cautiously – with older male adolescents (aged 16 or 17 years) and with adult female sex offenders. It is designed to guide the practitioner or team through a number of steps to identifying risk factors, their relevance, risk management scenarios and strategies. Pilot studies on the utility of the RSVP have been conducted, with a view to establishing inter-rater reliability and concurrent validity of ratings. However, it does not quantify behaviour or result in a final probability rating, and therefore its use in recidivism research is limited.

Clinical relevance of the dynamic domains

The cumulative evidence, described above, lends weight to the consideration of four core dynamic domains which have a growing evidence-base, and which appear to contribute significantly to static risk assessment. The domains are described more fully below.

Intimacy deficits/social competencies

These variables are closely associated with the static variables of never having had a live-in lover and the victim–perpetrator relationship (acquaintance/stranger). The importance of intimacy deficits has been widely reported (Marshall 1993; Ward *et al.* 1995) and are largely manifest by: an avoidance of adult intimacy in child molesters who fear negative evaluations or rapists who lack empathy for women, have multiple uncommitted sexual encounters or experience difficulties in managing assertiveness (Overholser and Beck 1986).

The Locus of Control Scale (Nowicki 1976) measures the extent to which an individual feels that events are contingent upon their own behaviour and the extent to which they feel that events are outside their control. Child molesters with an external locus of control are less likely to respond to treatment, more likely to have previous sexual convictions and more likely to re-offend sexually (Fisher, Beech and Browne 1998). It is not clear how far locus of control is a relevant risk predictor for rapists. Low self-esteem has been found to distinguish child molesters from comparison groups. Emotional loneliness seems to distinguish sexual offenders more generally, and appears to be the only aspect of inadequacy that seems to distinguish rapists (Thornton 2002).

Pro-offending attitudes

The relationship between sexual attitudes supportive of sexual assault – attitudes or values that excuse, permit or condone sexual offending – and sexual offence recidivism seems to be significant, but only to a very limited extent (Hanson and Bussiere 1998). An assessment of pro-offending attitudes by means of clinical interview will be heavily influenced by the circumstances in which the offender is being assessed, the degree of shame – rather than distorted belief – that they experience, and the motivational interviewing skills of the assessor (Craissati 1998). There is likely to be some difficulty in differentiating between child molesters and rapists in terms of pro-offending attitudes. Hanson and Harris (1998) found that there was no significant difference between the two groups in the extent to which they endorsed rape myths or held attitudes which sexualised children. However, these authors also found that justification for the sex crimes, sexualising children and feeling entitled to express their strong sexual drive, were all significant in differentiating between recidivists and non-recidivists generally.

There is also a lack of clarity as to whether empathy deficits are general (as measured by the Interpersonal Reactivity Index) (Davis 1980) or specific to a class of potential victims or actual victims, as measured by the Rape Myths Scale (Burt 1980) or victim empathy distortions (Beckett and Fisher 1994). Thornton (2002) found that recidivist child molesters showed more distorted attitudes to sex with children and rape myths, suggestive of a more general tendency to distorted attitudes rather than minimisation of a specific kind of offending. Beech, Fisher and Beckett (1999), in contrast, found that child molesters did not demonstrate general problems in empathy deficits, although cognitive distortions in relation to their own offence victims contributed to a model of high deviancy.

Denial is often a preoccupation within the assessment, and the feature of an offender's presentation most likely to cause an impasse. The relationship between denial and risk is often misunderstood: essentially, total denial of the offence – either that nothing illegal took place, or that someone else committed the crime – has not been shown to be related to an enhanced risk of recidivism (Craissati 2004; Hanson *et al.* 2002). This is because denial is so often related to conscious and deliberate attempts to avoid responsibility, or to more complex feelings of shame in relation to offending, and not related to fundamental and entrenched psychological difficulties. Denial of the offence overlaps with refusal to enter treatment, and, again, this does not have a direct relationship to enhanced risk (Hanson *et al.* 2002).

Sexual self-regulation

There is strong evidence to support the view that sex offenders who present with a poorly controlled expression of sexual impulses are at a higher risk for re-offending. In assessing sexual preoccupation, it is important to differentiate between the direction (see deviant sexual interests below) and the strength of sexual interests; for example, how frequently the offender engages in sexual activity (not necessarily illegal) such as masturbation, consenting intercourse and frequenting prostitutes. High-risk sex offenders are more likely to respond sexually to stress or negative affect, or feel deprived or frustrated if they are unable to quickly satisfy their sexual urges (Hanson and Harris 2000). It appears that the experience of negative affect, especially that arising from interpersonal conflict (humiliation and resentment) seems to precipitate offence-related fantasies. Clinically, this is often referred to as 'sexualisation', that is, a preoccupation with sex as a necessary and persistent regulator of self-esteem (Rosen 1979), which comforts the individual in the face of anxiety-provoking internal conflicts.

Deviant sexual interest may be defined as a distortion in aim (e.g. children as victims) or in means (e.g. coercion in the 'courtship disorders' of rape). It does *not* refer to sexual arousal during the course of the offending episode, but should be based on an assessment of *persistent* erotic interests over time. Hanson and Bussiere (1998) concluded that deviant sexual interest – as measured by PPG – was the single most important dynamic factor in predicting sex offender recidivism. Around 25–40 per cent of child molesters and 10 per cent of rapists exhibit deviant sexual interests; yet the area is not without controversy and inconsistency, in particular in relation to rapists.

General self-regulation

General self-regulation concerns the offender's ability to self-monitor and inhibit antisocial thoughts and behaviours. This cluster of variables – also related to the static variables of violent and general previous offending – incorporates many of the elements of personality disorder. Lifestyle impulsivity is not referring primarily to a lack of planning in the index offence, but to a disorganised, irresponsible lifestyle and poor impulse control established prior to adolescence, likely to result in negative consequences. It refers to an individual's ability to plan, problem-solve and regulate impulses so as to better achieve long-term goals.

Co-operation with supervision – or compliance – warrants particular consideration. Compliance may be interpreted in several ways, including poor attendance at supervision or treatment, being excluded from treatment or dropping out (for whatever reason) or failure on conditional release. Non-compliance has regularly been shown to be related to high recidivism rates (Cook *et al.* 1991; Craissati and Beech 2001; Marques 1999). Failure to complete treatment is *not* the same as failing to meet the treatment goals; a compliant sex offender is one who attends and co-operates with the structure of treatment, regardless of whether that offender has made any demonstrable progress in improving his offence attitudes or social competencies. Difficulty with complying with statutory expectations is likely to relate to psychological difficulties or personality factors, in particular impulsivity and hostile attitudes.

THE SPECIFIC CONTRIBUTION OF CLINICAL APPROACHES

There are three broad areas where clinical approaches to risk assessment are of paramount importance. First, a clinical approach is implicit in many of the psychometric measures detailed above. Thus clinical judgement is informed by and anchored within actuarially driven approaches to risk assessment.

Second, the aim of clinical approaches is to move from the general to the specific; to create an individualised account of offending which pays attention to the minutiae as well as the patterns of behaviour. The practitioner will seek to understand the situations which trigger problematic behaviours, and the cognitions and affects which mediate them. This involves an understanding of the meaning of the offence to the individual offender, and the way in which it regulates his sense of self in relation to the world around him. This is considered further in Chapter 7.

Third, the role of clinical approaches is to consider risk issues in individuals who have committed offences outside the norm, that is, offences with unusual features, or rare offences which are not captured by the broad sweep of actuarially based risk assessments. This is not an opportunity for clinicians to override or ignore the evidence-based literature on risk assessment, but to enhance mainstream approaches with a more individualised approach.

SUMMARY AND CONCLUSIONS

There is no single approach to the procedure of risk assessment that is superior over all others. However, there are key steps which can be approached sequentially to ensure that a comprehensive and defensible approach is adopted, one which is transparent, methodical and replicable.

- Gather as much corroborative information as is feasible and reasonable within the limitations of time and resources.

- An interview with the offender is usually necessary to provide meaning to the risk variables and to shape a risk management plan; however, extreme caution should be used in emphasising self-report and expressed attitudes in interview in comparison to the weight of 'factual' information available.

- Start with a consideration of diagnostic issues and/or psychological formulation; that is, understand the offence and the offender before being distracted by risk considerations.

- Chose your risk assessment tools with reference to their psychometric properties, their advantages and their limitations. Draw on the evidence base to guide your professional judgement.

- Start with a baseline assessment of static risk; know which risk grouping the offender falls into.

- Consider the dynamic risk factors and, in particular, pay attention to risk variables that appear within most of the dynamic risk tools.

- Ensure that you have differentiated between the likelihood of re-offending, concerns for the seriousness of victim impact and public interest concerns.

- Consider whether there are unusual features to the offender or the offence which give legitimate (evidence-based) cause to adjust the risk assessment.

- Develop a risk management plan that takes into account all of the above, prioritising: the highest risk factors and/or those factors most amenable to intervention.

- Always measure any change in relation to the original static baseline assessment; that is, demand more evidence of change in more areas of functioning for a high-risk than a low-risk offender.

REFERENCES

Abel, G. G., Mittleman, M., Becker, J., Rathner, J. and Rouleau, J. (1988) 'Predicting Child Molesters' Response to Treatment.' In R. A. Prentky and V. L. Quinsey (eds) *Annals of the New York Academy of Science.* New York, NY: New York Academy of Science, 223–235.

Alexander, M. (1999) 'Sexual offender treatment efficacy revisited.' *Sexual Abuse: A Journal of Research and Treatment 11,* 101–116.

Bard, L. A., Carter, D. L., Cerce, D. D., Knight, R. A., Rosenberg, R. and Schneider, B. (1987) 'A descriptive study of child molesters, development, clinical and criminal characteristics.' *Behavioral Sciences and the Law 5,* 203–220.

Beckett, R. and Fisher, D. (1994) 'Assessing victim empathy: a new measure.' 13th Annual Conference of the Association for the Treatment of Sexual Abusers (ATSA). San Francisco, CA, USA.

Beech, A. (1998) 'A psychometric typology of child abusers.' *International Journal of Offender Therapy and Comparative Criminology 42,* 319–339.

Beech, A., Fisher, D. and Beckett, R. (1999) *An Evaluation of the Prison Sex Offender Treatment Programme.* London: HMSO.

Boer, D., Hart. S., Kropp, P. and Webster, C. (1997) *Manual for the Sexual Violence Risk-20: Professional Guidelines for Assessing Risk of Sexual Violence.* Vancouver, BC: Institute against Family Violence.

Burt, M. (1980) 'Cultural myths and support for rape.' *Journal of Personality and Social Psychology 39,* 217–230.

Cann, J., Friendship, C. and Gozna, L. (2007) 'Assessing crossover in a sample of sex offenders with multiple victims.' *Legal and Criminological Psychology 12,* 149–163.

Cook, D., Fox, C., Weaver, C. and Rooth, F. (1991) 'The Berkeley Group: 10 years' experience of a group for non-violent sex offenders.' *British Journal of Psychiatry 158,* 238–243.

Craig, L. A., Beech, A. and Browne, K. D. (2006) 'Cross-validation of the risk matrix 2000 sexual and violent scales.' *Journal of Interpersonal Violence 21,* 5, 612–633.

Craissati, J. (1998) *Child Sexual Abusers: A Community Treatment Approach.* Hove: Psychology Press.

Craissati, J. (2004) *Managing High Risk Sex Offenders in the Community: A Psychological Approach.* Hove: Brunner–Routledge.

Craissati, J. and Beech, A. (2001) 'Attrition in a community treatment program for child sexual abusers.' *Journal of Interpersonal Violence 16,* 3, 205–221.

Craissati, J. and Beech, A. (2003) 'A review of dynamic variables and their relationship to risk prediction in sex offenders.' *Journal of Sexual Aggression 9*, 1, 41–55.

Craissati, J., Falla, S., McClurg, G. and Beech, A. (2002) 'Risk, reconviction rates and pro-offending attitudes for child molesters in a complete geographical area of London.' *Journal of Sexual Aggression 8*, 1, 22–38.

Craissati, J., McClurg, G. and Browne, K. (2002) 'Characteristics of perpetrators of child sexual abuse who have been sexually victimized as children.' *Sexual Abuse: A Journal of Research and Treatment 14*, 3, 225–239.

Davis, M. (1980) 'A multidimensional approach to individual differences in empathy.' *JSAS Catalog of Selected Documents in Psychology 10*, 85.

Elliott, M., Browne, K. and Kilcoyne, J. (1995) 'Child sexual abuse prevention: what offenders tell us.' *Child Abuse and Neglect 19*, 579–594.

Firestone, P., Bradford, J., McCoy, M., Greenberg, M., Curry, S. and Larose, M. (2000) 'Prediction of recidivism in extrafamilial child molesters based on court-related assessments.' *Sexual Abuse: A Journal of Research and Treatment 12*, 203–221.

Fisher, D. and Thornton, D. (1993) 'Assessing risk of reoffending in sexual offenders.' *Journal of Mental Health 2*, 105–117.

Fisher, D., Beech, A. and Browne, K. (1998) 'Locus of control and its relationship to treatment change and abuse history in child sexual abusers.' *Legal and Criminological Psychology 3*, 1–12.

Forth, A. and Kroner, D. (1995) The Factor Structure of the Revised Psychopathy Checklist with Incarcerated Rapists and Incest Offenders. Unpublished manuscript.

Furby, L., Weinrott, M. and Blackshaw, L. (1989) 'Sex offender recidivism: a review.' *Psychological Bulletin 105*, 3–30.

Glasser, M. (1998) 'On violence: a preliminary communication.' *International Journal of Psycho-Analysis 79*, 887–902.

Grubin, D. (1998) *Sex Offending Against Children: Understanding the Risk* (No. 99). London: Home Office.

Grubin, D. and Wingate, S. (1996) 'Sexual offence recidivism: prediction versus understanding.' *Criminal Behaviour and Mental Health 6*, 349–359.

Hanson, K. (2002) 'Recidivism and age: follow up data from 4,673 sexual offenders.' *Journal of Interpersonal Violence 17*, 1046–1062.

Hanson, K. (2006) 'Does Static-99 predict recidivism among older sexual offenders?' *Sexual Abuse: A Journal of Research and Treatment 18*, 343–356.

Hanson, K. and Bussiere, M. (1998) 'Predicting relapse: a meta-analysis of sexual offender recidivism studies.' *Journal of Consulting and Clinical Psychology 86*, 348–362.

Hanson, K. and Harris, A. (1998) *Dynamic Predictors of Sexual Recidivism*. Ottawa: Department of the Solicitor General of Canada.

Hanson, K. and Harris, A. (2000) *The Sex Offender Need Assessment Rating (SONAR): A Method For Measuring Change in Risk Levels*. Ottawa: Department of the Solicitor General of Canada.

Hanson, K. and Harris, A. J. R. (2001) 'A structured approach to evaluating change among sexual offenders.' *Sexual Abuse: A Journal of Research and Treatment 13*, 105–122.

Hanson, K. and Morton-Bourgon, K. (2004) *Predictors of Sexual Recidivism: An Updated Meta-Analysis*. Ottawa: Public Safety and Emergency Preparedness Canada.

Hanson, K. and Morton-Bourgon, K. (2007) *The Accuracy of Recidivism Risk Assessments for Sexual Offenders: A Meta-analysis.* Ottawa: Solicitor General of Canada.

Hanson, K. and Thornton, D. (1999) *Static 99: Improving Actuarial Risk Assessments for Sex Offenders.* Ottawa: Department of the Solicitor General of Canada.

Hanson, K. and Thornton, D. (2000) 'Improving risk assessments for sex offenders: a comparison of three actuarial scales.' *Law and Human Behaviour 24,* 119–136.

Hanson, R., Gordon, A., Harris, A., Marques, J., Murphy, W., Quinsey, V. *et al.* (2002) 'First report of the collaborative outcome data project on the effectiveness of psychological treatment for sex offenders.' *Sexual Abuse: A Journal of Research and Treatment 14,* 169–194.

Hare, R.D. (2003) *Hare Psychopathy Checklist – Revised* (PCL-R), Second edition. New York, USA and Newbury, UK: Multi-Health Systems Inc.

Harris, G. T., Rice, M. E. and Quinsey, V. L. (1993) 'Violent recidivism of mentally disordered offenders: the development of a statistical prediction instrument.' *Criminal Justice and Behaviour 20,* 313–335.

Hart, S. (2005) 'Dangerousness and Personality Disorder'. Paper presented at the International Conference on the Treatment and Management of Dangerous Offenders. Home Office and Department of Health, York.

Hart, S., Kropp, P., Laws, D., Klaver, J., Logan, C. and Watt, K. (2003) *The Risk for Sexual Violence Protocol (RSVP): Structured Professional Guidelines for Assessing Risk of Sexual Violence.* Vancouver, BC: Institute Against Family Violence.

Howitt, D. (1995) 'Pornography and the pedophile: is it criminogenic?' *Journal of Medical Psychology 68,* 15–27.

Lewis, P. (1991) *The Report of the Working Party on the Assessment and Treatment of Sex Offenders at Broadmoor Hospital.* Internal document.

Ly, L. and Howard, D. (2004) *Statistics of Mentally Disordered Offenders, 2003* (No. 16/04). London: Research Development and Statistics Directorate, Home Office.

MacCullough, M. J., Snowden, P. R., Wood, P. J. and Mills, H. E. (1983) 'Sadistic fantasy, sadistic behavior and offending behavior.' *British Journal of Psychiatry 143,* 20–29.

Marques, J. (1999) 'How to answer the question "Does sex offender treatment work?"' *Journal of Interpersonal Violence 14,* 437–451.

Marshall, W. L. (1993) 'The role of attachments, intimacy, and loneliness in the etiology and maintenance of sexual offending.' *Sexual and Marital Therapy 8,* 109–121.

McClurg, G. and Craissati, J. (1997) 'Public opinion and the sentencing of perpetrators of CSA.' *Journal of Sexual Aggression 3,* 30–34.

Murray, G., Briggs, D. and Davies, C. (1992) 'Psychopathic disordered/mentally ill, and mentally handicapped sex offenders: a comparative study.' *Medicine, Science and the Law 32,* 331–336.

Nowicki, S. (1976) *Adult Nowicki–Strickland Internal–External Locus of Control Scale.* Atlanta, GA: Department of Psychology, Emory University.

Overholser, C. and Beck, S. (1986) 'Multimethod assessment of rapists, child molesters, and three control groups on behavioural and psychological measures.' *Journal of Consulting and Clinical Psychology 54,* 682–687.

Quinsey, V. L., Lalumier, M., Rice, M. and Harris, G. (1995) 'Predicting Sexual Offenses.' In J. Campbell (ed.) *Assessing Dangerousness: Violence by Sexual Offenders, Batterers and Child Abusers.* Newbury Park, CA: Sage; 114–137.

Rice, M. and Harris, G. (1997) 'Cross-validation and extension of the violence risk appraisal guide for child molesters and rapists.' *Law and Human Behaviour 21*, 231–241.

Risk Management Authority. (2006) *Risk Assessment Tools Evaluation Directory*. Paisley: Risk Management Authority. Available at www.rmascotland.gov.uk, accessed on 15 November 2007.

Rosen, I. (1979) *Sexual Deviation*. London: Oxford University Press.

Sahota, K. and Chesterman, P. (1998) 'Sexual offending in the context of mental illness.' *Journal of Forensic Psychiatry and Psychology 9*, 267–280.

Seto, M. and Eke, A. (2005) 'The criminal histories and later offending of child pornography offenders.' *Sexual Abuse: A Journal of Research and Treatment 17*, 201–210.

Smallbone, S. W. and Dadds, M. R. (1998) 'Childhood attachment and adult attachment in incarcerated adult male sex offenders.' *Journal of Interpersonal Violence 13*, 555–573.

Street, R. (1998) *The Restricted Hospital Order: From Court to the Community* (No. 186). London: Research and Statistics Directorate Report, HMSO.

Thornton, D. (2002) 'Constructing and testing a framework for dynamic risk assessment.' *Sexual Abuse: A Journal of Research and Treatment 14*, 139–153.

Thornton, D. and Hanson, K. (1996) Do Sex Offenders Specialise in Particular Forms of Sexual Offence? Paper presented at the XXVIth International Conference of Psychology, Montreal.

Thornton, D., Mann, R., Webster, S., Blud, L., Travers, R., Friendship, C. *et al.* (2003) 'Distinguishing and combining risks for sexual and violent recidivism.' *Annals of the New York Academy of Science 989*, 225–235.

Ward, T., Hudson, S. M., Marshall, W. L. and Siegert, R. (1995) 'Attachment style and intimacy deficits in sexual offenders: a theoretical framework.' *Sexual Abuse: A Journal of Research and Treatment 7*, 317–335.

Webb, L., Craissati, J. and Keen, S. (2007) 'Characteristics of internet child pornography offenders: a comparison with child molesters.' *Sexual Abuse: A Journal of Research and Treatment 19*, 449–465.

Weeks, R. and Widom, C. (1998) 'Self-reports of early childhood victimization among incarcerated adult male felons.' *Journal of Interpersonal Violence 13*, 346–361.

3

Mental Disorder
and Sexual Offending

Andrew M. Aboud

INTRODUCTION

Most mentally disordered individuals do not sexually offend. However, high rates of personality disorder and certain mental illnesses have been found in populations that have offended (McElroy *et al.* 1999; Raymond *et al.* 1999). Mental health professionals, and in particular those working in forensic settings, frequently assess individuals with a mental disorder who have committed sexual offences or are thought to present a risk of doing so. Similarly, those working in criminal justice settings (such as court, prison and probation services) may request mental health assessment of sex offenders. Formulation, risk assessment and management planning are central components of this process, and should be based on a robust understanding of the relevant issues. Unfortunately empirical research regarding the associations between mental disorders and sexual offending has not been extensive. However, some of the theoretical models developed in relation to sex offenders in general may be applied to mentally disordered offenders, and may promote a better understanding of the relationship between disorder and offending. The purpose of this chapter is to shed light on this important area in a way that is useful to clinicians.

Mental disorder is a broad concept, and can include any condition listed in the *International Statistical Classification of Diseases and Related Health Problems* (10th edition) (ICD-10) (WHO 1994) or the *Diagnostic and Statistical Manual of Mental Disorders* (fourth edition) (DSM-IV) (APA 1994) diagnostic manuals. Although it is acknowledged that a range of mental disorders can potentially be found in individuals who sexually offend (e.g. organic brain disorder, learning disability, substance abuse disorders), this chapter focuses particularly on mental illness and personality disorder.

The relationship between mental disorders and sexual offending can sometimes seem unclear. The clinician must try to establish whether that relationship is direct and causal, whether the mental disorder lowers the threshold for offending (perhaps exacerbating it) or whether it is a coincidental occurrence. There may be treatment implications irrespective of the relationship, but the clinician must consider to what degree treatment of the mental disorder might modify the risk of re-offending, and to what extent other risk factors may need to be addressed.

PREVALENCE OF MENTAL DISORDER IN SEX OFFENDER POPULATIONS

Sexual offending and mental illness

Schizophrenia and other psychotic disorders do occur in sex offender populations, but possibly at rates no higher than in general criminal populations. In a study of 36 convicted sex offenders McElroy *et al.* (1999) found only one case of psychotic disorder. In a slightly larger retrospective study Curtin and Niveau (1998) found psychotic disorders in five per cent of offenders. This compares with a figure of 10 per cent for a 61 strong Australian prison population (Butler and Allnutt 2003). Wallace, Mullen and Burgess (2004) examined the pattern of criminal convictions in 2861 schizophrenic patients over a 25-year period, and found that the male patients were more than twice as likely than control subjects to be convicted of a sexual offence (1.8% versus 0.7%). Firestone *et al.* (1998) compared 48 homicidal sexual offenders with a group of incest offenders, finding much higher rates of psychosis (and also paraphilias, substance abuse and psychiatric comorbidity) in the study group.

Several researchers have specifically studied mentally ill sex offenders in terms of their mental state at the time of offending. Twenty patients in a medium secure unit were examined in this way retrospectively (Chesterman and Sahota 1998; Sahota and Chesterman 1998a). Twelve patients were considered to have been psychotic at the time. One patient had experienced command hallucinations and passivity phenomena. One-third had been suffering delusions and one-half paranoid ideation. Interestingly, only one patient gave his symptoms as an explanation or motivation for the offence. However, 90 per cent described irritability and some disturbance in cognition. Sixty per cent of the sample reported substance abuse, of which, for two-thirds, it was alcohol.

Craissati and Hodes (1992) studied 11 mentally ill sex offenders (of whom 10 had schizophrenia), finding that all had deteriorated mentally before offending, and this deterioration was primarily affective in nature (irritability, withdrawal, volatility or disinhibition). Around half of the subjects described a prominent sexual component to their mental state (increased sexual arousal and urge). Smith and Taylor (1999) examined the relationship between psychotic symptoms and offending in a group of schizophrenic sex offenders in a high-security hospital, concluding that, although the illness was relevant, a direct symptom relationship (or specific psychotic drive) was unusual. This finding was replicated in a secure hospital study of 15 schizophrenic men with sexual offending histories (Phillips et al. 1999).

Several studies have shown high rates of other Axis I psychiatric disorders in sex offender populations. McElroy et al. (1999) found a 97 per cent lifetime prevalence of 'any' Axis I disorder, with 78 per cent having three or more disorders. In a study of rapists (Hillbrand, Foster and Hirt 1990), two-thirds fulfilled criteria for alcohol abuse disorders and one-third for depressive disorder. Raymond et al. (1999) assessed psychiatric disorder in 45 paedophile offenders, finding high lifetime prevalence of mood disorders (67%), anxiety disorders (64%) and substance abuse disorders (60%).

High rates of anxiety, mood, alcohol and substance abuse disorders are seen in populations of individuals with paraphilias, with psychiatric comorbidity and the presence of multiple paraphilias being the norm (Kafka and Prentky 1994). Where present, abnormal sexual fantasies and interests may be associated with, or indeed drive, offending. It should be noted, however, that paraphilias are not uncommon in the non-offending population (Templeman and Stinnett 1991).

In summary:

- Psychotic disorders are not commonly seen in sex offender populations.

- Paraphilias and sexual offending are associated with elevated rates of mood, anxiety, alcohol abuse and substance abuse disorders.

- Comorbidity of psychiatric disorders is common.

- More serious offending may be associated with more severe psychopathology.

Sexual offending and personality disorder

It is not the case that all sex offenders suffer disorder of personality, though high rates are seen across various studies. McElroy *et al.* (1999) found that 94 per cent of their cohort had an Axis II disorder, with one-third meeting criteria for three or more personality disorders. The highest rates were associated with the Cluster B subtypes, namely antisocial (72%), borderline (42%) and narcissistic (17%). However, one-quarter of the study group fulfilled diagnostic criteria for a Cluster A disorder (i.e. paranoid or schizoid subtypes) and a similar proportion for a Cluster C disorder (i.e. anankastic, anxious/avoidant or dependent subtypes). Raymond *et al.* (1999) found lower rates of Axis II disorder (60%), with Cluster C variants (43%) being more common than Cluster B (33%) and Cluster A (18%). The most frequently occurring individual disorders were anankastic, antisocial, avoidant and narcissistic. Curtin and Niveau (1998) reported half their study group to be personality disordered, with the borderline subtype predominating. Such individuals are characterised by pervasive affective instability, poor impulse control, impairment of self-identity and a tendency towards engaging in unstable relationships associated with emotional crises underpinned by a fear of abandonment. This contrasts with antisocial personality disorder, which is hallmarked by a longstanding pattern of disregard for and violation of the rights of others and society's established norms.

These findings support previous evidence that every diagnosable personality disorder was represented in samples of rapists (Rosenberg 1981) and child molesters (Schneider 1981). Psychometric studies demonstrated the diversity of maladaptive personality traits among sexual offenders (Berner *et al.* 1992).

Proulx *et al.* (1994) suggested the particular blend of personality traits present was associated with the level of violence used during a sexual offence. Earlier work had already indicated that antisocial and hostile personality traits could lead to sexual coerciveness and sexual aggression (Malamuth *et al.* 1991). When Firestone *et al.* (1998) compared homicidal sex offenders to incest offenders, antisocial personality disorder was seen in half of the former yet only in four per cent of the latter. In the same study sadistic traits were seen in three-quarters of the study group but in only two per cent of the control subjects.

In summary:

- High rates of personality disorder are found in sex offender populations.

- All personality disorders are represented (not just Cluster B subtypes such as antisocial, borderline and narcissistic).

- It is likely that there is a relationship between personality traits and severity of offending.

RELATIONSHIP BETWEEN MENTAL DISORDER AND SEXUAL OFFENDING

Sahota and Chesterman (1998b) found that there were similarities in the psychosexual profiles of mentally ill and non-mentally ill sex offenders, with an apparent overlap in motivation to offend. In a subsequent paper (Sahota and Chesterman 1998a), the authors divided schizophrenic sex offenders into four groups: those where offending arose directly from delusions or hallucinations; those where offending was associated with features of illness such as heightened arousal, irritability or impaired cognitions; those where offending may have been related to negative symptoms of the illness such as emotional blunting, social withdrawal and impaired social skills; and those where offending was unrelated to illness. This is a useful start in ascertaining the significance of schizophrenia in an individual who has sexually offended. This section now considers theoretical concepts and models which help to understand how mental disorder in general can affect sexual offending. Of particular interest to the clinician is how the presence of a mental disorder might impact on an individual's risk for sexual offending.

Developmental concepts

As discussed in Chapter 1, issues related to adversity at key stages of the childhood developmental process have been implicated as part of the core aetiology in those who eventually offend sexually. The most important developmental factor cited is in relation to attachment, where erratic and rejecting parenting behaviours limit the individual's ability to form secure attachment bonds (Hanson and Bussiere 1998; Marshall 1989). These attachment problems can progress to difficulties in forming appropriate adult relationships (Hudson and Ward 1997). Although not equivocal, there is also some evidence to suggest that, for some individuals, their own experience of sexual victimisation may be significant in the development of later sexual offending against children (Craissati, McClurg and Browne 2002).

We could reasonably suggest that these developmental factors might predispose an individual to develop any number of mental disorders or disturbed behaviours. Equally, they might not lead to any maladaptive outcomes. The presence of these factors do not assure a causal pathway to sexual offending, but, rather, provide an understanding of the early experiences of many offenders.

Developmental concepts are useful in appreciating the role of attachment theory in the underlying aetiology of sexual offending. However, in the absence of a causal link, sexual offending and some mental disorders may simply have a shared aetiology.

Addictions model

Carnes (1983, 1990) argued that sexual activity could become an addictive behaviour, especially when the effect was one of regulating mood state. Marlatt (1985) described a model of relapse in addiction where lifestyle imbalance, urges and cravings played key roles in the pathway towards high-risk situations, and Pithers *et al.* (1983) developed the relapse prevention model specifically in relation to the treatment of sexual offending.

The addictions model highlights risk factors for sexual offending not dissimilar to the later-derived dynamic risk factors. Mental illnesses (such as affective disorders) and personality disorders can markedly affect such factors. The model also provides an understanding of the often compulsive nature of paraphilic behaviours.

Disinhibition theories

The relationship between mental disorder and sexual offending has often been considered in terms of disinhibition. Finkelhor and Araji (1986) described a theoretical model where 'disinhibiting factors' (alcoholism, psychosis, organicity or senility and mental retardation) circumvent normal behavioural controls, increasing the individual's probability of offending. Finkelhor (1984) expanded the concept of disinhibition to include any substance abuse, environmental disharmony, weakening of familial bonds, cultural influences, use of child pornography and poor impulse control.

Prentky, Cohen and Seghorn (1985) progressed this model by suggesting that these disinhibiting factors contributed to the relaxation of controls and allowed the expression of a 'pre-existing tendency' to engage in certain behaviours. Thus an individual was not considered at an increased risk of offending simply on account of his or her mental disorder.

A more dynamic model was proposed where 'motivation' to offend and 'disinhibitors' were balanced against 'inhibitors' (Schwartz 1988; Schwartz and Cellini 1995). A broader view of disinhibition was offered, including personal stress, peer pressure and lack of empathy and criminal thought processes, in addition to Finkelhor and Araji's (1986) disinhibiting factors. Inhibition was thought to act as a moderator for sexual aggression, especially when the motivation to offend was relatively low.

Hall and Hirschman (1991, 1992) described a four-component model where physiological sexual arousal was considered to be the motivating influence for offending. This motivation would then progress towards offending if influenced by cognitive distortions, affective dyscontrol and chronic personality difficulties.

Disinhibition theories are easily understood and allow for a broad conceptualisation of the relationship between mental disorders and sexual offending. However, if taken without reference to other models the described relationship is probably too simplistic. Nevertheless, clinicians have readily adopted such theories, appreciating that most mental illnesses and personality disorders (as well as organic brain disorders or learning disabilities) could act as acute or chronic disinhibitors.

Neurobiological models

Grubin (in press) reviewed the role of the hormone testosterone and the monoaminergic neurotransmitters, dopamine and serotonin, in the mediation of sexual arousal and behaviour. Their exact mechanisms of action are not fully understood. Testosterone is closely associated with levels of sexual interest and arousal, and is also thought to have an association with aggression and dominance among other influences. Dopamine pathways are thought to be 'activating' with respect to appetitive-type behaviours (including sexual arousal and behaviour), while serotonin pathways are thought to be primarily 'inhibitory' in nature (inhibiting mesolimbic dopamine release). Low serotonin levels have been implicated in depressive disorders, anxiety disorders, obsessive compulsive disorder, impulsive aggression and behavioural inhibition generally.

However, Grubin (in press) concluded that sexual behaviour was more than simply a manifestation of testosterone interacting with certain neurotransmitter systems in the central nervous system. It is influenced by a complex array of factors, including personality characteristics, learning experiences, social factors and the environment.

Neurobiological models aid our understanding of how balance of specific chemicals may underpin (or reflect) sexual interest, arousal and behaviour. The fact that certain neurotransmitter pathways are associated with both sexual behaviour as well as various psychiatric conditions may help explain the prevalence of certain mental disorders within sex offender populations. Nevertheless, given the array of other factors involved, and with an appreciation that the sexual offending itself represents a complex behavioural endpoint, one suggests that taken in isolation these models only provide partial understanding of the relationship between disorder and offending. At very least such models provide a basis and rationale for the use of certain medications as a component of sex offender treatment strategies.

Models based on risk-related variables

Actuarial instruments are probabilistic risk prediction tools which combine *historical* or *static* factors, such as age of offender and broad details of previous sexual and non-sexual offences. Examples of instruments in current use are the Risk Matrix 2000/S (Thornton *et al.* 2003) and the Static 99 (Hanson and Thornton 1999). Recently, aetiological models of sexual offending have been based on dynamic risk-related variables (e.g. Ward and Siegert's (2002) Pathways model). In order to understand the potential role of mental disorder in aetiology and risk management, it is necessary to briefly review the main dynamic risk factors discussed in detail in the previous chapter.

Hanson and Harris (1998) found evidence for key *stable dynamic variables* that related to risk for sexual offending, and listed these as intimacy deficits, attitudes, sexual self-regulation, general self-regulation and social influences. Thornton (2002) suggested that the main dynamic factors identified by researchers fell into four dynamic risk domains: sexual interests; distorted attitudes; socio-affective functioning; and self-management problems.

The *acute dynamic variables* are primarily related to the work of Hanson and Bussiere (1998), who found that substance abuse, negative mood, anger, hostility and opportunities for victim access were important in predicting 'when' an individual might re-offend, as opposed to their likelihood of re-offending. These items are captured in the Sex Offender Need Assessment Rating (SONAR) (Hanson and Harris 2000). Recent revisions of these variables have included collapse of social supports, increase in sexual preoccupations and increased propensity to reject supervision.

Unless a history of mental illness or personality disorder is specifically listed as an item in the actuarial instrument, it is likely that mental disorder, at most, only indirectly affects the *static* risk factors. However, the cognitions, emotions and behaviours manifest in more pervasive mental disorders (e.g. personality disorder, chronic mental illness, longstanding substance abuse, learning disability) would certainly affect items underpinning certain *stable dynamic* risk factors, such as emotional regulation and intimacy deficits. It is also clear that, for an individual who is mentally ill, some of the *acute dynamic* risk factors correlate closely with deteriorations in mental state, social circumstances and co-operation with treatment.

An integrated theoretical model

Beech and Ward (2004) developed a comprehensive model of sexual offending by integrating the potential aetiological factors with the known static and dynamic risk variables (Figure 3.1).

In this model the developmental factors are conceptualised as 'distal factors'. The static factors act as 'markers' for vulnerability. The stable dynamic factors denote psychological vulnerabilities, and are the surface representation of underlying traits. Taken together the stable dynamic factors incorporate the static factors and reflect 'trait factors'. Some of the acute dynamic factors can act as triggering events (or contextual risk factors), pushing the trait factors into 'state factors' (which are, in fact, a different cluster of acute dynamic factors). It is upon these state factors that the level of risk is based. The model thus provides a temporal picture showing risk variables affecting a pathway towards offending.

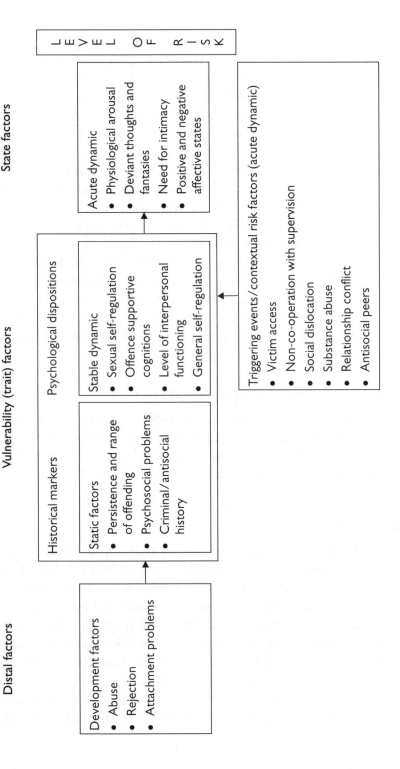

Figure 3.1 Aetiological model of risk (Beech and Ward 2004, reproduced with permission of Elsevier. Copyright © Elsevier 2004.)

Progressing the model

Beech and Ward's (2004) model may readily be progressed to an understanding of the impact of mental disorders on risk of sexual offending. It seems that trait factors relate to the 'likelihood' of re-offending, whereas state factors relate to the 'immediacy' (interfacing directly with the risk behaviour). Most mental disorders, in accordance with their specific symptoms and manifestations, have effects on both the trait and the state variables. It is likely that the more pervasive disorders (such as personality disorders, chronic mental illness, cognitive impairment or learning disability) would impact more heavily on the traits, while more acute conditions (e.g. hypomania or psychosis) would largely affect the state factors. In addition, disorders with childhood onset (such as conduct disorder, autistic spectrum disorders or learning disability) are likely initially to affect the distal factors, heightening vulnerability for parental rejection and attachment difficulties.

One suggestion is that the manner in which each symptom and manifestation of a mental disorder (or any stressor) impacts on each risk-related variable, in both the long and short terms, might further explain the mechanism underpinning the disinhibition theories.

Application of the model to hypothetical cases

In these examples consideration will primarily be given to the factors related to mental disorder. Case formulation and risk analysis must also take into account factors that do not relate to mental disorder, and these are discussed in more detail in the examples in Part II of this book.

CASE EXAMPLE 1

This is a 19-year-old man with diagnoses of mild learning disability and schizophrenic illness. He spent his childhood in a series of care homes, and demonstrated insecure attachment behaviours with occasional aggressive outbursts. Poor social skills left him with few friends and no intimate relationships. His psychotic disorder was first noted at age 18 years, and has been characterised by auditory hallucinations (running commentary), thought disorder, incongruity of affect and sexual disinhibition. He has no history of antisocial behaviour or previous offending.

Recently, when unwell with psychosis, he committed an act of indecent assault, by following a stranger adult female down an isolated lane, holding her from behind in a bear-hug, and rubbing his pelvis against her. When arrested he told police that he had hoped she would be his girlfriend.

The following risk-related variables appear to have been, at least in part, influenced by his mental disorders.

- *Distal factors*: His mild learning disability and history of being in care may have affected his ability to form secure childhood attachments.

- *Trait factors*: His learning disability may be related to vulnerability for low self-esteem, emotional loneliness and rehearsal of negative emotions. He has a history of poor aggression control. His developing schizophrenic illness probably affected his psychosocial functioning, level of interpersonal functioning and emotional self-management many years in advance of the actual onset of positive symptoms.

- *State factors*: His acute psychotic disturbance was associated with physiological arousal and affective instability, which may have heightened his need for intimacy.

Thus, having a learning disability probably played a role in the aetiology of this man's underlying vulnerability and, in combination with his developing schizophrenic illness, also increased his potential 'likelihood' of offending. When acutely psychotic, however, his risk of offending became more 'immediate'. Triggering factors may have included perceived social dislocation as well as victim access. Other factors that are highly likely to be relevant are his attitudes towards women and sex, as well as any underlying problems of general and sexual self-regulation.

CASE EXAMPLE 2

This is a 35-year-old man with diagnoses of mixed personality disorder (borderline and antisocial), harmful use of alcohol and recurrent depressive disorder. As a child he was physically and sexually abused by his stepfather. At that time he displayed evidence of mixed disorder of conduct and emotions. He developed a pattern of binge-drinking alcohol from his late adolescence. He has suffered several episodes of mild depression as an adult, primarily in relation to social difficulties. His four-year marriage has been fraught with frequent arguments and domestic violence. He has a long history of acquisitive offending.

Recently his 11-year-old stepdaughter disclosed that he had been sexually abusing her intermittently for a period of two years. In psychiatric interview he described a pattern of marital conflict, depressed mood and alcohol intoxication preceding offending behaviours.

The following risk-related variables appear to have been, at least in part, influenced by his mental disorders.

- *Distal factors*: His mixed disorder of conduct and emotions in childhood may have heightened his vulnerability for being victimised, rejected by his parents and forming poor attachments.

- *Trait factors*: His mixed personality disorder was associated with his persistent and diverse offending, psychosocial problems and criminal or antisocial history (static factors). His mixed personality disorder may also have been associated with his self-esteem, emotional loneliness, benign control and control of aggression. Similarly, his alcohol misuse will have affected his benign and aggressive control.

- *State factors*: His depressed mood and alcohol intoxication will have heightened his negative affective state, need for intimacy and possibly his physiological arousal.

Thus, having a mixed disorder of conduct and emotions in childhood probably played a role in the aetiology of this man's underlying vulnerability. His mixed personality disorder and alcohol misuse increased his overall potential 'likelihood' of offending. When depressed and intoxicated by alcohol, however, his risk of offending became more 'immediate'. Triggering factors may have included relationship conflict, substance misuse and victim access. Other relevant factors are likely to include intimacy deficits, distorted attitudes in relation to sexuality of children, as well as any underlying problems of general and sexual self-regulation.

The 'weather analogy'

Beech and Ward's (2004) model neatly lends itself to being conceived in terms of a straightforward analogy of the weather system (author's own), where the underlying developmental factors are represented by the 'climate', the trait variables by the 'weather', and the state variables by 'variations in the weather' (such as a storm) (see Figure 3.2). In this simple conception the damage inflicted by a storm on the environment represents a sexual offence.

Thus, if the climate is poor, the weather is more likely to be generally unfavourable and there may be frequent and dramatic variations in the weather, with occasional storms. Alternatively, it is possible, though unlikely, to experience a solitary storm which might never recur. At very least this would suggest something untoward in the underlying climate and weather.

The role of most mental disorders can be conceived as one of 'amplification' (or 'moderation') of both the weather and its variations. The more chronic and pervasive the disorder the more impact it will have on the weather; the more acute and florid the condition the more impact it will have on the variations in the weather.

ASSESSMENT

Assessment of an individual who has sexually offended, or behaved in a sexually inappropriate way, is discussed in detail in Chapter 7. Specialised mental health assessment of a sex offender might occur when a known offender is being screened for psychiatric disorder, or when a known psychiatric patient has committed a sexual offence, has engaged in inappropriate sexual behaviour, or is thought to present with a heightened risk of doing so. Assessment should always include a thorough evaluation of the offending behaviour in addition to assessment of the psychiatric condition. This should include exploration of cognitions, perceptions and fantasies (Sahota and Chesterman 1998b). It must encapsulate issues of diagnosis, an understanding of the relationship between the mental disorder and the sexual behaviour, a formulation of risk and a plan for management. Taking a thorough history, including psychosexual history, is imperative. Corroborative information from other sources (file, police records, family members, other healthcare professionals) is vital. Specialist psychometric assessment can be particularly informative, and employing standardised risk assessment instruments to account for both static and dynamic variables is recommended. Physical examination and associated clinical tests should not be neglected where indicated. Occasionally, referral for PPG should be considered. In the UK PPG is only available within specialist services such as the high-secure hospitals and sex offender treatment programmes in certain

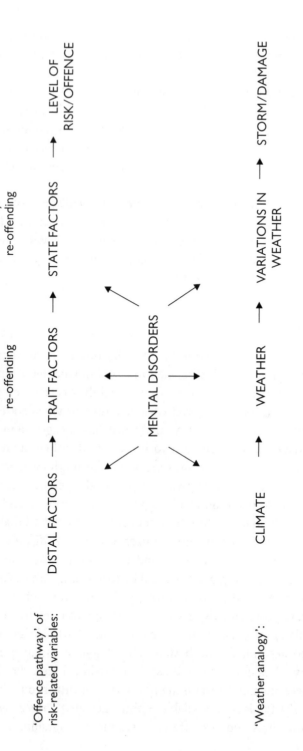

Figure 3.2 Theoretical model demonstrating the influence of mental disorder on the pathway to sexual offending

prisons (Gordon and Grubin 2004). PPG may usefully be employed to help offenders overcome denial in relation to areas of sexual interest and arousal. As in any clinical investigation, phallometry should only be undertaken voluntarily under conditions of appropriate informed consent.

Psychiatric disorders associated with higher rates of sexual offending are worth noting during assessment. These include the paraphilias, personality disorders, alcohol and substance misuse, organic brain disorder, learning disability, mood disorders where negative emotional states or, alternatively, sexual disinhibition are prominent, and psychotic disorders where positive symptoms link closely to inappropriate sexual thoughts and behaviour.

TREATMENT

As it is unusual for mental disorder alone to fully account for sexual offending, treatment should address the latter as well as the former, and this is specifically addressed in Chapter 8. However, understanding the relationship between the offending and the disorder is crucial, and will help direct treatment. In the case of mentally ill individuals, treatment will also involve the accepted therapies for those conditions (e.g. antidepressant medication for depression or neuroleptics for psychotic illness). In the acutely unwell, stabilisation of mental state will probably be necessary in order to enable the subject to meaningfully engage in psychological therapy. For the chronically unwell, cognitively impaired or learning disabled, standard offender therapies may need to be modified or adapted to accommodate the subject's individual needs.

There are, however, some medications that are thought to be useful in the treatment of sex offenders, often as an adjunct to psychological therapy. These include various psychotropic medications as well as the anti-libidinal medications.

Psychotropic medications

It has been suggested that paraphilic and non-paraphilic compulsive sexual behaviour may be related to imbalances in serotinergic pathways (Bradford 2001). There is growing, but still limited, evidence for the efficacy of selective serotonin reuptake inhibitors (SSRIs) in modifying these behaviours (Kafka 2000). Possible explanations of their mode of action include anti-obsessive, anti-impulsive, anxiolytic and anti-depressant effects. One explanation suggests that benefits are more likely to be achieved by pre-scribing the SSRI at a relatively high dose, such as that recommended in the treatment of obsessive-compulsive disorder or anxiety disorders. SSRIs may be particularly useful when obsessive-compulsion or impulsivity is a feature, when comorbid anxiety or depression is diagnosed, and also when the aim is to reduce deviant sexual interests while sparing the non-deviant interests. There is some limited evidence that tricyclic anti-depressants, such as lithium and buspirone, may also have some similar beneficial effects.

Sexual dysfunction is, of course, a not uncommon side-effect of many psychotropic medications. This is true for the SSRIs, tricyclic antidepres-sants, mood stabilisers and also for the various antipsychotic agents. Antipsychotic medications may be considered where symptoms of relevant mental illness are present, or where a more general reduction in arousal is sought (Grubin, in press).

Anti-libidinal hormonal medications

Anti-libidinal hormonal medications are thought to be particularly effective in reducing deviant sexual arousal, associated fantasies and frequency of sexual urge in subjects suffering hypersexuality or sexual deviancy, or both, whether paraphilic or non-paraphilic. Cyproterone acetate (CPA) is a testos-terone antagonist with progestogenic effects, and is widely used in Europe and Canada. Medroxyprogesterone acetate (MPA) is a progestational agent that reduces testosterone production, and is used in the USA where CPA is unavailable. Administration may be oral or by depot injection, though in the UK CPA may only be given as a depot injection on a named basis. Unfortu-nately, these medications have side-effect profiles that somewhat limit their use and certainly reduce compliance. CPA can lead to gynaecomastia, weight gain, general weakness, depression, osteoporosis, thrombo-embolism and liver damage, whereas MPA can cause lethargy, malaise, weight gain, nightmares, headaches, muscular cramps, diabetes and testicular atrophy. More recent research has shown that long-acting luteinis-ing hormone-releasing hormone (LHRH) or gonadotrophin-releasing hormone (GnRH) agonists, such as leuprolide, triptorelin and goserelin, may offer treatment options with more favourable side-effect profiles (Briken, Hill and Berner 2003).

There is robust evidence that recidivism rates in surgically castrated sex offenders was less than 10 per cent (Freund 1980), and in some studies as low as three per cent (Sturup 1972), with follow-up lasting for many years post-surgery. Findings for the chemical equivalent has been, at worst, inconclusive (White *et al.* 2005), but in general highly favourable (Krueger and Kaplan 2002; Maletzy and Field 2002; Rosler and Witztum 2000). It has proved difficult to conduct research on this population, owing to the untoward side-effects of the drugs and high drop-out rates. When compliance is achieved sexual recidivism is greatly reduced (APA 1999), with rates below five per cent cited in the literature (Grubin, 'in press'). It is important to remember that these treatments are invariably recommended for use in conjunction with appropriate psychological therapies, rather than on their own.

SUMMARY AND CONCLUSIONS

Sexual offending seems to represent a maladaptive cognitive/emotional/ behavioural solution to a complex interplay of distal and proximal bio-psycho-social issues, the seeds of which may have been planted at a key stage of the developmental process in a vulnerable individual. The influence of the mental disorders upon risk of sexual offending appears to be one of variable effect across this causal pathway, and thus affecting important risk-related variables. Most mental disorders are associated with changes in an individual's thoughts, emotions and behaviour, but are unlikely to represent the underlying offending drive. Clearly, it is the nature and degree of the symptoms and manifestations of the disorder that is relevant, rather than the actual psychiatric diagnosis. In a somewhat rhetorical generalisation the more chronic (and unfluctuating) disorders may be associated with longer-term influences on risk, whereas the more acute (and rapidly fluctuating) disorders may be associated with shorter-term influences on risk.

It is important to stress that it remains the responsibility of the assessing clinician to exercise professional judgement in deciding to what degree each symptom or manifestation of a particular mental disorder (or comorbid disorder) affects a particular individual at a particular point or period in time, and how it relates to the risk factors for offending. It is broadly recommended that efforts should be made to treat the mental disorder and also address the sexual offending. Careful exploration and understanding of the relationship between the offending and the disorder will inform whether a proposed treatment might also achieve risk reduction.

Treatment of the mental disorder may or may not reduce risk, depending on the relationship between the disorder and the offending. The clinician must decide which of the risk-related symptoms and manifestations of the mental disorder have been ameliorated by treatments. Wherever possible, of course, interventions should be employed to also address risk factors that are not associated with mental disorder. We must evaluate to what degree these treatments and interventions have led to a scenario where the risk presented by the individual can be safely managed (e.g. in the community; in conditions of lesser security; with only one escort and so on). It may be, however, that significant risk issues remain, whether or not associated with the mental disorder. Consideration should then be given to utilising other strategies such as closer supervision and monitoring, specialist sex offender therapies, multi-agency approaches and liaison with public protection agencies.

REFERENCES

American Psychiatric Association. (1994) *Diagnostic and Statistical Manual of Mental Disorders*, (fourth edition). Washington, DC: APA.

American Psychiatric Association. (1999) *Dangerous Sex Offenders: A Task Force Report.* Washington, DC: APA.

Beech, A. R. and Ward, T. (2004) 'The integration of etiology and risk in sex offenders: a theoretical framework.' *Aggression and Violent Behavior 10*, 31–63.

Berner, W., Berger, P., Gutierez, K., Jordan, B. and Berger, J. (1992) 'The role of personality disorder in the treatment of sexual offenders.' *Journal of Offender Rehabilitation 18*, 25–37.

Bradford, J. M. (2001) 'The neurobiology, neuropharmacology, and pharmacological treatment of the paraphilias and compulsive sexual behaviour.' *Canadian Journal of Psychiatry 46*, 26–33.

Briken, P., Hill, A. and Berner, W. (2003) 'Pharmacotherapy of paraphilias with long-acting agonists of luteinizing hormone-releasing hormone: a systematic review.' *Journal of Clinical Psychiatry 64*, 890–897.

Butler, T. and Allnutt, S. (2003) *Mental Illness among New South Wales' Prisoners.* Sydney: NSW Corrections Health Service.

Carnes, P. (1983) *Out of the Shadows: Understanding Sexual Addiction.* Minneapolis, MN: Comp Care Publications.

Carnes, P. (1990) 'Sexual Addiction.' In A. L. Horton (ed.) *The Incest Perpetrator.* Beverly Hills, CA: Sage.

Chesterman, P. and Sahota, K. (1998) 'Mentally ill sex offenders in a regional secure unit. I: psychopathology and motivation.' *Journal of Forensic Psychiatry 9*, 150–160.

Craissati, J. and Hodes, P. (1992) 'Mentally ill sex offenders: the experience of a regional secure unit.' *British Journal of Psychiatry 161*, 846–849.

Craissati, J., McClurg, G. and Browne, K. (2002) 'Characteristics of perpetrators of child sexual abuse who have been sexually victimized as children.' *Sexual Abuse: A Journal of Research and Treatment 14*, 225–239.

Curtin, F. and Niveau, G. (1998) 'Psychosocial profile of Swiss sexual offenders.' *Journal of Forensic Sciences 43*, 755–759.

Finkelhor, D. (1984) *Child Sexual Abuse: New Theory and Research.* New York, NY: Free Press.

Finkelhor, D. and Araji, S. (1986) 'Explanations of pedophilia: a four factor model.' *Journal of Sex Research 22*, 145–161.

Firestone, P., Bradford, J., Greenberg, D. and Larose, M. (1998) 'Homicidal sex offenders: psychological, phallometric and diagnostic features.' *Journal of the American Academy of Psychiatry and Law 26*, 537–552.

Freund, K. (1980) 'Therapeutic sex drive reduction.' *Acta Psychiatria Scandinavia 287*, 1–39.

Gordon, H. and Grubin, D. (2004) 'Psychiatric aspects of the assessment and treatment of sex offenders.' *Advances in Psychiatric Treatment 10*, 73–80.

Grubin, D. (in press) 'Medical Models and Interventions in Sexual Deviance.' In R. Laws and W. O'Donohoe (eds) *Sexual Deviance: Theory, Assessment and Treatment* (2nd edition). New York, NY: Guilford Press.

Hall, G. and Hirschman, R. (1991) 'Towards a theory of sexual aggression: a quadripartite model.' *Journal of Consulting and Clinical Psychology 59*, 662–669.

Hall, G. and Hirschman, R. (1992) 'Sexual aggression against children: a conceptual perspective on etiology.' *Criminal Justice and Behavior 19*, 8–23.

Hanson, R. K. and Bussiere, M. T. (1998) 'Predicting relapse: a meta-analysis of sexual offender recidivism studies.' *Journal of Consulting and Clinical Psychology 86*, 348–362.

Hanson, R. K. and Harris, A. (1998) *Dynamic Predictors of Sexual Recidivism.* Ontario: Department of the Solicitor General.

Hanson, R. K. and Harris, A. (2000) *The Sex Offender Need Assessment Rating (SONAR): A Method for Measuring Change in Risk Levels, User Report 1998–01.* Ontario: Department of the Solicitor General.

Hanson, R. K. and Thornton, D. (1999) *Static 99: Improving Actuarial Risk Assessments for Sex Offenders.* Ontario: Department of the Solicitor General.

Hillbrand, M., Foster, H. and Hirt, M. (1990) 'Rapists and child molesters: psychometric comparisons.' *Archives of Sexual Behavior 19*, 65–71.

Hudson, S. M. and Ward, T. (1997) 'Intimacy, loneliness and attachment styles in sexual offenders.' *Journal of Interpersonal Violence 12*, 323–339.

Kafka, M. P. (2000) 'Psychopharmacological treatment for nonparaphilic compulsive sexual behaviour.' *CNS Spectrums 5*, 49–59.

Kafka, M. P. and Prentky, R. A. (1994) 'Preliminary observations of DSM-III-R axis I comorbidity in men with paraphilias and paraphilia-related disorders.' *Journal of Clinical Psychiatry 55*, 481–487.

Krueger, R. B. and Kaplan, M. S. (2002) 'Behavioral and psychopharmacological treatment of the paraphilic and hypersexual disorders.' *Journal of Psychiatric Practice 8*, 21–32.

Malamuth, N. M., Sockloskie, R., Koss, M. P. and Tanaka, J. (1991) 'The characteristics of aggressors against women: testing a model using a national sample of college students.' *Journal of Consulting and Clinical Psychology 59*, 670–671.

Maletzy, B. M. and Field, G. (2002) 'The biological treatment of dangerous sexual offenders: a review and preliminary report of the Oregon pilot depo-Provera program.' *Aggression and Violent Behavior 8*, 391–412. ·

Marlatt, G. A. (1985) 'Relapse Prevention: Theoretical Rationale and Overview of the Model.' In G. A. Marlatt and J. R. Gordon (eds) *Relapse Prevention: Maintenance Strategies in the Treatment of Addictive Behaviors.* New York, NY: Guilford Press.

Marshall, W. L. (1989) 'Intimacy, loneliness and sexual offenders.' *Behaviour Research and Therapy 27*, 491–503.

McElroy, S. L., Soutullo, C. A., Taylor, P., Nelson, E. B. *et al.* (1999) 'Psychiatric features of 36 men convicted of sexual offenses.' *Journal of Clinical Psychiatry 60*, 414–420.

Phillips, S. L., Heads, T. C., Taylor, P. J. and Hill, M. (1999) 'Sexual offending and antisocial sexual behaviour among patients with schizophrenia.' *Journal of Clinical Psychiatry 60*, 170–175.

Pithers, W. D., Marques, J. K., Gibat, C. C. and Marlatt, G. A. (1983) 'Relapse Prevention with Sexual Aggressives: A Self-control Model of Treatment and Maintenance of Change.' In J. G. Greer and I. R. Stuart (eds) *The Sexual Aggressor: Current Perspectives on Treatment.* New York, NY: Van Nostrand Reinhold.

Prentky, R. A., Cohen, M. L. and Seghorn, T. K. (1985) 'Development of a rational taxonomy for the classification of sexual offenders: rapists.' *Bulletin of the American Academy of Psychiatry and the Law 13*, 39–70.

Proulx, J., Aubut, J., McKibben, A. and Cote, G. (1994) 'Penile responses of rapists and non-rapists to rape stimuli involving physical violence or humiliation.' *Archives of Sexual Behaviour 23*, 295–310.

Raymond, N. C., Coleman, E., Ohlerking, M. A., Christenson, G. A. and Miner, M. (1999) 'Psychiatric comorbidity in pedophilic sex offenders.' *American Journal of Psychiatry 156*, 786–788.

Rosenberg, R. (1981) 'An empirical determination of sexual offender subtypes.' In R. A. Prentky (Chair) *Assessment of Subtypes of Rapists and Pedophiles: Implications for Treatment.* Symposium presented at the meeting of the American Psychological Association, Los Angeles.

Rosler, A. and Witztum, E. (2000) 'Pharmacotherapy of paraphilias in the next millennium.' *Behavioral Sciences and the Law 18*, 43–56.

Sahota, K. and Chesterman, P. (1998a) 'Sexual offending in the context of mental illness.' *Journal of Forensic Psychiatry 9*, 267–280.

Sahota, K. and Chesterman, P. (1998b) 'Mentally ill sex offenders in a regional secure unit. II: cognitions, perceptions and fantasies.' *Journal of Forensic Psychiatry 9*, 161–172.

Schneider, B. (1981) 'Validation of sex offender subtypes through personality assessment.' In R. A. Prentky (Chair) *Assessment of Subtypes of Rapists and Pedophiles: Implications for Treatment.* Symposium presented at the meeting of the American Psychological Association, Los Angeles.

Schwartz, B. K. (1988) *A Practitioner's Handbook for Treating the Incarcerated Male Sex Offender.* Washington, DC: National Institute of Corrections, Department of Justice.

Schwartz, B. K. and Cellini, H. R. (eds). (1995) *The Sex Offender: Correction, Treatment, and Legal Practices.* Kingston, NJ: Civic Research Institute.

Smith, A. D. and Taylor, P. J. (1999) 'Serious sex offending against women by men with schizophrenia: relationship of illness and psychotic symptoms to offending.' *British Journal of Psychiatry 174*, 233–237.

Sturup, G. K. (1972) 'Castration: The Total Treatment.' In: H. P. L. Resnick and M. D. Wolfgang (eds), *Sexual Behaviors: Social, Clinical, and Legal Aspects.* Boston, MA: Little, Brown.

Templeman, T. L. and Stinnett, R. D. (1991) 'Patterns of sexual arousal and history in a "normal" sample of young men.' *Archives of Sexual Behavior 10*, 137–150.

Thornton, D. (2002) 'Constructing and testing a framework for dynamic risk assessment.' *Sexual Abuse: A Journal of Research and Treatment 14*, 139–153.

Thornton, D., Mann, R., Webster, S., Blud, L. *et al.* (2003) 'Distiguishing and combining risks for sexual and violent recidivism.' *Annals of the New York Academy of Sciences 989*, 225–235.

Wallace, C., Mullen, P. and Burgess, P. (2004) 'Criminal offending in schizophrenia over a 25 year period marked by deinstitutionalization and increased prevalence of comorbid substance abuse disorders.' *American Journal of Psychiatry 161*, 716–727.

Ward, T. and Siegert, R. J. (2002) 'Toward a comprehensive theory of child abuse: a theory knitting perspective.' *Psychology, Crime, and Law 8*, 319–351.

White, P., Bradley, C., Ferriter, M. and Hatzipetrou, L. (2005) 'Managements for people with disorders of sexual preference and for convicted sexual offenders (review).' Cochrane Collaboration: The Cochrane Library, Issue 4.

World Health Organization. (1994) *International Statistical Classification of Diseases and Related Health Problems* (10th edition). Geneva: WHO.

4

Sexual Offending

Ethnicity, Culture and Diversity Issues in Assessment and Management

Olumuyiwa J. Olumoroti

INTRODUCTION

Ethnicity and culture have not often been taken into account in previous sexuality-related research, unlike in non-sexual criminal offending, (Wiederman, Maynard and Fretz 1996). This increases the risk for overgeneralisation of results from research conducted with majority ethnicity samples to minority groups. There is evidence to suggest that different ethnic and cultural groups vary in their views of what constitutes sexual aggression and what to disclose, and deal differently with behaviours that others might consider sexually inappropriate (Alaggia 2001). These differences are rooted in different cultural beliefs and attitudes, and it is therefore important for clinicians to understand how cultural values and beliefs might affect the full range of responses to sexual offending (e.g. of mothers of sexually abused children), the factors contributing to those responses and the context in which the responses took place.

This chapter will consider the evidence for the prevalence of sexual offending among different ethnic and cultural groups, and will examine the available literature on the ethnic and cultural backgrounds of sex offenders. It will discuss factors contributing to sexual behaviour and offending in different groups, the attitude, practices and sanctions for sexually inappropriate behaviour in different cultures, factors affecting disclosure and the response to disclosures of sexual offending. It will examine the role of ethnicity and culture in child sexual abuse and rape, and concludes by commenting on the role of ethnicity, culture and other diversity issues in assessment and management of sex offenders and their victims. American literature and research findings have provided useful insight for this work and references to specific countries and cultures are made without any malice or prejudice. Major ethnic groups and cultures are largely referred to in this chapter and the reader's attention is drawn at this point to the heterogeneity that exists in individual ethnic categories, which should be borne in mind throughout.

DEFINITIONS

'Race', 'ethnicity' and 'culture' are used interchangeably by many people and are rarely defined in many articles. 'Race' refers to genetic heritage, at least in theory and is typically assigned based on biological traits that are presumed to be inherited and visibly evident to others (such as skin colour, hair texture and eyelid folds). 'Ethnicity', however, refers to cultural rather than genetic heritage. An ethnic group may be defined by its shared place of origin, history, language, religion, arts, cuisine and other factors. 'Culture' may be defined as a full range of human values, behaviour and social structure indigenous to specific groups that are passed on from one generation to the next. Culture is more than ethnicity and includes beliefs, values, religion, personal relationships, family life, sexuality and politics. Culture greatly influences whether certain beliefs, behaviours or symptoms are considered pathological or merely lie along the spectrum of normality. Culture is also important in the interaction between individuals and social systems such as law and medicine.

All societies have forms of sexual violence that are socially proscribed and others that are tolerated, or encouraged by social customs and norms. Sexual assaults vary in severity from molestation, which involves touching, stroking, fondling or grabbing of any part of the victim's body, through to rape where the victims suffer severe emotional trauma. Most societies condemn sex between adults and children, and forced sexual intercourse with an unmarried virgin. Some, however, openly accept forced sex within marriage or against women who are sexually experienced, passive or viewed as provocative. What are usually absent, surprisingly, from most cultural definitions of abuse are the volition, perception and feelings of the victim involved. The victim's perception of abuse is also influenced by cultural beliefs and values. Occasionally, the context of an act (who did what to whom and under what circumstances) is more important in defining what is more acceptable than the act itself or the effect on the victim. For instance, some individuals argue that there is no such thing as marital rape in their culture, and that marriage, by definition, grants men unrestricted sexual access to their wives. Others argue that women have a right to refuse unwanted sex regardless of what male-defined norms of marriage and culture might say. Unfortunately, the former position, which was the case in the USA until the late 1970s (Bennice and Resick 2003), continues to be the case in many parts of the world today.

DATA ON ETHNICITY

Within the literature on sex offending, details on the ethnicity of sex offenders are scarce, as is what type of offence a particular ethnic or cultural group commits. Such data, if not supported by very robust evidence, are likely to be subject of not only intense but also fierce criticism. In any case, and owing to under-reporting of sexual offending behaviour, such data are likely to be far from the truth. It has been found in a few studies that a disproportionate number of convicted child molesters in a men's prison population were white while a disproportionate number of rapists were black (West and Templer 1994). In addition, a disproportionate number of white inmates were child molesters, rapists and sex offenders. The reasons for the ethnic differences were not clear. The demographics of people referred to an outpatient SOS in south-west London over a six-year period (2001–2006) also revealed the majority to be white (77%), with seven per cent black Caribbean, four per cent black African, five per cent Asian Indian, five per cent Asian Pakistani and 'other' two per cent (including people whose information was not collected or who refused to assign an ethnicity to themselves) (Scoales and Houston 2006). When this figure is compared to the catchment area population for the London Boroughs of Wandsworth, Sutton, Richmond, Kingston and Merton: (white – 76%; black Caribbean – 2%; black African – 2%; Asian Indian – 3%; Asian Pakistani – 1%; and 'other' – 16%), although the proportion of white men referred was representative of the population, some of the specific ethnic minority groups were over-represented. The population in this sample was not categorised into offence types or child molesters versus rapists. The author is not aware of literature on the ethnic characteristics of people involved in, cautioned or convicted of internet sex offending, a growing worldwide problem.

CULTURAL CONSIDERATIONS IN SEXUAL BEHAVIOUR AND COERCION

Ethnicity and culture do not necessarily create a risk for sexually coercive behaviour but do affect how women are viewed in different cultures. The effect of race and ethnicity on psychiatric diagnosis and formulation could result from clinicians' different interpretations of behaviours, practices and symptoms exhibited in different ethnic groups. This may be especially true when clinicians are unfamiliar with the beliefs and practices of cultural minority groups. Most cultures include elements of patriarchy (of social organisation in which a male is the head of the family and descent, kinship and title are traced through the male line) and misogyny (relating to hatred of or having negative attitudes towards women) (Sanday 1997), but cultural groups also vary in the extent to which their behaviour is influenced by intrapersonal and interpersonal determinants. For example, European Americans tend to be more individualistic and less collectivistic than people of Chinese ancestry (Oyserman, Coon and Kemmelmeier 2002). Thus, the behaviour of a person of Chinese ancestry may be more influenced by how it might have an impact on group harmony than would the behaviour of a European American person, which may be more influenced by concerns about establishing independence from others.

People in particular ethnic groups may be relatively individualistic, for example Asian Americans. For relatively individualistic people, intrapersonal variables, including misogynous beliefs, are most directly associated with sexually coercive behaviour. For relatively collectivistic people, interpersonal variables, including concerns about the effects on one's social reputation of perpetrating sexual coercion, are most directly associated with sexually coercive behaviour. Being a member of a group is taken seriously in collectivist contexts and a pro-social reference group may discourage sexual coercion, whereas a misogynous reference group may encourage it. Moreover, many ethnic minority Americans are bi-cultural in that they are both individualistic and collectivistic. Individual beliefs that justify sexual coercion may outweigh concerns about the acceptability of inappropriate sexual behaviour towards others. Where independence is more valued, the individual is the main decider of whether or not to engage in a particular behaviour. Sexual coercion among bi-cultural people may therefore be influenced by both intrapersonal and interpersonal variables.

It has been suggested that misogynous beliefs (and negative attitudes towards women) are associated with men's sexual coercion against women (Malamuth et al. 1991, 1995). This has also been found as a risk factor for both European American and Asian American men (Hall, Teten and Sue 2003). However, the consideration of misogynous beliefs alone offers an incomplete explanation for Asian American men's sexual coercion. In addition to misogynous beliefs, loss of face, perceived effect of sexual coercion on one's reputation, number of sexual partners and alcohol use were components of Asian American men's sexual coercion. The study by Hall et al. (2003) also supports the view that European American men's sexual coercion is primarily a function of intrapersonal variables. Conversely, Asian American men's sexual coercion is a combination of intrapersonal variables (rape-myth acceptance, hostility towards women), interpersonal variables (loss of face, perceived effect of sexual coercion on one's reputation) and situational variables (availability of sexual partners, alcohol use). It was concluded that there are bi-cultural influences on Asian American sexual coercion, in that there was ethnic overlap in intrapersonal determinants, but ethnic specificity in interpersonal and situational determinants.

DISCLOSURE OF SEXUAL ASSAULTS AND RESPONSES

The definition of child sexual abuse varies from one place to another, depending on the culture, values and beliefs of the individuals in a community or society. Sub-cultures may define child and spouse abuse in varying ways and these would markedly affect the manner in which abuse can be effectively assessed and treated by professionals. Child sexual abuse may mean anything from child pornography to genital mutilations or sexual intercourse between a child and adult. One of the most widely referred definitions is that given by Schechter and Roberge (1976, pp. 127–142) which refers to the sexual exploitation of children as: 'the involvement of dependent, developmental immature children and adolescents in sexual activities that they do not fully comprehend, are unable to give informed consent to and that violate the social taboos or family roles.'

Cultural and sub-cultural factors can have a marked effect upon the reporting, assessment and treatment of abuse and family violence. The physical and sexual abuse of children within their own families is a culture-bound issue and sub-cultural variations create special problems related to assessing and intervening in intrafamilial abuse. Russell (1986) found that girls growing up in the company of stepfathers were seven times more likely to be sexually abused by their stepfathers than girls growing up in the company of a natural father. In many closely knit sub-cultures, in particular those with low population density, confidentiality is a major issue of concern. Intrafamilial child sexual abuse can continue because older people believe that nobody will tell. The initial determination of whether or not such abuse is identified as a problem, subsequent decisions about the actions that constitute sexual abuse, situations that excuse or mitigate abuse, and the types of interventions that are appropriate for the abusing family or victims are all made within the context of a specific group's attitudes, values and beliefs system.

People from black and white ethnic backgrounds are over-represented, and Asians are under-represented, relative to the ethnic or racial distribution in the prevalence of sexual abuse in different studies (Rao, DiClemente and Ponton 1992). Cultural differences in sexual restraint have been cited as one of the reasons. Meston, Trapnell and Gorzalka (1996) reported that Asian students were significantly more sexually conservative and less sexually experienced than their non-Asian counterparts. An alternative explanation is that people from Asian ethnic backgrounds are reluctant to report being sexually abused. In a study of sexual abuse among Asian refugees (Wong 1987) most participants stated that they would keep sexual abuse as a family secret for fear of blame and rejection by their communities. Asian American sexual coercion may not be considered as a serious problem because of the unwillingness to report sexual coercion to authorities and the low rates of arrests from such limited reporting. However, sexual coercion appears to be as serious a problem in Asian American communities as it is in European American men, with both groups reporting similar experience of the perpetration of sexual coercion on others (Hall *et al.* 2000).

AFRICAN AND OTHER DEVELOPING WORLDS

The impression that child sexual abuse does not occur in the traditional African society is a myth fostered by the sociological concept of the extended family as a system, which provides love, security and care to the child within the cultural milieu. Sexual abuse in these regions is often attributed to the 'forces of modernisation, foreign influence and rapid social change', although studies from a variety of countries suggest that child sexual abuse is an international problem (Lalor 2004). Recent concerns about commercial sexual exploitation of children in south-east Asia, Africa and other parts of the developing world has meant that the more pervasive sexual abuse of children in their own homes, neighbourhoods and communities, frequently in the hands of peers, teachers, parents and other relatives, has been neglected. Le Vine and Le Vine (1981), studying the Gusii in Kenya, observed the sexual molestation of girls at the hand of father figures. These authors also commented on the seduction of pubescent girls by male school teachers in Nigeria and Kenya. Intrafamilial child sexual abuse occurs in many parts of Africa and in most known cases of defilement the assailants were related to their victims. In most West African cultures the extended family tends to cover up such cases so as not to spoil the family's name. Some men from parts of West African sub-region believed that sex with a virgin could cleanse a man from infection and young girls have been infected with sexually transmitted diseases and HIV because of these practices (Meursing et al. 1995).

Of the 35 perpetrators of child sexual abuse identified in a study by Haffejee (1991), the majority, 23 (67%) were fathers, stepfathers and uncles. When the ethnicity breakdown was looked at, most of the perpetrators among a Malay population were fathers, uncles and cousins in that order. Among the Chinese, most perpetrators were fathers, whereas among Indians they were uncles and brothers-in-law. Some of these differences could be explained by socio-cultural factors. Among Indians, marriage between a maternal uncle and niece is allowed, irrespective of the age of the niece. Practices of this nature have allowed some maternal uncles to take advantage of their nieces by having a sexual relationship without marriage. Issues of this nature have caused difficulties in bringing cases to court whenever such a perpetrator is identified. A breakdown in the clan authority, a male-dominated social structure and different practices and beliefs are also partly to be blamed. For instance, it is appropriate to marry girls as young as 13 years old in certain cultures without this being considered as sexual abuse. Armstrong (1998) described the remedies enacted by families from the Shona tribe in Zimbabwe, to compensate for the rape of a girl-child. These include the payment of fines or marrying of the rapist and the victim in order to fulfil the girl's *lobola* (bride price). The economic consequences for the family are grave as a girl who has had sexual intercourse, whether consensual or not, has less chance of contracting a marriage that will contribute the lobola to the family. Of more concern is the report, although evidence is anecdotal, that some traditional healers in Zimbabwe advise clients seeking luck in farming, business or gambling to secure this by having sex with very young girls, often the client's own daughter (Meursing *et al.* 1995).

A culture in which sex is perceived as an activity where the woman gives and the man receives is likely to perpetuate impersonal sex and sexual exploitation in any society. Rajani and Kudrati (1996), who analysed the sexual behaviour of street children in Mwanza (a large city on the shores of Lake Victoria in Tanzania), noted that only five per cent of boys' and 15 per cent of girls' sexual behaviour could be described as 'stereotypical prostitution' (selling of sexual favours to external clients – people with whom the children had no prior relationship). More widespread was the initiation ritual of anal sex with new boys in the group, described as 'an important rite of passage in identity formation' and experienced by virtually all street boys in Mwanza. These street boys also initiate anal intercourse on one another, typically on a more docile boy for the relief of sexual tension and mutual 'comfort sex'.

For girls, sexual relations typically involve a degree of material gain or practical benefits, such as food, shelter and clothes. The girls typically adopt the stereotypical social role of women as sexual beings with a primary responsibility to satisfy one's male partner sexually. Their relationships have little mutuality, are frequently rough or violent and are characterised by power, intimidation and practical exchange. Unfortunately, these relationships may be perceived by these girls as 'family' or 'marriage' as a way to recreate the families they have lost or never had, explaining some of the apparently self-destructive behaviour of the street girls. Because the continuum between love and abuse is so blurred, and because they have very low self-esteem, street girls often accept violence and humiliation in the pursuit of love and connection. Alternatively, girls may pursue love in a cynical and calculated attempt to gain resources while continuing to think that the sexual experience needs to be 'something special'. This confusion often seriously undermines the ability of these girls to seek and create alternative healthy options. One particularly disturbing effect suggested by Rajani and Kudrati (1996) seems to be a complete numbing out – separating one's mind from one's body and being incapable of refusing sexual advances and the abuse of one's body.

CULTURE AND RELIGION

Cultural and religious influences have been noted to influence maternal responses to intrafamilial child abuse. Alaggia (2001) explored facets of maternal response and aspects of more or less supportive responses to children who were sexually abused by the mother's intimate partner. Cultural and religious influences affected how mothers made meaning of the sexual abuse and the actions they took. Mothers from cultural backgrounds which adhered to rigid patriarchal norms demonstrated intense value conflicts about family preservation, loyalty bind between the abusive partner and child victim, and anxieties around being alienated from their extended family and ethnic community. Cultural beliefs about preserving the family unit and value system conflicts between mothers and service providers were significant factors affecting how they understood the child sexual abuse and how they acted after their child's disclosure. Mothers who believed that they could support both the partner-perpetrator and the child victim maintained strong beliefs about forgiveness, sacrifice and redemption. These mothers were guardedly optimistic about the perpetrator's ability to change and viewed forgiving the perpetrator as a 'good Christian act'. This approach strikes some resemblance to the response by some churches to child sexual abuse perpetrated by clergymen and priests in many parts of the world.

Mothers who experienced intense loyalty issues between their children and partners expressed more adherences to patriarchal structures. For these mothers, separation or divorce was not a realistic outcome for their situation since their church and ethnic community did not accept divorce. The culturally embedded belief system was so strong that these mothers had enormous difficulties leaving their abusive partners under any circumstances, including intrafamilial child sexual abuse. These groups of mothers questioned the need for separation because of their desire to keep their families together and believed they could protect their children from re-abuse. When there were value system conflicts with service providers, mothers who were deemed less supportive by social providers felt misunderstood, judged and isolated. The more the service providers tried to highlight problems associated with mediating the competing needs of the child and the perpetrators, the more the mothers defended their positions. For the mothers who were very much influenced by their cultural and religious beliefs, tensions arose from divergent values about the institutions of marriage and attitudes towards divorce. These mothers wanted to focus on strategies for keeping their children safe in the context of re-uniting with their partners. This places enormous stress on women, who are put in the position of trying to keep the family together at all costs, or separating and suffering negative repercussions, thereby raising obvious questions for child protection.

Despite the prevalence of male dominance and abuse of male sexual power among those following all major and minor religions, no religion or social code of ethics condones or supports sexual violence. However, legal practices in some parts of the world have been subjected to scrutiny by some authors. In Pakistan, courts have ruled that testimonies of women of 'easy virtue' have less weight. To assess a woman's virtue the court uses, among other things, a finger test to see if her vagina accommodates two fingers easily. If so, sex is said to be habitual and a woman's testimony loses weight (Jahangir and Jilani 1990). Hadi (2003) cited one of the six sub-laws in Hadood Ordinance, (Government of Pakistan 1979) dealing with sexual offences. The law, which repealed the offence of rape to two offences, 'zina' and 'zina-bil-jabr' required the evidence of at least four Muslim male witnesses (whom the court is satisfied are faithful people who abstain from major sins), saying that they were eye witnesses to the act of penetration, necessary for the proof of the offence of 'zina' and 'zina-bil-jabr'. The consequence of this standard of proof according to Hadi (2003) is that scientific evidence and examination are totally ignored, with the cases being tried later for a lesser offence. Many scholars agree that the requirement of the four witnesses is a requirement by Islamic religion which cannot be disputed. As the punishment for the offences of 'zina' and 'zina-bil-jabr' is death by stoning, it has to be proved beyond doubt that a rape has occurred in order not to wrongly kill anyone. Fortunately, a recent Presidential Order (Government of Pakistan 2006) rectified some of the deficiencies contained in the 1979 Hadood Ordinance, and has now given more protection to women.

RAPE

Rape is an act of sexual violence that is deemed unacceptable in almost all ethnic and cultural groups, yet many of the behaviours that lead to rape are rooted in cultural myths, beliefs, attitudes, practices, interpretations and responses. The classification of rape as 'transgressive' or 'normative' in some literature (Heise, Moore and Toubia 1995) highlights some of these problems. Transgressive or non-normative rape is defined as 'illicit, uncondoned genital contact that is both against the will of the woman and in violation of social norms for expected behaviour'. This definition depicts the stereotypical rape that consists of a surprise attack on a virtuous woman. The wrongness of rape is determined not by the nature of the act committed but by the marital or moral status of the woman. Tolerated or normative rape is defined as 'genital contact that the female does not choose, but that is supported by social norms'. The authors added further that coercive sex is supported by social norms when 'there is no punishment of the male or only the female is punished; if the rape itself is condoned as a punishment of the female; if the genital contact is embedded in a cultural ritual such as an initiation ceremony, or when refusal is disapproved or punished by the community'. Cultural responses to rape frequently reflect the attitude that only women of good character deserve protection from rape. Heise *et al.* (1995) suggested that this notion is codified in certain Latin American countries, including Costa Rica, Ecuador and Guatemala, whose laws recognise rape of only honest and chaste women. This idea that rape only occur to 'honest' women may exist in more subtle ways in the UK when issues are played out in court on the history or sexual experience of a victim.

RAPE MYTHS AND THEIR IMPLICATIONS

Rape myths have been described as 'attitudes and beliefs that are generally false but are widely and persistently held and that serve to deny and justify male sexual aggression against women'. (Lonsway and Fitzgerald 1994, p. 134). Rape myths that encourage and support sexual assault also contribute to victims' reluctance to report rapes. People who accept rape myths are less likely to believe women who report being raped and are more likely to blame victims for the assault (Estrich 1987). One common rape myth is that 'real rapes' mirror those represented in the media (Estrich 1987), typically involving a woman who is walking alone at night when a stranger pulls her behind some bushes or into an alley, holds her at gun- or knife-point, and rapes her. Such rapes by strangers represent fewer than 25 per cent of all rapes (Matlin 1993), the remaining 75 per cent occurring between acquaintances. Most rapes occur indoors and do not involve the use of weapons.

Another myth alleges that the typical rape involves a black male rapist assaulting a white female (Epstein and Langenbaum 1994). The origin of that myth can be traced to the days of slavery when the rape of a black female slave by her white owner was ignored or condoned. In contrast, a black man, having sexual relations, even if consensual, with a white woman was severely punished and often executed. Unfortunately, vestiges of those reactions to rape remain. Black men accused of rape have received disproportionately severe punishment and black women have remained particularly vulnerable to rape by white men (Wriggens 1983). Most rapes involve people of the same race and the myth of the black rapist and the white victim continues to influence reactions to rape. White women who report being raped by black men are believed more often than those with white assailants. Black women reporting being raped are less likely to be believed by white women (Wyatt 1992) regardless of the perpetrator's race. Rape myths have serious implications for the legal system, with many victims reluctant to report rapes to the police because of concerns that the authorities will not believe them or, even worse, will blame them for the incident. Black women compared to white women are particularly reluctant to report a rape to the police (Feldman-Summers and Ashworth 1981), although all ethnic groups are likely to report the crime to hospital staff.

BLACK AND WHITE PERCEPTIONS OF INTER-RACIAL AND INTRARACIAL DATE RAPE

Race, gender and class have historically played a role in the definitions and consequences of rape. These inter-related systems have influenced societal perceptions of sexuality and, consequently, sexual relations. For example, diametrically opposed conceptions of women's sexuality were used to define black and white women during slavery. Compared with white women, who were perceived as pure, virtuous and disinterested in sex, black women were characterised as lascivious and sexually uninhibited (Getman 1984; Higginbotham 1992). An interesting finding in a US study (Varelas and Foley 1998) highlighted the different perceptions held by undergraduate psychology students (mostly females) who were asked to read a scenario describing an acquaintance rape in which the researchers varied the races of the victim and the perpetrator. The participants assessed the victims and perpetrators responsibility for the incident and reported their personal reactions to it. The white participants generally had more negative reactions to the rape than the black participants and were more likely than the black participants in thinking the incident was rape and that the victim should notify the authorities. They attributed more responsibility to the perpetrator and less to the victim than the black participants.

There was very limited support for the hypothesis that the respondents would attribute more responsibility to the perpetrator of a different race who raped a victim of their race. The white participants attributed less responsibility to a white woman raped by a black man than to a black woman raped by a black man. In contrast to the white participants, the black participants attributed the most responsibility to the black woman raped by a white man, much more than if she were raped by a black man. These data further support the perceptions of black women that they are not believed if they report being raped. The race of the perpetrator was a much more important predictor of the participants' reactions to the scenario than the race of the victim. If the perpetrator was a black man, the participants reacted more negatively than if the perpetrator was a white man, and they also attributed more responsibility to the perpetrator and less to the victim. This has implication for how the ethnic and cultural backgrounds of professionals (and jurors) may influence perception of what constitutes a rape or other sexual assaults.

GENERAL AND CULTURE-SPECIFIC FACTORS INFLUENCING REPORTING OF SEXUAL ASSAULTS

African American women report rape to the police and public services agencies less frequently than white women do (Feldman-Summers and Ashworth 1981; Kidd and Chayet 1984). Examination of barriers to reporting sexual assault is a critical component of post-assault recovery, and not reporting sexual assaults to police may have deleterious effects on survivors, assailants and the broader community. Women who do not report rape most likely will not be told about the support available to rape victims. Additionally, non-reporting reduces the prospect that offenders will be rehabilitated or imprisoned (or both) which may, in turn, enable them to re-offend (Bachman 1993). Lower reporting rates among African American rape survivors have been attributed to the strained relationship between the police and black communities nationally (Wyatt 1992). Several factors have also been found to affect a woman's perception of victimisation, including her relationship to the assailant, whether stranger or acquaintance

(Feldman-Summers and Ashworth 1981; Feldman-Summers and Norris 1984), the degree of force used, whether medical attention was received and the level of self-blame for the incident (Binder 1981). Fear of not being believed, being blamed or socially stigmatised also affect whether or not a woman reports a crime. The implication is that black women rape survivors may disclose rape less frequently because they do not perceive other African Americans as supportive of sexual assault victims. Perceived police insensitivity, in addition to the general distrust of the police, globally appears to contribute moderately to decisions not to report sexual assaults.

ACCESS AND SERVICE ISSUES

The predominantly white ethnicity of most samples in several studies reflects a more widespread problem in dealing with sexual offending. Black men who have sexually offended are over-represented in the UK prison population and this over-representation becomes greater in the longer sentence groups. Cowburn (1996) examines these facts in the context of white constructions of black sexuality, arguing that racist stereotypes about the predatory and dangerous nature of black male sexuality have pervaded Western clinical, police and judicial responses to sexual crimes for years. Such stereotyping (racism) may result in black sex offenders being given less opportunity to attend treatment facilities and their unwillingness to make use of what are overwhelmingly white-dominated services. Clinicians dealing with sex offenders should therefore give particular considerations to cultural and cross-cultural issues if some of the often insidious stereotypic prejudices, ways of thinking and cultural misperceptions are to be avoided.

ASSESSMENT AND ASSESSMENT TOOLS

The importance of cultural competency in sexual offending work cannot be overemphasised. Results in testing and assessments are subject to influences of language fluency, variability of verbal and visual concepts across cultures, the level of the subject's acculturation, the setting and the interpersonal process between the interviewer, clinicians and the subject. Cross-cultural evaluation of victims and perpetrators should put into consideration that reports of feelings about sexual traumas, depression, guilt and shame vary widely among different cultures and ethnic groups. Also, actuarial procedures for the assessment of recidivism in criminal offenders have become increasing popular. However, the promising predictive validity of some assessment tools may not generalise across offenders of different ethnicity, and migration status and co-variates of ethnicity may better explain different rates of offending. Even the 'Psychopathy Checklist – Revised' (PCL-R), a heavily weighted item in most risk assessment instruments, showed small differences in scores in individual items in whites and African Americans who have similar overall scores (Cooke, Kosson and Michie 2001).

Two of the most well-known actuarial tools for assessment of recidivism risk in sexual offenders are the Static-99 (Hanson and Thornton 1999, 2000) and its precursor, the Rapid Risk Assessment of Sexual Offense Recidivism (RRASOR) (Hanson 1997). Langstrom (2004), in a retrospective study of all adult men released from prison in Sweden between 1993 and 1997 with a sentence related to a sexual offence, found that both the RRASOR and the Static-99 exhibited moderate predictive accuracy for sexual reconvictions among Nordic and European offenders, whereas there was no association between the scores and sexual recidivism among African Asian offenders. When confounders were explored in offenders of African Asian descent by comparison of sociodemographic, criminological and psychiatric characteristics across ethnic groups, statistically significant differences emerged across ethnic sub-groups with the highest rating found in African Asian offenders. Compared to European offenders, African Asian offenders had more often sexually victimised a non-relative or stranger, had higher Static-99 scores, were younger, more often single and more often homeless. Although this finding emphasises the need for caution in the use of actuarial tools, the author also suggested that the differences might be more related to factors reflective of recent immigration from distant cultures rather than belonging to an ethnic group *per se*. It is therefore essential that psychological testing cross-culturally should be interpreted with great caution.

TREATMENT ISSUES

Even when offenders have had access to treatment and services, the need to consider cultural beliefs and values continue to be very relevant. The author is reminded of two important examples in clinical practice. A man in his late twenties was admitted into a medium-secure hospital following conviction for raping his ex-girlfriend. The diagnosis became an issue and there were different opinions on whether this man's behaviour was largely attributable to a personality disorder or mental illness, which was not clearly demonstrable at the time of the offence. The man's formative years were in Africa where he was conscripted into the army at the age of nine years to fight rebel soldiers attempting to overthrow the government. Soldiers from both sides perpetrated atrocities, including physical and sexual assaults and rapes. Unfortunately, sexual assault and rapes of girls and women were 'currencies' that different factions used to dominate, humiliate or even punish people belonging to other groups. The subject reported his initial reluctance to be involved with groups which carried out some of the atrocities, but rapes became regular features for which fighting soldiers were acknowledged and praised for their manliness and brutality. That was the 'culture' in which the subject grew up before fleeing 14 years of civil war. It was argued that his personality could not be considered as abnormal or largely contributory as the use of sexual violence was not out of keeping with the 'cultural beliefs and practices' of the environment in which this offender grew up. Others argued that the rape of his ex-girlfriend in a foreign land was a very serious crime and his culture should not be used to 'excuse' or 'justify' his heinous crime.

Another man was convicted of a sexual assault against a child. He was required as part of his treatment to consider hypothetically potential risky scenarios in his mind, in order to help him recognise situations when seemingly non-threatening contact with a child might lead to a risk of further sexual offending. The man refused to co-operate, citing that his religion forbade him to imagine potentially sinful acts in his mind and that doing that for the purpose of treatment was not acceptable. While this concern was taken seriously in this man, others argue that a convicted sex offender who did not consider that his religion forbade certain behaviour, such as sexual activities with a child, should not be allowed to cite his religion as an excuse to avoid treatment in which reference to avoiding future inappropriate or abusive sexual behaviour is part and parcel of overall therapy. Advancing cultural competence and taking culture into consideration are proposed in the assessment and treatment of child sexual abuse (Heras 1992), but respect for culture should not be allowed to compromise the ultimate goal of treatment which is voluntary, safe sexuality for all people.

SUMMARY AND CONCLUSIONS

In conclusion, understanding of ethnic and cultural factors that contribute to sexual offending is important in ensuring that clinicians adequately and sensitively deal with perpetrators in order to achieve the best outcome for all. There is a need to consider context in the prevention of sexual coercion, for example modifying misogynous beliefs, which is a basic element of prevention programmes. Modifying peer group influences may also be important in men who are concerned about their social standing. Cultural competence is necessary in handling cross-cultural issues particularly in intrafamilial abuses. We need to be mindful of the cultural and social realities of non-Western children and their families if more harm is to be prevented. Professionals need to remember that in many parts of the world organised legal and statutory services are lacking. Professionals therefore sometimes have to look beyond the legal and discipline-specific prescriptions in order to assess, understand and intervene in abuse situations in different cultural groups. The best outcome is likely to be achieved if treatment strategies are thoughtfully evaluated to fit within a sub-cultural context, while continuing to maintain ethical and legal principles essential to protecting abuse victims and restraining and helping abuse perpetrators.

ACKNOWLEDGEMENT

The author is grateful to many colleagues from other cultures who provided useful insights into cultural and religious practices other than his own.

REFERENCES

Alaggia, R. (2001) 'Cultural and religious influences in maternal response to intrafamilial child sexual abuse: charting new territory for research and treatment.' *Journal of Child Sexual Abuse 10*, 2, 41–60.

Armstrong, A. (1998) 'Consent and Compensation: The Sexual Abuse of Girls in Zimbabwe.' In W. Ncube (ed.) *Law, Culture, Tradition and Children's Rights in Eastern and Southern Africa.* Aldershot: Ashgate.

Bachman, R. (1993) 'Predicting the reporting of rape victimizations: have rape reforms made a difference?' *Criminal Justice and Behaviour 20*, 254–270.

Bennice, J. A. and Resick, P. A. (2003) 'Marital rape: history, research, and practice.' *Trauma, Violence, and Abuse 4*, 228–246.

Binder, R. L. (1981) 'Why women don't report sexual assault.' *Journal of Clinical Psychiatry 42*, 437–438.

Cooke, D. J., Kosson, D. S. and Michie, C. (2001) 'Psychopathy and ethnicity: structural, item and test generalisability of the Psychopathy Checklist – Revised (PCL-R) in Caucasian and African American participants.' *Psychological Assessments 13*, 531–542.

Cowburn, M. (1996) 'The black male sex offender in prison: images and issues.' *Journal of Sexual Aggression 2*, 2, 122–142.

Epstein, J. and Langenbaum, S. (1994) *The Criminal Justice and Community Response to Rape.* Washington, DC: US Department of Justice.

Estrich, S. (1987) *Real Rape.* Cambridge, MA: Harvard University Press.

Feldman-Summers, S. and Ashworth, C. D. (1981) 'Factors related to intentions to report a rape.' *Journal of Social Issues 37*, 53–70.

Feldman-Summers, S. and Norris, J. (1984) 'Differences between rape victims who report and those who do not report to a public agency.' *Journal of Applied Social Psychology 14*, 562–573.

Getman, K. (1984) 'Sexual control in the slaveholding South: the implementation and maintenance of a racial caste system.' *Harvard Women's Law Review 7*, 115–153.

Government of Pakistan. (1979) *Hadood Ordinance, including Shariat Laws.* Lahore: Kausar Brothers.

Government of Pakistan. (2006) 'Protection of Women (Criminal Laws Amendment) Bill.' Available at www.pakistani.org/pakistan/legislation/hudood.html, accessed on 4 February 2008.

Hadi, S. (2003) 'Womens rights in Pakistan: a forensic perspective.' *Medicine, Science and the Law 43*, 2, 148–152.

Haffejee, I. E. (1991) 'Sexual abuse of Indian (Asian) children in South Africa: first report in a community undergoing cultural change.' *Child Abuse and Neglect 15*, 147–151.

Hall, G. C. N., Sue, S., Narang, D. S. and Lilly, R. S. (2000) 'Culture specific models of mens' sexual coercion: intra- and interpersonal determinants.' *Cultural Diversity and Ethnic Minority Psychology 6*, 252–267.

Hall, G. C. N., Teten, A. L. and Sue, S. (2003) 'The cultural context of sexual aggression – Asian American and European American perpetrators.' *Annal of New York Academy of Science 989*, 131–143.

Hanson R. K. (1997) 'The Development of a Brief Actuarial Scale for Sexual Offending Recidivism.' *User Report No. 1997–04.* Ottawa, Canada: Department of the Solicitor General of Canada.

Hanson R. K. and Thornton, D. (1999) 'Static 99: Improving Actuarial Risk Assessments for Sex Offenders.' *User Report No. 1999–02.* Ottawa, Canada: Department of the Solicitor General of Canada.

Hanson R. K. and Thornton, D. (2000) 'Improving risk assessments for sex offenders: a comparison of three actuarial scales.' *Law and Human Behaviour 24*, 119–136.

Heise, L., Moore, K. and Toubia, N. (1995) 'Defining Coercion and Consent Cross Culturally.' *Siecus Report 24*, 2, 12–14.

Heras, P. (1992) 'Cultural considerations in the assessment and treatment of child sexual abuse.' *Journal of Child Sexual Abuse 1*, 3, 119, 124.

Higginbotham, E. B. (1992) 'African-American women's history and the metalanguage of race.' *Sign 17*, 251–274.

Jahangir, A. and Jilani, I. (1990) *A Divine Sanction?* Lahore: Rhota Books.

Kidd, R. F. and Chayet, E. F. (1984) 'Why do victims fail to report? The psychology of criminal victimization.' *Journal of Social Issues 14*, 39–50.

Lalor, K. (2004) 'Child sexual abuse in Tanzania and Kenya.' *Child Abuse and Neglect 28*, 833–844.

Langstrom, N. (2004) 'Accuracy of actuarial procedures for assessment of sex offender recidivism risk may vary across ethnicity.' *Sexual Abuse 16*, 2, 107–120.

Le Vine, S. and Le Vine, R. (1981) 'Child Abuse and Neglect in Sub-Saharan Africa.' In: J. Korbin (ed.) *Child Abuse and Neglect: Cross Cultural Perspectives.* Berkeley, CA: University of California Press.

Lonsway, K. A. and Fitzgerald, L. F. (1994) 'Rape myths: in review.' *Psychology of Women Quarterly 18*, 133–164.

Malamuth, N. M., Sockloskie, R. J., Koss, M. P. and Tanaka, J. S. (1991) 'Characteristics of aggressors against women: testing a model using a national sample of college students.' *Journal of Consulting and Clinical Psychology 59*, 670–681.

Malamuth, N. M., Sockloskie, R. J., Koss, M. P. and Tanaka, J. S. (1995) 'Using the confluence model of sexual coercion to predict mens conflict with women: a 10-year follow-up study.' *Journal of Personality and Social Psychology 6*, 353–369.

Matlin, M. (1993) *The Psychology of Women.* New York, NY: Holt, Rinehart & Winston.

Meston, C. M., Trapnell, P. D. and Gorzalka, B. B. (1996) 'Ethnic and gender differences in sexuality: variations in sexual behaviour between Asian and non-Asian university students.' *Archives of Sexual Behaviour 25*, 33–72.

Meursing, K., Vos, T., Coutinho, O., Moyo, M., Mpofu, S., Oneko, O. *et al.* (1995) 'Child sexual abuse in Matabeland, Zimbabwe.' *Social Sciences and Medicine 41*, 12, 1693–1704.

Oyserman, D., Coon, H. M. and Kemmelmeier, M. (2002) 'Rethinking individualism and collectivism: evaluation of theoretical assumptions and meta-analyses.' *Psychological Bulletin 128*, 3–72.

Rajani, R. and Kudrati, M. (1996) 'The Varieties of Sexual Experience of the Street Children of Mwanza, Tanzania.' In S. Zeidenstein and K. Moore (eds) *Learning about Sexuality: A Practical Beginning.* New York, NY: Population Council.

Rao, K., DiClemente, R. J. and Ponton, L. E. (1992) 'Child sexual abuse of Asians compared with other populations.' *Journal of the American Academy of Child and Adolescent Psychiatry 31*, 880–886.

Russell, D. (1986) *The Secret Trauma: Incest in the Lives of Girls and Women.* New York, NY: Basic Books.

Sanday, P. R. (1997) 'The Socio-cultural Context of Rape: A Cross-cultural Study.' In L. L. O'Toole and J. R. Schiffman (eds) *Gender Violence: Interdisciplinary Perspectives.* New York, NY: New York University Press.

Schechter, M. D. and Roberge, L. (1976) 'Sexual Exploitation.' In R. E. Helfer and C. H. Kempe (eds) *Child Abuse and Neglect, the Family and Community.* Cambridge, MA: Ballinger.

Scoales, M. and Houston, J. (2006) 'A descriptive study of personality disorder traits and offence-related factors in an outpatient sex offender sample.' Internal research report commissioned by the South West London and South East Region Forensic Consortium. Available from the second author.

Varelas, N. and Foley, L. (1998) 'Blacks' and Whites' perception of interracial and intraracial date rape.' *Journal of Social Psychology 138*, 3, 392–400.

West, J. and Templer, D. I. (1994) 'Child molestation, rape, and ethnicity.' *Psychological Reports 75*, (3 Pt 1) 1326.

Wiederman, M. W., Maynard, C. and Fretz, A. (1996) 'Ethnicity in 25 years of published sexuality research: 1971–1995.' *Journal of Sexual Research 33*, 339–342.

Wong, D. (1987) 'Preventing child sexual abuse among South-East Asian refugee families.' *Child Today 16*, 18–22.

Wriggens, J. (1983) 'Rape, racism and the law.' *Harvard Women's Law Journal 6*, 103–141.

Wyatt, G. E. (1992) 'The sociocultural context of African American and White American women's rape.' *Journal of Social Issues 48*, 77–91.

5

The Law and Sex Offending

Sarah Galloway and Sandra MacPhail

INTRODUCTION

Sex offending is often seen by the public as 'different' to other forms of offending, and sex crimes and their management have moved up the political agenda over the last decade. In 1997 a newly elected Labour government gave an undertaking to help victims of sexual crimes, given that the existing laws were outdated for modern society and technology, and, in 1999, the Sexual Offences Review began. The key difference seen in today's society is that the public now has greater understanding of sexual offending behaviour and media coverage of the subject is high fuelled by high-profile cases.

Intense media coverage of rare but notable cases of sexual murder, especially those involving child victims, such as Sarah Payne, Holly Wells and Jessica Chapman (in Soham) resulted in criticism of the criminal justice agencies.

Government officials have stated that tragedies of this kind 'should never happen again', but, unfortunately, a promise of absolute safety can never be delivered (Kemshall 2003). The government has responded to the message of absolute safety with increasing rigorous legislation in relation to dangerous and sexually violent offenders and has even commented, 'The risks to children from sexual abuse are now better understood than ever before' (Home Office 2004).

In June 2006, the Home Secretary commissioned a review of the management of child sex offenders, the premise being that serious child sex offenders should be in custody and remain there for as long as they pose a threat to the public.

This chapter provides an overview of the legislative framework and reflects upon it, it also discusses the challenges of an agency 'duty to co-operate' whilst acknowledging that different agencies have different thresholds and perspectives on issues such as disclosure. It will also evaluate how proposed changes in legislation which discloses convictions to potential partners, may work in practice.

MODELS OF LEGISLATION

In a review of the literature on serious, violent and sexual offenders Connelly and Williamson (2000) classified the introduction of legislation relating to sex offenders into two broadly defined models: the 'community protection model' and the 'clinical or therapeutic model'. These models are discussed below.

The community protection model

This model is most commonly in use in Australia, Canada, New Zealand and the USA where indeterminate sentences for serious sex offenders may be imposed. However, the USA is different from the other jurisdictions in that indeterminate sentence for sex offenders take the form of a civil commitment that is applied after the completion of a prison sentence. The legislation, which exists in different states, is of 'sexual predator' statutes.

In 1996 the Sex Offender Registration Act, commonly known as 'Megan's Law', was implemented in the USA. It allows the State discretion to establish the criteria for disclosure, but compels them to make private and personal information on registered sex offenders available to the public. The Act provides legal grounds to detain known sex offenders, claims that enactment of this law assists law-enforcement agencies in investigations and deters offenders from committing new offences. It also claims that the public can protect children from registered sex offenders. If these claims are to be achieved it is necessary for offenders to be known to their communities and to acknowledge that they are known and 'under watch' (Tewksbury 2005).

The Sex Offender Registration Act (1996) states that the amount of information that may be divulged depends on the level of risk of re-offending. For high-risk offenders a considerable amount of information is publicly available. This includes the offence, the 'modus operandi' and special conditions imposed by the court or parole board. The offender's exact address may be disclosed along with their photograph.

In Australia, Canada and New Zealand, indeterminate sentencing, similar to that used in the USA is available, although legislation in these countries does not make a distinction between sexual and non-sexual violent offences. The decision to impose an indeterminate sentence is made at the point of disposal for the index offence and not at the completion of the prison sentence as in the USA. Constitutional and human rights challenges to this legislation have highlighted that a system of regular review of detention is essential (Connelly and Williamson 2000).

The clinical or therapeutic model

Denmark, England, Germany, Switzerland, the Netherlands and Wales are described as having a more clinical approach to dangerous offenders, which is orientated away from punishment and public protection. In the Netherlands the 'TBS Order' (roughly translated as 'detention at Government's pleasure') provides for post-trial detention for treatment in a secure forensic mental health hospital and is regularly reviewed. If the offender does not wish to participate they will receive a normal prison sentence.

Germany also provides hospital detentions. The focus here is on 'dangerousness' and previous convictions rather than on illness. Surgical castration is available for sexual offenders, and indeterminate commitment, although rarely implemented, may be used for offenders who are dangerous and mentally unwell.

Switzerland provides preventative detention for serious personality-disordered offenders who have committed a serious sexual or violent offence. The detention is aimed at preventing future offending. The most serious offenders in Denmark receive a 'Dangerous Order' if there is evidence of future offending. The order lasts for a fixed period but can be renewable. In Denmark surgical castration has been replaced by chemical castration and psychotherapy.

England and Wales are considered to fit into the clinical model because of the availability of hospital orders and limitation directions for convicted offenders with a mental disorder. Sex offenders with mental health problems (mental illness or personality disorder) may be detained under the Mental Health Act 1983 in low-, medium- or high-secure forensic mental health hospitals. However, recent legislation identifies a shift towards the public protection model (Connelly and Williamson 2000) and at least 10 statutes have been established since 1991 (Brown 2005).

Internationally, a considerable number of offenders in receipt of inderterminate sentences or detention are sex offenders. Many countries have introduced legislation after a high-profile crime was committed by a recently released offender with a history of offending. Overall, there appears to be a move away from the emphasis on treatment and rehabilitation towards prioritising public safety, with a growth in new forms of indeterminate sentencing.

Each of the above jurisdictions are required to comply with the protections contained within their national equivalent of the European Convention on Human Rights. The position of the USA in this regard was outlined in the case of Kansas v Hendricks (1997), in which the Supreme Court approved the Kansas sexual predator statute. The Court's disposal of constitutional issues raised may only be interpreted as providing approval for the validity of a model of community protection within a country and for a legal system that is strongly founded on the principles of liberty and due process. In the European Convention on Human Rights the essential element appears to be the absence of inhuman treatment or punishment, which may, in Europe, affect the lawfulness of compulsory castration. The American model, whereby indeterminate sentencing is imposed after a prison sentence, is unique. If such a system existed in Europe it would probably be deemed to be in breach of European Convention on Human Rights legislation.

THE LEGISLATION IN ENGLAND AND WALES

The introduction of legislation that is relevant to sex offenders during the last decade includes the following Acts.

Sex Offender Act 1997

The Sex Offender Act (Home Office 1997) placed a duty on police services to establish and maintain a Violent and Sex Offender's Register. Sex offenders were required to inform the police of their name and addresses, and to provide any changes in these details. There was also a requirement between the police and the Probation Service to manage sex offenders via risk management panels.

Crime and Disorder Act 1998

The Crime and Disorder Act (Home Office 1998) introduced the sex offender order, a civil order. The police may apply to the Courts for a sexual offender order with evidence showing risk behaviours and prohibitions. These orders are not widely used. This Act also introduced extended supervision for up to 10 years for sexual offences.

Protection of Children Act 1999

The Protection of Children Act (DfES 1999) came into force in 2000 and established a list that places a duty on the Secretary of State to record the names of individuals unsuitable to work with children.

The Protection of Children Act 1999 criteria require organisations which work with children to check this list before employing staff and to make additions to the list for those candidates whose history make them unsuitable to work with children.

The Act ensures that any individuals included in the Protection of Children Act 1999 list are barred from working in child-care positions in the education area and are also included on 'List 99'. Employment has been defined as work which is paid or unpaid.

Criminal Justice and Court Services Act 2000

The Criminal Justice and Court Services Act (Home Office 2001) established the multi-agency public protection arrangements on a statutory basis and placed a duty on police and the probation services, as responsible authorities, to make arrangements for the assessment and management of the risk posed by sexual and other violent offenders. The Act placed a duty to consult with the victims of both violent and sexual offenders with sentences over 12 months. The multi-agency public protection panel framework and contact with victims are discussed in more detail later in this book.

It is an offence under the Criminal Justice and Court Services Act 2000 to both knowingly offer work or employ an individual in a 'regulated' position, or to place those who are subject to the Protection of Children Act 1999 list and List 99 in such positions.

Criminal Justice Act 2003

The Criminal Justice Act 2003 (Home Office 2003) included provisions for the Prison Service to be a responsible authority along with the police and the probation services. It also introduced direct public scrutiny of multi-agency public protection panel by requiring the Secretary of State to appoint two lay advisers to each of 42 strategic boards and placed a 'duty to co-operate' on a number of agencies:

- local authority housing, education and social services
- health service bodies
- job centres
- youth offending teams
- registered social landlords who accommodate multi-agency public protection panel offenders
- electronic monitoring providers.

Representatives from each of these agencies who have a 'duty to co-operate' should be people of sufficient standing and expertise to command respect and support of partner agencies and they must have a firm grasp of local operational issues. They need to have sufficient superiority within their agency to be able to make decisions on behalf of their organisation and be able to allocate resources to manage the risk where necessary.

Sexual Offences Act 2003

The Sexual Offences Act 2003 (Home Office 2003) was the first major overhaul of the sex offending legislation since 1956. It was intended to provide a comprehensive framework that reflected the current nature of sexual offending. It repealed all relevant legislation and re-introduced most of the provisions with improvements. As well as updating the list of sexual offences, the Act also reformed the sex offender registration legislation.

The Sexual Offences Act 2003 imposed more stringent requirements on sex offender registration, offenders having to inform police of a change in their notified details on the register within three days rather than the previous 14 days and having to provide their National Insurance number, and for all offenders to confirm their details on an annual basis even if there are no changes to them. The Act also introduced a number of new civil pre-ventative orders. In addition to statutory supervision and the imposition of conditions, the Courts could now impose civil orders (see below) which contain prohibitions to restrict the activities of certain sexual offenders. The Criminal Justice and Court Services Act 2000, together with the Criminal Justice Act 2003 and the Sexual Offences Act 2003 have extended the power of the courts to impose these orders upon sexual offenders who pose the highest risk to the public, recently eliminated discrimination by applying sexual offences to males and females of any sexual orientation.

The Sexual Offences Act 2003 clarified a number of definitions, and now 'consent' has a legal definition and children under the age of 13 cannot legally consent to sexual activity. The definition of rape has also expanded and now includes penetration of the vagina, anus or mouth. The Act created new offences protecting children from indecent text messages, and online and offline 'grooming'; that is, 'Communication with a child with an intention to meet and commit a sex offence'. It has also created new offences, with the objective of protecting people with mental disorders. All of these changes are designed to enhance community protection.

Safeguarding Vulnerable Groups Act 2006

The Safeguarding Vulnerable Groups Act 2006 (Home Office 2006a) was introduced after the Bichard Inquiry Report (2004), which found systematic failures in the vetting and barring systems. Some of the criticisms made by the Report were:

- inconsistencies between List 99, the Protection of Children Act 1999 list and the Protection of Vulnerable Adults list

- inconsistencies in police disclosure between police authorities

- barring systems based on harmful behaviour not preventative measures.

The Safeguarding Vulnerable Groups Act 2006 brought about a legislative framework for a new vetting and barring scheme for individuals working with children and vulnerable adults. The Act will be discussed later on in this chapter.

Mental Health Act 2007

Revising the mental health laws has caused significant controversy and subsequent reviews and as a result this process took nine years to become the Mental Health Act 2007 (DoH 2007). This Act made numerous changes, and the following list is a broad description of the changes.

- Removal of categories of mental disorder with new generic definition.

- Exclusions and principles in the application of the Mental Health Act 2007 – has removed 'promiscuity or other immoral conduct' and 'sexual deviancy'.

- The treatability test has been compromised with a replacement of 'treatment should be *likely* to improve condition'.

- Professional roles have changed with the introduction of non-medical practitioners who could be Section 12 approved and take on the registered medical practitioner role. The role would be assigned on competency not professional status.

- Safeguards for patients – a duty to provide advocacy for all detained patients, 'nearest-relative' status has been expanded and patients can now apply to legally displace their nearest relative.

- Supervised community treatment, which is a version of supervised discharge, requiring compliance with a treatment regimen and powers to recall on default.

CIVIL PREVENTATIVE ORDERS

Sexual Offences Prevention Order

A 'Sexual Offences Prevention Order' may be implemented at the time of conviction, or by the police submitting an application to a Magistrates or Crown Court under civil proceedings. The Sexual Offences Prevention Order is designed to include prohibitions to an individual's risk and will, and is exclusive to that offender. Prohibitions in a Sexual Offences Prevention Order could include the barring of an offender from entering school playgrounds or from visiting swimming baths and so on. A breach of a Sexual Offences Prevention Order is punishable with a maximum of five years' imprisonment, and the number of years a Sexual Offences Prevention Order lasts for may be specified.

Risk of Sexual Harm Order

The 'Risk of Sexual Harm Order' may be applied for by the police against any person thought to pose a risk to children under the age of 16 years. The defendant may not necessarily have a prior conviction for a sexual offence.

The courts can make an order if they are satisfied that it is necessary for the purpose of protecting either an individual child or children in general from the defendant.

Notification Order

A Notification Order is intended to protect the public in the UK from the risks posed by sex offenders who have been convicted or cautioned for sexual offences committed overseas. Offenders can be British citizens or foreign nationals who are resident in the UK. The Notification Order requires offenders to register their details with the police and, once implemented, carries sex offender registration requirements. An application for a Notification Order by the police is made to the Magistrates Court acting in its civil capacity.

Foreign Travel Order

A Foreign Travel Order is intended to prevent offenders with convictions for sexual offences against children from travelling abroad when there is evidence that they intend to commit sexual offences against children abroad.

Disqualification Order

The senior courts, for example the Crown Court, the Appeal Court, a court martial and its appeal court have the legislative authority to impose a Disqualification Order. Certain offenders, who have been convicted of a specific sexual offence against a child or of supplying Class A drugs to a child, may be eligible for the implementation of a Disqualification Order. This prevents an offender from working with children and includes baby-sitting or working as a schoolteacher, plus work in a local authority or social services department or voluntary work at a youth club. It also includes positions where supervision or management of others who are working directly with children, for example being a member of a school governing body.

The court must impose a Disqualification Order upon adult offenders unless it is satisfied that it is unlikely the offender will commit any further offences against a child and makes this statement in open Court. The Disqualification Order may be implemented for offenders under the age of 18 years at the discretion of the court. It applies for life; however, there is an appeals procedure.

ROLE OF THE INTERNET

For most people the internet has transformed their ability to access knowledge and improve communications. For others, whose behaviours are sexually inappropriate, it has facilitated a growing and sophisticated abuse system. The Sexual Offences Act 2003 (Home Office 2003) sought to protect children from online and offline 'grooming' by introducing new offences.

The government has continued to target abuse via the internet and has proposed legislation in its Criminal and Immigration Bill Ministry of Justice (2007) to tackle extreme pornography carrying a three-year custodial sentence.

The Criminal and Immigration Bill will ensure that pornographic images will be illegal on- or offline, and will include those images which contain not only photographs but realistic pictures. Such material is currently illegal under the Obscene Publications Act (1964), but the Criminal and Immigration Bill will now include possession.

MULTI-AGENCY PUBLIC PROTECTION ARRANGEMENTS

Following a number of high profile serious offences The Criminal Justice and Court Services Act 2000 (Home Office 2001) led to the formation of the multi-agency public protection panel and placed them on a statutory basis. The Criminal Justice Act 2003 (Home Office 2003) subsequently re-enacted and strengthened these provisions. The legislation requires the police, probation and prison services acting as the 'responsible authority' in each of 42 areas in England and Wales to:

- establish arrangements for assessing and managing the risks posed by sexual and violent offenders

- review and monitor the arrangements and, as part of the reviewing and monitoring arrangements, prepare and publish an annual report on their operation.

The multi-agency public protection panel now have 42 strategic management boards, which are composed of senior managers from the relevant agencies that have a 'duty to co-operate' with as a result of legislation in the Criminal Justice Act 2003 (Home Office 2003). Direct public scrutiny of the multi-agency public protection panel is present in the role of two lay advisers, who are intended to bring an ordinary person's perspective to each of the strategic management boards. These advisers are recruited locally and appointed by the Secretary of State. Their role is to ask fundamental questions of the senior representatives of the agencies and to bring a community perspective to a process which could lose sight of its main function: to protect members of the public from serious harm.

The strategic management boards are responsible for monitoring and reviewing the multi-agency public protection panel and for ensuring that risk assessment and management arrangements are reviewed and revised to reflect changes in legislation and criminal justice. They have a statutory responsibility to publish an annual report on the progress of the multi-agency public protection panel. The local criminal justice board continues to oversee the multi-agency public protection panel and has a role in receiving and approving the annual report from the Strategic Management Board.

The multi-agency public protection panel framework

The multi-agency public protection panel is underpinned by a responsibility to victims and the enhancement of public safety. They have four core functions, which are dynamic and overlap:

- identification of offenders who fit the multi-agency public protection panel profile
- sharing relevant information among agencies involved in risk assessment
- assessment of the risk of serious harm
- management of that risk.

Multi-agency public protection panel co-ordination requires:

- systemic co-ordination for coherence and contribution to public protection
- good administrative arrangements to maintain records of referral or management
- co-ordination of different levels of managements, such as multi-agency public protection panel and local risk management arrangements
- provision of data and support to the strategic management board.

The criteria for inclusion or categories of offenders subject to multi-agency public protection panel are divided into three categories.

Category 1

Registered sex offenders and those under a hospital order or guardianship order under the Mental Health Act 1983 (DoH 1983).

Category 2

Offenders on licence for a sexual or violent offence for which they have received sentence of imprisonment of 12 months or more.

Category 3

There are two considerations to be included under this category:

- conviction for an offence which indicates the offender is capable of causing serious harm
- the responsible authority must reasonably consider that the offender may cause serious harm.

Certain sexual and violent offenders are automatically included in categories 1 and 2 by virtue of their registration on the Sex Offenders Register or the length of their custodial sentence. Other offenders, identified by previous offending behaviour and assessed because of current behaviour, may be included under Category 3. They can be identified and referred by any agency and often provide the most significant challenge to ensuring their inclusion in the multi-agency public protection panel.

Police now also have access to the Violent and Sexual Offenders Register, to the Cross Regional Information Sharing Project and to the Impact Nominal Index. This access allows police forces to exchange information on 'known' offenders and is accessible 24 hours a day 365 days a year. It is used by all police forces throughout the UK.

MANAGING RISK

Managing the risk that is presented by an offender who is referred under the multi-agency public protection panel is assessed under three levels.

Level 1 (ordinary risk management)

This level includes individuals whose level of risk can be managed by a single agency without actively or significantly involving other agencies (and is only applicable to categories 1 and 2 offenders). Usually, these individuals will be monitored by either the police or probation service.

Level 2 (multi-agency)

This involves local inter-agency risk management, where the active involvement of more than one agency is required, but the offender does not present so great a risk as to warrant referral to the multi-agency public protection panel. These arrangements, known formally as risk management panels, include a permanent membership of local agencies that have an active role in risk and management, such as the police, social services, housing and health departments.

Level 3 (a critical few)

This level involves a small number of offenders 'the critical few' who are a major risk to public safety and who are subject to the management of the multi-agency public protection panel. This level of risk management involves case management, sharing information, discussing confidentiality issues and devising risk management plans. There is also a responsibility to monitor and review offenders under its remit. Kemshall (2003) identified public protection as depending upon:

- defensible decisions
- rigorous risk assessment
- the delivery of risk management plans that match the identified public protection need
- evaluation of performance to improve delivery.

Kemshall (2003) also suggests that multi-agency public protection panel represent a strengthening of public protection and provide effective risk management. This should not be understood as 'zero risk' as this position can never be reached because 30 per cent of serious sexual offenders had no previous convictions. Risk management should be understood as 'harm reduction', either through the reduction of the likelihood of a risk occurring or through the reduction of its effect should it occur. Risk assessment is not infallible and in its place we must put defensibility – making the most reasonable decisions and carrying them out professionally in a way, that may be seen as reasonable and professional.

Kemshall (2003) summarised the criteria for a defensible decision as:

- all reasonable steps have been taken
- reliable assessment methods have been used
- information has been collected 'and thoroughly evaluated'
- decisions are recorded (and subsequently carried out)
- policies and procedures have been followed
- practitioners and their managers adopt an investigative approach and are pro-active.

NATIONAL SEXUAL OFFENCES STATISTICS

The total number of sexual offences recorded in England and Wales in the year ending March 2006, was 62,081 (Home Office 2005/2006). This figure shows a 17 per cent rise since the years 2003/2004. It is unclear whether this increase had been caused by an increase in actual offences or because more offences are being reported.

The multi-agency public protection panel is currently monitoring 48,000 offenders in England and Wales. There are 30,000 sex offenders on the Sex Offenders Register. In London less than one per cent of offenders are rated at Level 3. The number of sex offenders has increased by four per cent in the last year. This increase was foreseen as the length of sentence or disposal fixes the length of time offenders remain on the Sex Offenders Register. The registration requirement varies between five years and life, therefore the number of registered sex offenders is cumulative.

INFORMATION-SHARING AND DISCLOSURE AND CONFIDENTIALITY

The 'duty to co-operate' required of the agencies involved in the multi-agency public protection panel process is a key element in their function. Each agency involved will have its own criteria or policies for disclosure and confidentiality of information. The duty to co-operate should improve sharing of information and, as a result, improve interpretations and analysis of information.

Crucial to information-sharing are necessity and proportionality. The *necessity* criterion requires that there is a 'pressing need'. The *proportionality* criterion requires that the information shared must be only that necessary to achieve the purpose for which it is being shared. Information-sharing must have lawful authority, be necessarily proportionate and be done in ways that ensure the safety and security of the information shared; it must be accountable and information should not be held for longer than is necessary.

When an offender is referred to the multi-agency public protection panel consent is obtained, whenever possible, for information to be sought and shared. Consent is not always given and this situation can present a dilemma for agencies with a duty to co-operate, especially mental health trusts, as this agent will involve mentally disordered offenders residing both in hospital and the community.

'Sharing' information may cause particular dilemmas for professionals, as information is often gained during the course of a sensitive and delicate therapeutic relationship. Professionals need to balance the duty to co-operate and the requirement to share information, whilst maintaining a therapeutic relationship which may be jeopardised if the patient feels he or she cannot trust the clinician; this, in turn, may increase potential risk if the relationship is terminated.

There are benefits for mental health trusts in co-operating in the multi-agency public protection panel with patients, as the arrangements annual report summarises:

- a source of information about patients
- a conduit and framework for joint working
- a useful source of advice on the appropriacy and implications of various medical treatments and interventions
- help in the management of risk in complex cases.

Disclosure

The multi-agency public protection panel guidance (Home Office 2003), together with a Royal College of Psychiatrists (2000) publication, states several situations in which patient information may be passed on without consent, these include:

- where serious harm may occur to a third party
- where a doctor believes a patient to be a victim of abuse and the patient is unable to give or withhold consent
- where, without disclosure a doctor would not be acting in the overall best interests of a child or young person who is his or her patient and incapable of giving consent when, without disclosure, the task of preventing, detecting or prosecuting a serious crime by the police would be prejudiced or delayed.

Good practice requires that personal information is obtained and processed fairly and lawfully; is only disclosed or shared in appropriate circumstances; is accurate, relevant and not held for any longer than is necessary; and is kept securely (Data Protection Act 1998).

Information-sharing must have lawful authority, be necessarily proportionate and done in ways that ensure the safety and security of the information shared and are accountable.

If disclosure happens it must be:

- an exceptional measure
- part of a risk management plan for levels 2 and 3 of the multi-agency public protection panel
- meet the proportionality requirement and criteria such as no other practicable means of protection or failure to disclose would put a person in danger.

EDUCATION

Legislation relating to the protection of children in the education sector dates back to 1926. Over the years subsequent legislation has resulted in the introduction of what has been called 'List 99'. This list contains information about individuals who are barred or restricted from providing education (including voluntary work) that involves contact with children under 18 years of age in a school, a local education authority or further educational institutions after a direction made by the Secretary of State, under Section 142 of the Education Act 2002. In March 2007 the Department for Education and Skills (DfES) estimated that there were almost 5000 names on List 99, of which the vast majority are barred from working with children indefinitely.

List 99 is maintained by the DfES, (now known as the Department for Children, Schools and Families [DfCSF]), and is separate from the Sex Offenders Register, which is maintained by the criminal justice agencies. As a result of concerns, including lack of communication between agencies and media coverage of a small number of serious sexual offenders against children, the Office for Standards in Education (OFSTED), in collaboration with the DfES, published a report, *Safeguarding Children: An Evaluation of the Procedures for Checking Staff Appointed by Schools,* in 2006. In essence, this report identified that more needed to be done to ensure that schools, colleges and local authorities kept proper records of all List 99 and Criminal Records Bureau (CRB) checks on potential staff.

The Safeguarding Vulnerable Groups Act 2006 (Home Office 2006) introduces a new vetting and barring scheme that will significantly strengthen safeguarding children. The Act provides for a central vetting process based on the CRB checks. It will combine List 99 and the Protection of Children Act 1999 (DfES 1999) lists into a single list to form the Independent Barring Board (IBB), which will come into force in late 2008. The IBB will be responsible for making decisions about barring individuals from working in contact with children which previously had been the responsibility of ministers.

The IBB will expand the scope of List 99 by automatically including anyone convicted or cautioned of a sexual offence against a child, as well as those convicted of serious sexual offences against adults.

Sir Michael Bichard, who headed the review prompted by the Soham murders (Bichard Inquiry Report 2004) stated that the new register: 'will not guarantee that all unsuitable people are prevented from working with children but it should ensure that no one about whom relevant intelligence is held be able to "slip through the net" in the future'.

VICTIMS

The Sexual Offences Act (Home Office 2003) puts victims first. It reflects the reality of life in the 21st Century and sets out clear boundaries about what is and is not acceptable. (Home Office 2004)

The Sexual Offences Act 2003 (Home Office 2003) attempts to address the gap between actual offences, reported crimes and conviction rates by making a number of provisions to support victims. The Act will allow evidence to be given for some victims via remote links, consultation before offenders' release and specialist rape prosecutors.

The Criminal Justice and Court Services Act 2000 (Home Office 2001) places a statutory duty upon probation boards to consult and notify victims about the release arrangements of offenders serving a sentence of 12 months or more for a serious violent or sexual offence. The Domestic Violence, Crime and Victims Act 2004 (Home Office 2004) extended this duty to the victims of mentally disordered offenders where the offender is subject to a hospital order with restrictions (MHA 1983 S.37/41) for a serious violent or sexual offence.

Probation staff gather information from victims about their concerns relating to the release from prison or hospital of the offender. With consent, a written report giving victims' views is presented to the Parole Board and to the Mental Health Unit at the Home Office. As a result of the information provided conditions can be placed upon the offender, for example arrangements in the community and can influence post-release licence conditions.

The national target is that 85 per cent of victims are to be contacted within eight weeks of a sex offender receiving a relevant-length sentence. Victim liaison officers are integrated into relevant meetings of the multi-agency public protection panel and they are able to identify and present the views of the victim. This provides an opportunity for re-victimisation, as seen in abusive relationships within a family or domestic violence, to be reduced. The victim liaison officers can keep victims informed of developments, and provide general support or can refer them to a specialist agency.

HOW DO WE MOVE FORWARD?

In the UK the horrific abduction and murder of Sarah Payne in July 2000, by Roy Whiting, led to the campaign to introduce legislation known as 'Sarah's Law', which is comparable to 'Megan's Law' in the USA. Megan's Law makes personal and private information on registered sex offenders available to the public. Roy Whiting was a known sex offender, but his crimes were committed in 1995 and therefore did not require registration.

The UK government has decided, at present, not to implement a 'Sarah's Law' that will give the public a 'right' to some public disclosure to find out if a 'paedophile' lives in their street, and children's charities, senior police officers and other professionals have contended that a move of this kind may have forced individuals 'underground'.

The discourse has acknowledged that single mothers who enter new relationships are vulnerable to those who wish to exploit them for the purposes of abusing their children. These women often have little knowledge of 'grooming' for both children and potential partners and may unwittingly start families with sexual offenders or men with problematic behaviours who are currently beyond 'legislative measures' as they have no cautions or convictions.

SUMMARY AND CONCLUSION

The effect of the Sexual Offences Act 2003 (Home Office 2003) and the introduction of orders which limit and prohibit the activities and behaviour of offenders who pose a risk of serious harm to the public has resulted in an increase in 'external control' available to the multi-agency risk management of offenders (HM Inspectorate of Probation/HM Inspectorate of Constabularies 2005). The Act was intended to strengthen statutory provision in order to enforce the provisions for the protection of the public. External control is intended to be supported by the development of 'internal control' through the offender's completion of nationally accredited offender treatment programmes. Attendance on these programmes may be imposed as a condition of a community order or post-release licence, and failure to comply is rigorously enforced.

Many professionals view the legislation as helpful, but it views sexual offenders as a homogenous group and not as individuals.

It is important to balance the external controls with individual approaches to assessment and treatment, as discussed in later chapters of this book. However, we may now have a society that is more able to identify sexually deviant behaviour but which may not have sufficient information to manage the risks.

REFERENCES

Bichard Inquiry Report. (2004) Available at www.bichardinquiry.org.uk, accessed on 19 November 2007.

Brown, S. (2005) *Treating Sex Offenders: An Introduction to Sex Offender Treatment Programmes.* Uffculme: Willan Publishing.

Cobley, C. (2003) 'The Legislative Framework.' In: A. Matravers (ed.), *Sex Offenders in the Community: Managing and Reducing the Risks.* Uffculme: Willan Publishing.

Connelly, C. and Williamson, S. (2000) *A Review of the Research Literature on Serious, Violent and Sexual Offenders.* Edinburgh: Scottish Executive Central Research Unit. www.ofsted.gov.uk/assets/Internet_content/Publications_Team/File_attachments/saf eguarding.2467.pdf, accessed on 5 February 2008.

Data Protection Act. (1998) London: HMSO.

Department for Education and Skills (DfES). (1999) *Protection of Children Act.* London: HMSO.

Department for Education and Skills (DfES). (2006) *Safeguarding Children: An Evaluation of the Procedures for Checking Staff Appointed by Schools.* Available at www.ofsted.gov.uk/assets/Internet-content, accessed on 5 February 2008.

Department of Health (DoH). (1983) *Mental Health Act.* London: HMSO.

Department of Health (DoH). (2007) *Mental Health Act.* London: HMSO.

Education Act. (2002) London: HMSO.

Her Majesties Inspectorate of Constabulary/Her Majesties Inspectorate of Constabularies. (2005) *Managing Sex Offenders in the Community – Joint Inspection on Sex Offenders.* Available at www.inspectorates.homeoffice.gov.uk/hmiprobation/inspect_reports/thematic-inspect ions1.html/sothematic.pdf, accessed on 19 November 2007.

Home Office. (1997) *Sex Offender Act.* London: HMSO.

Home Office. (1998) *Crime and Disorder Act.* London: HMSO.

Home Office. (2001) *Criminal Justice and Court Services Act 2000: Amendments to the Sex Offender Act 1997.* Home Office Circular 20/2001. London: HMSO.

Home Office (2003) *Criminal Justice Act.* London: HMSO.

Home Office. (2003) *The MAPPA Guidance. Multi Agency Public Protection Arrangements.* London: National Probation Directorate.

Home Office. (2003) *Sexual Offences Act.* London: HMSO.

Home Office. (2004) *Working within Sexual Offences Act 2003.* SOA/4. Available at www.voiceuk.org.uk/docs/care-workers.pdf.

Home Office. (2004) *Domestic Violence, Crime and Victims Act.* London: HMSO.

Home Office. (2006) *Crime in England and Wales. Statistical Bulletin.* London. Available at www.homeoffice.gov.uk/rds, accessed on 5 February 2008.

Home Office. (2006a) *Safeguarding Vulnerable Groups Act.* London: HMSO.

Home Office. (2006b) *MAPPA – The First Five Years: A National Overview of the Multi Agency Public Phrotection Arrangements 2001–2006.* Available at www.probation.homeoffice.gov.uk/files/pdf/MAPPA, accessed on 5 February 2008.

Kansas v. Hendricks (1997) Supreme Court. 117.2072.

Kemshall, H. (2003) 'The Community Management of High Risk Offenders.' *Prison Service Journal 126,* 2–5.

Minstry of Justice. (2007) *Criminal Justice and Immigration Bill.* Available at www.parliament.uk, accessed on 5 February 2008.

Obscene Publications Act. (1964) London: HMSO.

Royal College of Psychiatrists. (2000) *Good Psychiatric Practice: Confidentiality and Information Sharing.* (Council Report Cr 133). London: Royal College of Psychiatrists.

Tewksbury, R. (2005) 'Collateral Consequences of Sex Offender Registration.' *Journal of Contemporary Justice 1,* 67–81.

Part II:

Clinical Practice
Issues

A Sex Offender Service within a Mental Health Setting

Julia Houston and Malcolm Scoales

INTRODUCTION

In England, Scotland and Wales, work with men convicted of sexual offending has largely been provided by the criminal justice service, in particular the Prison and Probation Service (now the National Offender Management Service in England and Wales). Sex offenders with mental health problems are also detained and treated in inpatient forensic mental health settings, such as low-, medium- and high-secure hospitals (Fisher, Grubin and Perkins 1998) and historically have been treated as outpatients by some psychologists working in these services (Houston, Thomson and Wragg 1994). However, there are very few specialist, multidisciplinary or multi-agency sex offender services which provide a community service and have a mental health input. The notable exceptions are the Challenge Project at the Bracton Clinic in south-east London (Craissati and McClurg 1996), a partnership between health and probation, and the Sexual Behaviour Unit in Newcastle, a partnership between health, probation and Barnardo's (Kennington, personal communication). This chapter describes the development and operation of the multidisciplinary Sex Offender Service (SOS) based within the Forensic Mental Health Services at the Shaftesbury Clinic, South West London and St George's Mental Health

NHS Trust. It outlines current service provision and offers descriptive data about the men referred. A smaller sub-sample is studied in more detail in terms of specific offence characteristics, childhood experiences, sexual development and mental health or personality functioning.

THE HISTORY AND DEVELOPMENT OF THE SOS

The role of a forensic mental health service in working with sex offenders is important for a number of reasons. Individuals under the care of mental health teams, who have a history of sexual offending or sexually inappropriate behaviour, are likely to require additional input and expertise. Similarly, probation officers are not likely to have the expertise to work alone with personality-disordered sex offenders or those with mental health problems, and these men are also the ones more likely to continue to require treatment at the end of a community rehabilitation order or licence, as part of multi-agency risk management. Many individuals who are not under any statutory framework also require a risk assessment or assessment for treatment. These men may be unconvicted, having been the subject of allegations but not charged with any offence, or self-refer as they are worried about their own behaviour.

The SOS originated as a separate specialist multidisciplinary service within the Forensic Mental Health Services in 1993. Although, historically, clinicians had seen sex offenders for assessments and individual psychological treatment, the nature of those assessments varied according to the expertise of the individual clinician, and at that time there was no provision for group treatment. The aim of the SOS was to bring together a multidisciplinary team of individuals to focus expertise, allow for greater standardisation of the process of assessment and for the provision of group treatment as well as individual work.

The SOS has developed in three main phases, which have roughly paralleled national developments in the organisation of the treatment of sex offenders.

Phase I: 1993–1997

During the initial phase the SOS ran closed initial treatment groups for men who had offended against children and one to two 10-week closed relapse prevention groups each year. Individual psychological treatment continued to be provided, where appropriate, according to individual need. Sessional input to the team meeting was provided by a probation officer from the Inner London Probation Service.

A major initiative towards the end of this period was the development of a working partnership with the South West London Probation Service, which involved probation officers being available to facilitate treatment groups with members of the SOS for men referred from probation, social services and mental health sources.

Phase II: 1997–2000

The partnership with the South West London Probation Service prompted a re-assessment of the models of group treatment. These were opened up to men who had committed a range of sexual offences and changed to a modular structure to minimise waiting time. The relapse prevention group was re-designed to run as a rolling programme. Groups were based on one of the programmes that had received accreditation from the Home Office. However, the combination of mandatory and voluntary group members, and the inclusion of those with mental health problems and personality disorders, meant that the content of the groups had to have a degree of flexibility to reflect their differing needs, without losing treatment integrity.

In April 2000 the Probation Service was reorganised and the South West London Probation Service became part of the London Probation Service. Men on community rehabilitation orders were also required to attend Home Office-accredited treatment programmes. This led to the end of the local partnership, and a refocusing of service provision as outlined below.

Phase III: 2001–2007

Phase III has seen the SOS increase service provision to men referred from mental health teams and social services. There has been significant development in the liaison role of the forensic community psychiatric nurse within the SOS. The SOS is now specifically identified by commissioners from primary care trusts as part of the service provided by the Forensic Mental Health Services as a whole. The commissioners have been keen to include the assessment of the protective abilities of partners as part of this, and the subsequent provision of a psycho-educative group for partners (see Chapter 11). The SOS continues to offer individual or group treatment to men in the community who are not suitable for the London Probation Service-run Sex Offender Group Programme, and in recent years the initial treatment groups have been particularly aimed at men with histories of sexual offending and mental health or personality problems.

CURRENT SERVICE PROVISION

Clinical input to the SOS is provided by sessions from a range of disciplines (psychology, community psychiatric nursing, psychiatry and occasionally social work when resources allow), who all work within the Forensic Mental Health Services and also have a range of other roles in the service. A weekly team meeting is held to discuss all referrals, to feed back the outcome of assessments and consultations and discuss the progress of individuals in treatment. Service provision is as follows.

Assessment

The assessment of clinical formulation, risk and likely response to treatment is a core function of the service. Complex assessments are typically carried out jointly by different disciplines in order to bring complimentary perspectives to formulation and risk management. More details about the process and content of assessment are discussed in Chapter 7. Typical examples of questions addressed in assessment would be as follows.

- What is the risk posed by a man under the care of a mental health service who has behaved in a sexually inappropriate way towards a female stranger while on unescorted leave in the community?

- How suitable would the probation community group treatment be for attendance by an offender with a personality disorder?

- What treatment can the SOS provide for an offender with a personality disorder, who is under no statutory obligation to attend?

- What is the risk posed by a man who has a previous conviction for a sexual offence against a male child, and is now in a relationship with a woman who has a female child?

Treatment

The SOS aims to match treatment provided to individual need, and may be group, individual, or a combination of the two. The current initial treatment group runs as a closed group, weekly for 90 minutes, over the course of a year. It is attended by men who are inpatients of the medium-secure unit that hosts the SOS, discharged inpatients now living in the community, men from mental health services elsewhere in the Trust, and those who are unable to access or are unsuitable for the probation community group treatment programme. Chapter 8 focuses on treatment in more detail. The range of treatments provided include the following.

- Attendance at the weekly group treatment programme for men who present a potential medium to high risk of re-offending.

- Time-limited individual treatment focused on relapse prevention for men whose likelihood of re-offending is relatively low. This is provided by a psychologist or the community psychiatric nurse.

- Longer-term individual psychological or psychotherapeutic treatment, often as an adjunct to or subsequent to the group, for men who have severe personality disorders.

Advice, consultation and liaison

Following assessment of formulation and risk, advice on risk management is given to the referrer. This may be accompanied by treatment, as outlined above, or by consultation and liaison with the referrer, including joint working, attending care programme reviews, or both. Typical examples are as follows.

- Consultation with clinicians from a community mental health team about managing potential risk in a man living in a hostel, and developing a clear risk management plan that all staff are aware of.

- Joint working with a community psychiatric nurse to ensure that a mental health team are aware of a client's relapse prevention plan and can continue to monitor and support the client in the longer term.

- Consultation and advice to a clinician in a specialist service about their role in promoting an offender's self-esteem, positive social identity and appropriate social network, to complement the offence-specific work carried out by the probation service.

Research, teaching and continuing professional development

Finally, the theoretical background to the assessment of sexual offending, risk assessment, management and treatment is a constantly developing area, and the SOS aims to ensure both that these academic developments are integrated into clinical practice, and also to contribute via research and teaching. As discussed throughout this book, work with men who have sexually offended and behaved in sexually inappropriate ways is very much evidence-based, and it is essential to keep abreast of such developments.

REFERRALS TO THE SOS: APRIL 2001–MARCH 2006

Having described the development and operation of the SOS, we now focus on the details of the men who have been referred. The descriptive information given here refers to Phase III of the development of the SOS, as described above, and reflects the period from April 2001 to March 2006.

The SOS received 365 referrals over this period, with an average of 68 referrals per year at a fairly consistent level. About 15 per cent each year were re-referrals; for example, for a re-assessment of risk after a change of circumstances. Referrals were received from a variety of sources, and fairly equally from psychiatrists and mental health professionals (23%), social workers (24%) and probation officers (25%), although with an increasing trend towards the former two professional groups. Other referrals were received from the courts, young offender teams and learning disability services.

The location of individuals at the time of referral to the service varied (see Table 6.1). The majority (70%) were living in the community, 16 per cent were in prison, and eight per cent were inpatients in a psychiatric setting.

Eighty-five per cent of referrals received by the service were accepted. The service refused referrals of individuals who were aged under 17, who lived outside the area covered by the primary care trusts, or where there were no behaviours or concerns which were related to criminal behaviour (e.g. transvestism or sexual dysfunction). Referrals were also initially refused

Table 6.1 Location at time of referral ($n = 365$)		
Location	*n*	*(%)*
Community – home	230	(63)
Community – hostel	18	(5)
Community – other	6	(2)
Prison/young offenders institute	57	(16)
Open psychiatric ward	15	(4)
Forensic low secure	5	(1)
Forensic medium secure	6	(2)
Forensic high secure	1	(<1)
Private secure forensic facility	1	(<1)
Psychiatric intensive care unit	2	(<1)
No fixed abode	1	(<1)
Other	9	(2)
Unrecorded	14	(4)

if individuals were subject to an ongoing police investigation, although they were invited to be re-referred once the outcome of this was clarified.

The most common reason for referral was a request for a risk assessment or advice about risk management (48%). Just over a quarter of referrals (27%) included a request for treatment, or specific concerns about child protection issues. Other reasons for referral included the provision of a specialist report to court, or a request for consultation.

Demographic data

Of the 365 referrals, 87 per cent were male and 13 per cent female. The majority of the 46 women were referred by social services after concerns about their ability to protect their children from male offenders, usually their partner or relative who had also been referred to the service. Although we know that women also commit sexual offences (Kelly, Regan and Burton 1991; Saradjian and Hanks 1996), from the period April 2001 to the end of

2006, only five women were referred owing to concerns about their own alleged or actual sexually assaultative behaviour. One woman was also referred before this time period. This translates to less than two per cent of all referrals and is largely consistent with conviction rates, although, as discussed in the introduction to this book, not with historical reports from victims.

The average age of individuals referred to the service was 39 years, ranging from 15 (not accepted) to 81, with the median age being 37 years. The majority of individuals referred to the service were white (77%), followed by black-Caribbean (7%), Asian-Indian (5%), Asian-Pakistani (5%) and black-African (4%). This distribution is representative of the ethnic composition of the boroughs covered by the service (Merton *et al.*), and the general issue of access to treatment is discussed further in Chapter 4.

Offence data

Referrals are not accepted if there is no indication that the person has committed any offence. However, this does not mean that all individuals referred to the service have a conviction for a sexual offence. The service also sees individuals about whom there are allegations or concerns about sexually inappropriate behaviour, as well as those who are known to have offended, but who have not been charged for varying reasons (e.g. the victim was unable or did not want to press charges, or the police did not pursue a charge against someone with a known mental health problem).

Sixty per cent of individuals referred had a conviction for a sexual offence, that is, an 'index offence'. The majority were convicted for indecent assault (63%), followed by offences involving internet child pornography (14%), rape (12%) and indecent exposure (8%). The remaining 40 per cent had no convictions for sexual offences and were therefore described by the SOS as those who had a 'problem behaviour'. This is a heterogeneous group, and included individuals who completely denied allegations against them, and those who admitted committing sexual offences but whom had not been caught or convicted. It also included men who had not committed an actual offence but were concerned about their fantasies of doing so.

RESEARCH SAMPLE

This section describes data obtained from a specific study of 97 men referred to the service. The majority of these individuals ($n = 71$) were initially studied as part of a research project commissioned by the South West London and South East Region Forensic Consortium (Scoales and Houston 2006), with data from a further 26 men subsequently being added. This study focused on men who were assessed by the service, and for whom personality data was available from the Millon Multi-axial Clinical Inventory, 3rd edition (MCMI–III) (Millon 1994). The MCMI–III is the most recent version of a widely used self-report test of personality which all individuals referred to the service are asked to complete. Generally, about 75 per cent of assessed individuals complete an MCMI–III. Men who are unable to complete the questionnaire are primarily accounted for by those for whom English is not their first language (7% of all assessed referrals over one year examined) and those who are too mentally unwell (a further 7%). A few men refuse, or just fail to return the questionnaire. Given these figures, the MCMI–III data reported here are judged to be fairly representative of assessed referrals as a whole.

Referral sources largely mirrored those of all referrals to the SOS, although they reflected the more recent decrease in referrals from the probation service (18% compared to 23% from mental health sources and 26% from social services). Other referrals were received from the courts, general practitioners or counsellors, youth offender teams and the Multi-Agency Public Protection Panels.

Descriptive data were collected from the assessment reports based on individual's self-report during assessment interviews, and other available reports, and the reliability of the data checked with the author of the report or the team leader. As information was largely based on individual's self report it is therefore likely to represent a minimum, rather than a definitive level. For each section below, for a minority of individuals, data were unavailable, unknown or undisclosed. In general, the levels of missing or unknown data were approximately two to four per cent, with the exceptions being the presence of any childhood disturbances (6% missing data), the specific question of any history of prolonged hospitalisation (also 6%) and use of pornography (12%).

Comparisons of the data with other published research are considered at the end of the chapter.

Specific offence-related information[1]

Seventy-seven per cent of the 97 men ($n = 75$) within the current sample had an index conviction for a sexual offence, although they were not necessarily under any legal obligations at the time of the assessment. In fact, 41 per cent, ($n = 40$) of the sample were men who attended the assessment voluntarily. This reflects the nature of the service and its referral sources, as described earlier.

Fifty per cent of men ($n = 49$) had one index conviction, 19 per cent ($n = 18$) had two, and eight per cent ($n = 8$) three or more. The remaining 23 per cent ($n = 22$) of the men were unconvicted and their problem behaviours included sexual fantasies about children, allegations or actual contact sexual offences for which they had not been charged and sexually inappropriate behaviour towards women or children. The majority of convictions (49%, $n = 52$) were for indecent assault, 21 per cent ($n = 22$) were for offences involving indecent images (mainly internet child pornography), seven per cent ($n = 7$) each for rape, gross indecency and indecent exposure, and three per cent ($n = 3$) for each of buggery and unlawful sexual intercourse. Forty per cent of the convicted men ($n = 30$) had more than one victim.

The majority of men in the sample (72%, $n = 70$) had offended against children (i.e. under 18 years of age), with 20 per cent ($n = 19$) offending against adults. In terms of cross-over, eight per cent ($n = 8$) of the sample had both adult and child victims, with seven of those eight men being convicted of offences against both adults and children. One man had been convicted for an offence against children and had a problem behaviour involving sexually inappropriate behaviour towards adults.

Most of the victims were female (72%, $n = 70$), consistent with what is known about sexual offending in general, as discussed in the Introduction to this book. However, unusually, a greater proportion of the total number of victims were female strangers (37%, $n = 36$), compared to relatives (18%, $n = 17$) or acquaintances (11%, $n = 11$). This is likely to reflect the heterogeneous nature of the sample in terms of its inclusion of men who had offended against adults and those who had created or accessed indecent images on the internet (whose victims were classified as strangers).

1   In this section, victim data also includes the victims of problem behaviours as well as of formal offences unless otherwise specified.

Seventeen per cent ($n = 16$) of men offended against male victims. Of the total number of victims, nine per cent ($n = 9$) were male acquaintances, six per cent ($n = 6$) male strangers and two per cent ($n = 2$) male relatives. In terms of cross-over, nine men (9%) had both male and female victims, mostly children, in relation to allegations of abuse or possession of indecent images. Compared to age cross-over, a lower proportion of these men were convicted (four out of the nine), which may reflect difficulties in achieving convictions where allegations of abuse have been made by children.

The men in this sample had a range of offending histories. A third of the sample (33%, $n = 32$) had a conviction for a previous sexual offence and similar numbers were the subject of previous unsubstantiated allegations of sexual offending (38%, $n = 37$). Seventeen per cent ($n = 16$) had a previous conviction for a violent offence and just over a quarter (27%, $n = 26$) had four or more convictions of any kind.

Nine per cent ($n = 7$) of the convicted men totally denied their index offence. This compared to 27 per cent ($n = 6$) of the unconvicted men who denied their problem behaviour. These men all categorically stated that they had not committed the offence they were convicted of, or the allegations made against them. Total deniers did *not* include those who admitted to having sexual contact with a victim, but who maintained that this was consensual.

Childhood experiences

As discussed in Chapter 1, an individual's childhood experiences are likely to be significant contributory factors in the development of pathways to sexual offending. Almost half of the sample had some experience of separation from their parents before the age of 11 years (see Table 6.2) and only a third (32%, $n = 31$) had *no* indications of any childhood disturbances under the age of 16 years (see Table 6.3). Thirty-two per cent ($n = 31$) of the sample showed two or more disturbances.

Sexual development

Sexual development history is an integral component of assessment. Fifty-seven per cent ($n = 55$) disclosed use of pornography and 14 per cent had experienced sexual play with boys as a teenager. Eighty-three per cent ($n = 80$) of the sample had experience of heterosexual intercourse over their lifetime and seven per cent had sexual contact with men as an adult. This

Table 6.2 Presence of any separation experience (n = 97)

Separation experience	n	(%)
Ever in care	29	(29)
Parents separated or divorced	24	(25)
Removal into care	15	(16)
Prolonged hospitalisation	11	(11)
Parental death	6	(6)
Any separation from parents	47	(49)

Table 6.3 History of childhood disturbances (n = 97)

Childhood disturbance	n	(%)
Bullied by others	26	(27)
Truanting	19	(20)
Aggressive behaviour	17	(18)
Literacy problems	8	(8)
Bullying others	7	(7)
Acquisitive offending	6	(6)
Substance misuse	5	(5)
Fire setting	4	(4)
Other*	17	(18)
None	31	(32)

* 'Other' included unspecified antisocial behaviour, disruptive behaviour, emotional problems, cruelty to animals, being lonely and running away from home.

suggests that at least 10 per cent of the men had never had any adult sexual experience. Interestingly, 18 per cent (n = 17) disclosed a history of other paraphilias, such as voyeurism or exposing.

Forty-nine per cent ($n = 47$) of the sample had a history of either physical or sexual abuse. Twenty-six per cent ($n = 25$) had been physically abused, while 36 per cent ($n = 35$) had been sexually abused.[2] The majority of those who had been sexually abused were aged between six and 11 years at the time (66%), and the perpetrator was most likely to be an acquaintance (34%) or a family member (31%), rather than a stranger (9%).

Mental health problems

Thirty-three per cent ($n = 32$) of the men in the sample had a pre-existing mental health diagnosis at the point of being referred to the service, with 14 per cent ($n = 14$) having a psychotic disorder, 10 per cent ($n = 10$) a mood disorder, and nine per cent ($n = 9$) a personality disorder (see Table 6.4). The relatively high rate of mental illness reflects the location of the SOS within a forensic mental health service, rather than being representative of sex offenders in general (see Chapter 3).

There were high levels of self-harm and addictive behaviours, with almost a third of the sample having a history of either deliberate self-harm or attempted suicide (29%, $n = 28$), 31 per cent ($n = 30$) reporting a history of illicit drug use, and 49 per cent ($n = 47$) a history of alcohol abuse. This latter figure should be interpreted with caution, as it may not have been defined sufficiently clearly for the information obtained to be reliable. However, at minimum, it does suggest that a large number of the men in this sample have used alcohol significantly in the past, which is consistent with their self-reporting on psychometric testing (see below).

The majority of the men in the sample had received previous psychiatric or psychological treatment for mental health problems before their referral to the SOS (65%, $n = 56$). Thirty-two per cent ($n = 36$) had received outpatient treatment and 19 per cent ($n = 23$) had received treatment as an inpatient. However, in terms of treatment for sexual offending, 61 per cent ($n = 59$) had received no prior treatment, 21 per cent ($n = 20$) had completed treatment for sexual offending, and eight per cent ($n = 8$) had dropped out of previous treatment.

---

2   Some individuals had been both physically and sexually abused ($n = 13$) and are included separately in both the physical and sexual abuse categories.

Table 6.4 Mental health diagnosis at time of referral (n = 97)		
Mental health diagnosis	*n*	*(%)*
Psychotic disorders	14	(14)
Schizoaffective disorders	3	(3)
Schizophrenia	10	(10)
Paranoid psychosis	1	(1)
Mood disorders	10	(10)
Depression	8	(8)
Bipolar disorder	2	(2)
Personality disorders	9	(9)
Antisocial personality disorder	2	(2)
Borderline personality disorder	1	(1)
Unspecified personality disorder	6	(6)
Substance disorders	3	(3)
Substance misuse disorder	2	(2)
Alcohol dependence	1	(1)
Developmental disorder	2	(2)
Learning disability	1	(1)
Asperger syndrome	1	(1)
Other	1	(1)
Frontal lobe syndrome	1	(1)

Personality functioning

As mentioned earlier, part of the routine clinical assessment of sex offenders referred to the service involves the use of the MCMI–III (Millon 1994), a widely used self-report measure of personality disorders and clinical syndromes. It measures Axis I clinical syndromes (anxiety, somatoform, dysthymic and bipolar disorders, alcohol or drug dependence, post-traumatic stress, thought disorder, major depression and delusional disorder) as well as Axis II personality disorders (schizoid, avoidant, depressive, histrionic, narcissistic, antisocial, aggressive (sadistic), compulsive, passive-aggressive (negativistic), self-defeating, schizotypal, borderline and paranoid). In terms of the Axis II scales, a score of 75–84 indicates the presence of a clinically significant personality *trait*, while scores of 85 and above are likely to indicate pathology pervasive enough to suggest a personality *disorder*. In practice, a diagnosis of personality disorder would not be made solely on the basis of a single test score, but the cut-off indicators are useful for research purposes and to indicate the broad personality characteristics of the men referred to the SOS.

Forty per cent of the sample ($n = 39$) scored above the cut-off suggestive of a personality disorder, with elevations on the depressive, dependent, avoidant and schizoid scales being most common (see Table 6.5). High scores on these scales are indicative of individuals who are generally pessimistic and feel inadequate, with low self-esteem (depressive). They tend to lean on others for support and have a fear of abandonment, being overly compliant to ensure this does not occur (dependent). They are hypersensitive to rejection, fearing and anticipating being judged negatively, and therefore detach themselves from social contacts (avoidant). Individuals who score highly on the schizoid scale have severe relationship deficits, both in terms of establishing and maintaining relationships, and an apparent low need for social contact. If they are in a committed relationship, their partner may be likely to complain about a lack of emotional involvement or intimacy (Strack 1999).

The Axis I scales with the highest percentage of men scoring above the cut-off for the prominence of a clinical syndrome (i.e. 85 or above), were anxiety, which is likely to reflect the circumstances leading to the assessment, followed by followed by dysthymia (i.e. depression of two or more years duration) and alcohol and drug dependence. In terms of comorbidity, over a quarter of the sample (27%, $n = 26$) met the cut-off score of 85 for both an Axis I and Axis II disorder.

These findings are of interest, as the levels of personality disorder suggested are higher than that known at the time of referral. They suggest that a substantial proportion of the men assessed by the service may have significant underlying personality difficulties, at a level which may be approaching that which could be described as a personality 'disorder', yet without having any formal diagnosis or treatment. This would need to be confirmed in the clinical interview.

Table 6.5 Percentage and number of sample with scores above 74 and 84 on MCMI–III (n = 97)				
	Above 74		Above 84	
	n	*(%)*	*n*	*(%)*
Personality scales				
Schizoid	28	(29)	10	(10)
Avoidant	34	(34)	11	(11)
Depressive	39	(40)	20	(21)
Dependent	29	(30)	12	(12)
Histrionic	1	(1)	0	(0)
Narcissistic	9	(9)	6	(6)
Antisocial	13	(13)	5	(5)
Sadistic	2	(2)	0	(0)
Compulsive	4	(4)	1	(1)
Negativistic	26	(27)	8	(8)
Self-defeating	20	(21)	2	(2)
Schizotypal	10	(10)	4	(4)
Borderline	15	(16)	5	(5)
Paranoid	13	(13)	1	(1)
Clinical syndromes				
Anxiety	56	(58)	31	(32)
Somatoform	4	(4)	1	(1)
Mania	1	(1)	1	(1)
Dysthymia	33	(34)	11	(11)
Alcohol abuse	22	(23)	7	(7)
Drug abuse	10	(10)	7	(7)
Post-traumatic stress disorder	14	(14)	5	(5)
Thought disorder	7	(7)	1	(1)
Major depression	12	(12)	6	(6)
Delusional disorder	6	(6)	3	(3)

COMPARISON WITH OTHER SAMPLES

Much of the research which has reported descriptive information about sex offenders has been either North American (e.g. Abel *et al.* 1987; Olver and Wong 2006) or in the UK, based on men either in prison (e.g. Fazel *et al.* 2002; Oliver *et al.* 2007) or forensic mental health secure units (e.g. Baker and White 2002; Chesterman and Sahota 1998; Sahota and Chesterman 1998). One of the few UK studies that has included a community-based sample of men convicted of sexual offences is that reported by Craisatti and McClurg (1996) on the Challenge Project. This is a community-based sex offender assessment and treatment programme for men convicted of sexual offences against children in south-east London, and this study reported descriptive data on 80 men, both in the community and in prison.

The sample of 97 men described here is not directly comparable to the Challenge Project in terms of including men who had offended against adults, those who were unconvicted of any sexual offence and those with a diagnosis of major mental illness or current inpatients. However, in the precursor to the analysis of the sample above, Scoales and Houston (2006) compared data from 59 men in the community referred to the SOS who had offended against children (or where allegations had been made) to the Challenge sample. Similar patterns of offending were displayed, in that the most frequent type of offence was indecent assault against a female victim. However, lower levels of sexual and physical victimisation were experienced (51% of the Challenge sample reporting a history of sexual abuse and 44% of the SOS sample, with rates for physical abuse being 40% and 29%, respectively). The Challenge sample was found to have significantly higher levels of childhood parental separation, and of individuals with two or more childhood disturbances. The SOS sample had a significantly higher proportion of female stranger victims (reflecting the inclusion of men who committed offences of internet child pornography) and of a history of alcohol and drug abuse. The differences are likely to reflect the differing focus of the two services, with the Challenge Project focusing on men with personality disorders primarily referred from probation sources.

There are some features of the current SOS sample which are particularly unusual in terms of published research in the UK. First, just under a quarter of men in the sample were unconvicted of any sexual offence. There are very few studies which have looked at men with problematic sexual behavior who do not have a conviction, with McClurg and Craissati (1999) in the UK, and Abel and Rouleau (1990) and Black *et al.* (1997) in the USA being the notable exceptions. Scoales and Houston (2006) found that there were no major differences between the offence data from the 'index offence' and 'problem behaviour' groups, with the latter actually having a higher proportion of men with a history of unsubstantiated allegations against them (44% compared to 32%). This suggests that this group, although heterogeneous in itself, could be conceptualised as 'unconvicted offenders', and this issue will be explored further in a forthcoming paper.

Second, approximately one-third of the men in the sample had a pre-existing mental health diagnosis at the time of referral, including 13 per cent with a mental illness. Although this is not representative of levels of mental health problems in sex offenders in general (see Chapter 2), some of the specific sexual development information is still consistent with other published research. For example, 36 per cent of the men in the SOS research sample reported experiencing sexual abuse as a child, consistent with the general prevalence rates previously reported (Elliot, Browne and Kilcoyne 1995; Fisher, Beech and Browne 1998). The level of other paraphilias disclosed (18%) was consistent with that previously reported by men who had offended against children outside the family, although lower than in men whose primary sexual offence was against females within the family and rape (Abel and Rouleau 1990). Cross-over rates of eight per cent offending against adults and children and nine per cent offending against both males and females were consistent with those found previously in larger studies, which reported rates of 9–10 per cent for the former and eight to nine per cent for the latter (Bradford, Boulet and Pawlak 1992; Cann, Friendship and Gozna 2007).

Finally, information about the personality functioning of the SOS sample is also consistent with previous research. Forty per cent of the SOS sample reached the cut-off for a diagnosis of a personality disorder on the MCMI–III, with the nature of the elevated scales (depressive, dependent, avoidant, schizoid) being consistent with the intimacy deficits pathway of Ward and Siegert's (2002) aetiological pathways model (see Chapter 1). This may reflect the type of offence pathway found in individuals referred to a (primarily) community service, and it is likely that different scales may be elevated in a prison or high-secure sample.

The indication from the MCMI–III of the level of personality disorder is broadly consistent with the rates of between 30 per cent and 50 per cent reported elsewhere (Ahlmeyer et al. 2003; Cochrane, Grisso and Frederick 2001; Craisatti 2004; Madsen, Parsons and Grubin 2006). Higher rates of

66 per cent were found by Lehne (1994), and 87 per cent by Dunsieth *et al.* (2004). However, it should be noted that all these studies used a range of methods for assessing the presence of personality disorder (from psychometric assessment to structured clinical interview), in a range of types of sex offender (offenders against adults, children and undifferentiated sex offenders), in a variety of settings (prison and forensic mental health services). What does seem to hold true for all these studies, (and is supported by the data from the SOS sample), is that, regardless of how personality disorders are measured, or the composition and location of the sample, sex offenders as a group seem to be characterised by quite substantial levels of personality pathology. Aspects of personality functioning which have contributed to the development and maintenance of an individual's sexual offending are clearly important to identify in assessment, and to address in treatment and risk management.

SUMMARY AND CONCLUSIONS

This chapter has described the development, organisation and service provided by one of the few multidisciplinary, mental health-based services for sex offenders in the UK. Two unique features of this service are its availability to men who are unconvicted of any offence and also to those who have mental health problems and, specifically, a diagnosis of mental illness. Despite this, examination of detailed descriptive data of a sub-sample of men did not indicate any major inconsistencies with existing research on sex offenders outside of mental health settings, which could not be accounted for by the nature of the population and their offence histories. Although this was a widely heterogeneous sample, the men had offended primarily against females, had experienced high level of victimisation themselves and were characterised by high levels of personality pathology. It is important that this heterogeneity is reflected in an individualised approach to assessment, treatment and risk management, and these issues are discussed further in subsequent chapters.

REFERENCES

Abel, G. G., Becker, J. V., Mittelman, M. S., Cunningham-Rathner, J., Rouleau, L. L. and Murphy, W. D. (1987) 'Self reported sex crimes of non-incarcerated paraphiliacs.' *Journal of Interpersonal Violence 2*, 2–25.

Abel, G. G. and Rouleau, J. L. (1990) 'The Nature and Extent of Sexual Assault.' In W. Marshall, D. Laws and H. Barbaree (eds) *Handbook of Sexual Assault*. New York, NY: Plenum Press.

Ahlmeyer, S., Kleinsasser, D., Stoner, J. and Retzlaff, P. (2003) 'Psychopathology of incarcerated sex offenders.' *Journal of Personality Disorders 17*, 4, 306–318.

Baker, M. and White, T. (2002) 'Sex offenders in high-security care in Scotland.' *Journal of Forensic Psychiatry and Psychology 13*, 285–297.

Black, D. W., Kehrberg, L. L. D., Flumerfelt, D. L. and Schlosser, S. S. (1997) 'Characteristics of 36 subjects reporting compulsive sexual behavior.' *American Journal of Psychiatry 154*, 2, 243–248.

Bradford, J. M. W., Boulet, J. and Pawlak, A. (1992) 'The paraphilias: a multiplicity of deviant behaviours.' *Canadian Journal of Psychiatry 37*, 104–108.

Cann, J., Friendship, C. and Gozna, L. (2007) 'Assessing crossover in a sample of sexual offenders with multiple victims.' *Legal and Criminological Psychology 12*, 149–163.

Chesterman, P. and Sahota, K. (1998) 'Mentally ill sex offenders in a regional secure unit. I: Psychopathology and motivation.' *Journal of Forensic Psychiatry 9*, 150–160.

Cochrane, R. E., Grisso, T. and Frederick, R. I. (2001) 'The relationship between criminal charges, diagnosis and psycholegal opinions among federal pretrial defendents.' *Behavioral Sciences and the Law 19*, 565–582.

Craissati, J. and McClurg, G. (1996) 'The Challenge Project: perpetrators of child sexual abuse in south east London.' *Child Abuse and Neglect 20*, 11, 1067–1077.

Craissati, J. (2004) *Managing High Risk Sex Offenders in the Community*. Hove: Brunner–Routledge.

Dunsieth, N., Nelson, E., Brusman-Lovins, L., Holcomb, J. *et al.* (2004) 'Psychiatric and legal features of 113 men convicted of sexual offences.' *Journal of Clinical Psychiatry 65*, 3, 293–300.

Elliot, M., Browne, K. D. and Kilcoyne, J. (1995) 'Child abuse: what offenders tell us.' *Child Abuse and Neglect 19*, 5, 579–594.

Fazel. S., Hope. T., O'Donnell. I. and Jacoby. R. (2002) 'Psychiatric, demographic and personality characteristics of elderly sex offenders.' *Psychological Medicine 32*, 219–226.

Fisher, D., Beech, A. and Browne, K. (1998) 'Locus of control and its relationship to treatment change and abuse history in child sexual abusers.' *Legal and Criminological Psychology 3*, 1–12.

Fisher, D., Grubin, D. and Perkins, D. (1998) 'Working with Sexual Offenders in Psychiatric Settings in England and Wales.' In W. Marshall, Y. Fernandez, S. Hudson and T. Ward (eds) *Sourcebook of Treatment Programs for Sexual Offenders*. New York, NY: Plenum Press.

Houston, J., Thomson, P. and Wragg, J. (1994) 'A survey of forensic psychologists' work with sex offenders in England and Wales.' *Criminal Behaviour and Mental Health 4*, 118–129.

Kelly, L., Regan, L. and Burton, S. (1991) *An Exploratory Study of the Prevalence of Sexual Abuse in a Sample of 16–21 Year Olds*. London: CSAU, North London Polytechnic.

Kennington, R. (personal communication) Sexual Behaviour Unit, National Probation Service Northumbria, 14 Pitt Street, Newcastle upon Tyne NE4 5SU. Contact for further information.

Lehne, G. (1994) 'The NEO Personality Inventory and the Millon Clinical Multiaxial Inventory in the Forensic Evaluation of Sex Offenders.' In P. T. Costa and T. A. Widiger (eds) *Personality Disorders and the Five-Factor Model*. Washington, DC: American Psychological Association.

McClurg, G. and Craissati, J. (1999) 'A descriptive study of alleged sexual abusers known to social services.' *Journal of Sexual Aggression 4*, 1, 22–30.

Madsen, L., Parsons, S. and Grubin, D. (2006) 'The relationship between the five-factor model and DSM personality disorder in a sample of child molesters.' *Personality and Individual Differences 40*, 227–236.

Millon, T. (1994) *Manual for the MCMI–III*. Minneapolis, Minn.: National Computer Systems.

Oliver, C. J., Beech, A. R., Fisher, D. and Beckett, R. (2007) 'A comparison of rapists and sexual murderers on demographic and selected psychometric measures.' *International Journal of Offender Therapy and Comparative Criminology 51*, 298–312.

Olver, M. E. and Wong, S. C. P. (2006) 'Psychopathy, sexual deviance and recidivism among sex offenders.' *Sexual Abuse – A Journal of Research and Treatment 18*, 65–82.

Sahota, K. and Chesterman, P. (1998) 'Mentally ill sex offenders in a regional secure unit. II: cognitions, perceptions and fantasies'. *Journal of Forensic Psychiatry 9*, 1, 161–172.

Saradjian, J. and Hanks, H. G. I. (1996) *Women Who Sexually Abuse Children*. Chichester: John Wiley & Sons.

Scoales, M. and Houston, J. (2006) *A Descriptive Study of Personality Disorder Traits and Offence-related Factors in An Outpatient Sex Offender Sample*. Internal research report commissioned by the South West London and South East Region Forensic Consortium. (Available from the second author.)

Strack, S. (1999) *Essentials of Millon Inventories Assessment*. New York, NY: John Wiley & Sons, Inc.

Ward, T. and Siegert, R. J. (2002) 'Toward a comprehensive theory of child sexual abuse: a theory knitting perspective.' *Psychology, Crime and Law 9*, 319–351.

7

Clinical Assessment
and Formulation

Tim Green

INTRODUCTION

This chapter is about process and technique rather than theory. The purpose is to offer the reader a guide to approaching clinical assessment, in order to gain the best quality information and understanding of the psychological functioning of the individual, which can then guide an appraisal of risk factors and treatment targets. This chapter aims to guide the reader to develop a clinical assessment that goes beyond a comment on risk, and can offer a formulation-based understanding of the person, which can lead to useful recommendations about future risks, treatment options and management. This formulation-based model leads more readily to the strengths-based treatment framework recently described in the literature as the 'good lives' model (Ward and Stewart 2003) in which an augmented treatment framework offers patients not only an insight into their offending behaviour patterns but also an understanding of how to derive the greatest benefit from positive aspects of their lives in order to prevent further offending behaviour. In assessment, this framework encourages the individual to see the pathway or patterns to their offending, developing an understanding of the 'how' rather than just the 'what' of their behaviour (Ward *et al.* 2004).

Chapter 1 outlined the main models and theories of sex offending and Chapter 2 offered readers a comprehensive approach to risk assessment techniques and an understanding of the interplay between considerations of static and dynamic variables. The present chapter aims to provide a clear assessment pathway in order to understand the *individual* in relation to the theory.

CONTEXT

Within the rubric of mental health services, the clinical assessment of sex offenders does not differ greatly from the generic assessment of this population in other settings, although perhaps does place a greater emphasis on clinical formulation. As discussed in Chapter 3, mental health problems are rarely sufficient to 'cause' the sexual offending behaviour and are probably more usefully thought of as impacting on stable and acute dynamic risk factors (e.g. mental illness may disinhibit behaviour that is motivated by other psychological factors).

Within the Sex Offender Service (SOS) at the Shaftesbury Clinic sexual offending behaviour has typically been understood to represent, and be motivated by, some degree of psychological disturbance. Men referred from a wide range of sources, including mental health teams, and those who are unconvicted, are all considered within the same assessment process. Whether the individual has a criminal conviction or not, the clinical assessment procedure followed will be the same, although special attention must be given to issues of confidentiality (discussed later in this chapter).

PURPOSE OF ASSESSMENT

Assessment is often only thought of as establishing an individual's risk of further sexual offending. The energy put into the development of psychometrics to assess this aspect of the offender are testament to the emphasis placed on this by society and clinicians alike. Arguably, less effort has been dedicated to the development of specialist psychometry that might assist in understanding the offenders' insight into themselves, their readiness to change their behaviour or other aspects of their well-being, or lack of well being, that might have contributed to their offending. A clinical assessment of sex offenders seeks information that will assist in the development of a clinical formulation that will understand and explain the individual's behaviour, as well as offer an understanding of what factors make the individual vulnerable to future offending. This formulation-based approach allows clinicians to make sensible suggestions about management and interventions to ameliorate future risk.

Beckett (1994) usefully suggests that assessment has three goals: appraisal of risk; identification of treatment goals; and a baseline measurement against which treatment progress may be evaluated. To this I would add that assessment allows for the development of an understanding of the person's internal world and formulation of their behaviour and offers insights into the mental mechanisms that underpin their behaviour. This is an understanding that can be shared with the person and marks a cross-over between assessment and treatment.

Systemic issues

Risk does not exist in individuals alone, but also in the system surrounding them. Dynamics that exist in the offending behaviour may be mirrored or re-enacted in the assessment if care is not exercised. This might include an offender offering different information to different professionals so as to confuse the process of assessment, or attempting to tell some professionals or family members things in confidence, not to be shared with the rest of the assessing system. It is important that the assessing system is alive to this possibility and is supportively and clearly structured so as to guard against any manipulation or sabotage of a proper assessment. Critical to the process of successful assessment is the presence of team members who can think about the issues presented by this challenging client group and support each other in the process of assessment. Having a systematic procedure for consideration of referrals, allocation of assessors, feedback from assessments completed and opportunities for joint thinking and peer supervision makes for a safe and effective environment in which to undertake this complex work. Having a multidisciplinary health service team has been invaluable in developing a comprehensive formulation of the individual. Having an organisational structure in place that ensures weekly meetings with all the relevant professionals represented has been a critical part of forming a stable base from which to provide effective assessments. This structure helps to avoid the difficulties discussed in detail in Chapter 13 in terms of the impact of the work on professionals.

Along with having a properly structured team in place, it is also vital to involve all the relevant agencies in the assessment process. This includes liaison with the individual's referrer as well as other agencies who may be involved in their lives, such as probation, mental health services and social services. Of critical importance since the introduction of the Criminal Justice Act 2003 (Home Office 2003) may be the involvement of the multi-agency public protection panel. This raises specific issues about confidentiality that must be handled delicately and will be discussed further later in this chapter.

ASSESSMENT PROCESS

In order to obtain the most complete information in a safe and boundaried way, we have tended to follow the process outlined below.

- Step 1: Receive referral.

- Step 2: Consider with team appropriateness of referral. Specifically, decide if the referral is appropriate and be clear about the questions being asked by the referrer.

- Step 3: If accepted, discuss with referring team or agency the appropriateness of referral questions being posed and agree the purpose of assessment.

- Step 4: Identify team members most appropriate to undertake assessment, including consideration of who is most appropriately qualified and clarify access to appropriate supervision.

- Step 5: Locate and read all relevant documentation.

- Step 6: Discuss case with relevant individuals as appropriate, including other informants.

- Step 7: Interviews with person referred.

- Step 8: Score relevant psychometrics to assess attitudinal and personality factors and use appropriate actuarial risk assessment tools (see Chapter 2).

- Step 9: Discuss assessment information with team and develop a formulation in relation to models of sex offending and factors known to affect risk.

- Step 10: Decide whether further assessment required, such as more information-gathering or specific assessment, such as neuropsychological functioning or psychopathic personality functioning.

- Step 11: Report to referrer with formulation, risk assessment and treatment or management recommendations.

- Step 12: Accept for treatment, suggest risk management options to referring team, suggest further specialist assessment or referral (e.g. neurorehabilitation, substance abuse service) or discharge from caseload, as appropriate.

Some of the steps listed above are self-explanatory, others need further consideration as new information may have been raised that are not covered in the steps above.

Develop a clear understanding of the questions being posed by the referrer

It is important to decide if the referral is appropriate and if an assessment can offer some new information or useful understanding to the referrer. It is also important to clarify who holds responsibility for the person referred, particularly when there is a mental health issue, as it will be appropriate for the community mental health team to hold the care programme approach and keep the patient on its caseload. Some cases will be handled more appropriately through a consultancy model offering management advice to the referrer, rather than a full-scale assessment. Other referrals may be inappropriate for reasons such as sexual deviancy not being the primary problem or that the behaviour is not illegal or causing any harm. In cases of those who may be facing charges but have not yet been convicted, or referrals from social services where allegations have been made but no charges have been proceeded with, individuals may be reluctant to be open about their behaviour. Consideration of what can be reasonably provided at this point given the resources available should be made.

Consideration of setting or context of assessment

Before meeting the individual referred it is useful to consider the physical setting and context of the interview. Assessment settings will vary from outpatient consulting rooms to prisons and psychiatric hospitals. In each case it is important to have a quiet room, free from distractions and interruptions. It is important to gain some understanding early in the assessment process

about how many assessment interviews may be required so that this information can be communicated to the individual at the outset of the interview
process. This decision can be guided by team discussion when the referral is
received and by the presentation of the individual in interview. There
appears to be no specific consensus regarding the number of sessions that
are optimal to see an individual to complete assessment. O'Reilly and Carr
(2004) advocate four assessment interviews when assessing young people
who sexually abuse. Where time and resources allow, there are certainly
advantages in allowing two sessions of interviewing, of at least two hours in
length each, with two members of the team, depending on the circumstances. This allows for an assessment that covers an understanding and formulation of the individual from more than one professional perspective and
also allows for the observation and assessment of an individual on more
than one occasion. This is useful as individuals with personality disorder
may present differently on different occasions and two assessment appointments offers an opportunity for this to be assessed. Two assessment sessions
also allow for the large amount of material that must be covered in sufficient
detail. Much of the material is obviously of a very sensitive nature. It may
also be helpful to explain to the person that you will be asking them about
their sexual and offending behaviour, but that you will ask them about their
background history. This allows for an initial session in which a rapport may
be established offering the person a better platform from which to discus
their sexual and offending behaviour in greater detail.

Some consideration of the meaning the individual makes of their circumstances will guide the clinician in understanding the reluctance of the
interviewee. When the clinician understands the issues that are worrying
the interviewee these can be discussed and the positive aspects of engaging
in the assessment may be highlighted, such as it may offer them an opportunity to give their account and possibly to access professional help for their
behaviour. It is also important to consider the context of the referral for both
the referring agency and the individual. Those referred for assessment as
part of legal proceedings may be more reluctant to disclose information that
they feel may result in a punitive disposal at court, those who have
self-referred may feel that they are being unfairly punished when questioned in great detail about their sexual behaviour and fantasies.

Considerations for the assessor

Before agreeing to undertake an assessment it is important to be clear not only about the nature of the referral questions, the setting and context but also one's own internal preparation. It is vital when undertaking this type of work that assessors are clear that they are appropriately qualified to carry out this work and have access to adequate support and supervision. This is crucial for two reasons: first, there are many issues of assessment that may potentially have serious consequences for the person being assessed, such as losing access to their children or being deprived of their liberty. Second, assessing sex offenders is a highly emotionally charged area of psychotherapeutic work, which can lead to difficult and mixed emotions in the clinician. It is important that assessors feel clear that they are emotionally and psychologically able to withstand and survive undertaking this work and that there is appropriate support and supervision for them.

Collateral information

The next stage of the assessment process is to ensure that all relevant collateral information has been collected. This may include probation reports, psychiatric reports, list of previous convictions, social services reports, witness statements and any other reports from other sources that will offer important information. These must be read thoroughly before the assessment interview takes place. Knowledge from these sources highlights inconsistencies, when individuals are minimising or omitting their previous documented actions and also alerts the clinician to important aspects of their history that should be discussed in detail at interview.

Psychometric personality assessment

In addition to the actuarial assessment tools outlined in Chapter 2 concerning risk, it is important to think about the individual's personality functioning when building up a formulation of their offending behaviour. Psychometric measurement of personality variables is helpful in this regard. Psychometric personality data allow the assessment team to understand the particular patterns of thinking and behaviour an individual may have that are reflected in their offending behaviour and may be related to assessment of the stable and dynamic factors affecting their future risk. Personality assessment measures can also alert the assessing team to the presence of personality disorder, which will be important in decision-making with regard to risk and treatment recommendations. The Shaftesbury Clinic team routinely obtains these data from the MCMI–III (Millon 1994). This is a self-report psychometric measure with indexes of personality functioning that corresponds with the *Diagnostic and Statistical Manual of Mental Disorders* (fourth edition) (APA 1994) nosological format for personality disorders, making a formulation of a person's mental disorder difficulties clearer and helping with making useful recommendations.

Informants

Where possible, it may prove useful to interview others who are close to the individual who is being assessed. This may include a care co-ordinator and a responsible medical officer (if referred from a mental health team), parents, partners or other significant individuals in the person's life who share their concerns. Some informants may, similarly to the individual, be angry with the assessment process and may prove hostile and collude with minimisation or denial of deviant behaviour. As it is important to consider the presence of risk in the system this will also be important information, as the presence of support systems that collude with offender minimisation, or the presence of deviant peers may act as a maintaining factor in their offending behaviour.

THE ASSESSMENT INTERVIEW

Confidentiality

Under the Criminal Justice Act 2003 (Home Office 2003) health services have a duty to co-operate and share information with the multi-agency public protection panel, a panel consisting of housing, social services, health, probation and the police (see Chapter 5). Clinicians need to be mindful of this with regard to informing the individual being assessed. If the person is already known to their local multi-agency public protection panel, then he or she needs to be aware that the outcome and recommendations of the assessment will be shared with those professionals. If the individual is unconvicted, the assessor needs to anticipate (and discuss in supervision) whether he or she is likely to disclose any information about identifiable offences or information which would lead to concern about significant imminent risk, either of which would need to be disclosed to other professionals. Discussions about the limits of confidentiality *must* take place near the beginning of the assessment interview, which should emphasise that this interview is unlike other consultations with mental health professionals. In practice, most people being assessed will understand this, but extra reassurance that if any information needs to be disclosed this will be done in a sensitive manner, will be needed for those who have self-referred or otherwise come for treatment voluntarily.

Therapeutic style

When the interviewee arrives for the assessment he or she is likely to be extremely nervous. This may present itself as anxiety, hostility, or in some other way. From the outset it is important to establish 'ground rules' for the interview process, being clear about how many times you are likely to meet, what will be asked and what will be fed back to the referrer, what will happen to information from the interview. It is also important to be clear with the interviewee at the outset what your role is and what information you have had access to already. Establishing this framework offers the individual a greater sense of containment in what may be an uncomfortable process for them. Establishing a rapport from the outset will maximise the opportunities for the interviewee to feel safe with you and therefore feel able to tell you more. O'Reilly and Carr (2004) suggest that adopting the therapist features identified by Marshall, Anderson and Fernandez (1999) allow for the most positive outcomes (see Table 7.1).

In addition to taking this therapeutic stance, useful aspects of the assessment process for the individual may also be highlighted. For example, this will be an opportunity for the interviewee to offer their account of events, it may be a place where they could receive some help for something that has been affecting their life for some time, and have an opportunity to gain greater insight into their behaviour and what might be motivating it. This stance offers some hope and also allows the interviewer to acknowledge that the current assessment is part of a current life-crisis that the person is experiencing, which, again, may help build rapport. It is also helpful to maintain a non-collusive but non-blaming stance throughout the interview process and to focus on the behaviour as being problematic rather than on the person being 'bad'.

Often the interviewee may take a defensive strategy to manage their anxiety, for example presenting themselves as a victim. This can lead to interviewees frequently coming with a rehearsed explanation of events that

Table 7.1 Therapist features related to positive intervention outcomes (Marshall, Anderson and Fernandez 1999)	
Empathic	Encourages active participation
Non-collusive	Directive and reflective
Respectful	Encourages pro-social attitudes
Appropriately self-disclosing	Confident
Warm and friendly	Asks open-ended questions
Appropriate use of humour	Interested
Sincere and genuine	Deals with frustrations and difficulties
Communicates clearly	Non-confrontational challenging
Rewarding and encouraging	Spends appropriate time on issues

they may seek to offer to you at the beginning of the interview. Whilst it is important not to interrupt their flow in the initial stages, which could damage building a rapport, it is also important not to go into great detail at the beginning of the interview. Often, it is helpful to allow the person a short amount of space at the beginning of the interview to vent their anxiety by way of presenting you with their view, then return to offending behaviour in greater detail later in the interview.

Questioning techniques

Many practitioners in this field have advocated the use of a 'yes set' questioning style (Beckett 1994). This technique suggests that initial questions are framed so that they are less threatening and the respondent is confident about offering a 'yes' answer, putting them more at their ease, as shown below.

In order to maintain a less threatening atmosphere in the interview, it is helpful to begin with more basic information and build up to more complex and detailed information over time. This may take the form of beginning with basic practical 'who?, what?, when?, where?' information and building up to the more difficult 'why?' questioning that asks the person to describe their motivations.

Therapist: I understand that you have been to court twice now, is that right?

Interviewee: Yes.

Therapist: OK, and those appearances at court have both been for the two charges of indecent assault on the same woman, is that right?

Interviewee: Yes.

Therapist: Right, and am I right in thinking that you were found guilty by the jury and you are going to be going back to court next month for the judge to pass sentence?

Interviewee: Yes, it's on the 18th.

Therapist: OK, so, I am sure that is leaving you feeling quite anxious about this assessment today, seeing as the court has requested it.

Interviewee: Yes, very much so!

Therapist: Sure, well, perhaps you could tell me a bit more about that feeling and then we could go from there.

Content of the interview

Areas that should be covered in the interview are specifically designed to lead to a formulation of the interviewee's personality functioning and behaviour. This should include information that might also be assessed by actuarial measures of risk (see Chapter 2), such as previous convictions, and information about dynamic variables. It should include detailed descriptive information about the person's psychosexual history and development, their social life (to assess the nature and degree of intimacy deficits), their means of coping with different moods and impulsivity (assessing general self-regulation). It is also important to assess what strengths and positive factors are present in order to complete a more full formulation, as there may be details about a person's life, such as hobbies or relationships, which could be built upon as risk management strategies for the future.

In order to gather sufficient information for a complete formulation it is important to gather detailed information about the individual's personal history. This should include the topics described below.

- *Early life experiences:* including details of any conflict experienced as a child and how this was managed, details of how women or children were treated in the family home and how this may have shaped subsequent attitudes and behaviour.

- *Education history:* including details of bullying (victim or perpetrator) and conflict with authority figures, ability to form and sustain friendships.

- *Occupational history:* including information about any conflict with employers and colleagues, how long they spent in jobs and why they left.

- *Psychosexual history and relationships:* how they learnt about sexual boundaries, first sexual experiences, unwanted sexual experiences, patterns of sexual relationships, development of fantasy material, frequency of sexual fantasy or behaviour.

- *Hobbies, interests or friends:* how they spend their leisure time constructively.

- *Previous forensic history:* including non-sexual offending history. Specific information about what?, when?, who? and so on is important; develop an understanding of the pattern of their offending behaviour.

- *Previous and current psychiatric treatment:* including any referral as a child to a psychiatrist or psychologist, current mental state, mental state at the time of offence and its contribution to offending behaviour.

- *Substance misuse history:* including current substance use and details of substance use in relation to offending behaviour.

- *Head injury:* to assess whether organic damage may influence their behaviour.

- *Self-harm:* or any other maladaptive means of coping they have as a result of depressive ruminations.

- *Self-image:* leading to depressive ruminations and maladaptive coping behaviours such as substance mis-use or self-harm.

- *Previous offending behaviour treatment:* including what their feelings about this treatment are and what they can remember about it, including examples of when they have put such learning into practice.

- *Current psychological functioning*: are they facing significant stress (financial, physical, social and so on), how are they coping, have they just been arrested, do they have any sources of support?

- *Current attitudes*: what way do they think about their behaviour, what is their current attitude to women or sex with children, and so forth?

- *Barriers to treatment*: motivation to change, practical difficulties.

Two of these areas require more detailed description in this chapter: psychosexual history and development and analysis of offending behaviour.

Psychosexual history and development

This should include a history of the individual's first sexual experiences, what messages they learnt about sex and sexuality at home, what sex education they received, information about unwanted sexual experiences they had as a child and adult, fantasies they have had through their life, material they have used to masturbate to, both in fantasy and reality, use of pornography (types and frequency), detailed questions about sexual practices and paraphilias, including those that might be thought unusual by the majority of the community. It is also important to obtain detailed information about the individual's relationship history, what sexual practices they engaged in, the quality of the relationship, the occurrence of any violence between them, why the relationships ended.

Offending behaviour

In a functional analysis of an individual's offending behaviour, it is important to gain an understanding of the attitudes he or she holds towards the behaviour. This can be achieved by asking the interviewee to recall what they were thinking leading up to their offence. This has the benefit of discovering something about the pro-offending attitudes the person may hold, the justifications he or she may use to facilitate the offending and also demonstrate further how thinking affects behaviour. Talking the individual through the fantasies and arousal pattern they had prior to the offending behaviour will also demonstrate to them how this process of thinking escalates to physical acting out. This can be emphasised by next asking the individual about how they planned the offending, including how they overcame environmental constrains (e.g. how did they ensure that they were alone with the victim) and overcoming the victim's resistance, either through physical force or through some other form of manipulation. It is useful to discuss with them how they selected their victim and what that person represented to them, in order to gain further insight into their offending attitudes. Part of the discussion of planning should include gaining information about any significant life events, stressors or any other event (internal or external) that might have acted as a precipitant or 'trigger' to the offending behaviour. Another part of offence analysis interviewing includes asking about how they avoided detection and what plans they made for this before offending. Ward *et al.* (2004) suggest asking individuals what the goal of their behaviour was, what did they expect to gain from the behaviour (improved mood and so forth).

Offence analysis should include information about the behaviour in the first instance:

- Where did it occur?

- Who was the victim? Why them?

- What did the victim do/say?

- What *exactly* did the offence involve, what did *they or the victim do and say*

- How did they think or feel about their behaviour at the time? Immediately afterwards?

- How did victim react?

- How did they ensure compliance? Threats, bribes, etc.

- How did they justify their behaviour at the time? Afterwards? Do they hold implicit theories or distorted ideas about entitlement to take sex? Do they see children as sexual objects? (See Chapter 1.)

- What was their pattern, how did their behaviour escalate?

- Have they had similar patters of offending before?

- Is there evidence of their behaviour escalating up to offending?

- What triggered their behaviour or triggered the pattern that culminated in the behaviour?

- What are their current circumstances now? Are similar trigger factors currently present?

Next, is it useful to discuss the consequences of the behaviour:

- Immediate thought and feelings after offending.
- What did they do to avoid detection?
- Longer-term thoughts and feelings (fear, guilt, victim empathy).
- Fantasies about behaviour later?
- Affect, including suicidal thoughts.

Denial and motivational interviewing

Denial, at some point on a continuum from mild minimisation to outright denial, is extremely common among sex offenders. It will, therefore, be an almost inevitable feature of an assessment interview. In order to keep the momentum of rapport optimal, it is often thought useful to ignore answers you know to be untruthful in the early stage of the interview, returning to them later with a reframed question. Denial may represent the only means that the person has of coping with the shame about their behaviour at the time they see you for interview, and it is more important to keep the individual engaged in a process of assessment that might lead to treatment than it is to challenge denial at this stage. Added to this is the fact that denial is not actuarially related to increased risk of re-offending (Craissati 2004). Beckett (1994) suggests that denial is used by offenders during the course of abuse to help minimise guilt and anxiety, and it has become an entrenched strategy, therefore, interviewers should moderate the amount of fear and anxiety experienced in the interview in the hope that this will lessen the need for the person to use this method of defence.

When managing denial in a clinical assessment it is important to identify clearly the discrepancies in the account the individual gives to you and the information available from other sources. It is not necessary to challenge this immediately, but it can be accepted initially without collusion and returned to for further questioning later in the interview, when a question can be posed, such as: 'You said earlier that you were not alone with her in the house, yet other reports have said that you were – how do you make sense of that?'

Motivational interviewing is a technique designed to lessen the need for defensiveness in a hostile or anxiously self-protective interviewee and is described by Miller and Rollnick (1991). This is derived from Prochaska and DiClemente's (1982) trans-theoretical model of motivation to help engage problem drinkers in examining their behaviour with the hope they would enter treatment. Prochaska and DiClemente (1982) suggest that contemplating behavioural change is difficult for people who have had a long history with a specific means of coping. They offer a model in which the individual moves through stated of pre-contemplation (denial of having a problem), to contemplation (accepting they have a problem but remaining ambivalent about change), to determination (the person decides that change is needed), to action (engaging in treatment), to maintenance (staying free of relapse). Sexual offending has also been described as an 'addiction', in terms of being a repetitive, self-reinforcing behaviour often used to counter a negative mood state (Mann 1996).

Motivational interviewing techniques include the interviewer maintaining a therapeutic stance in which they continue to express empathy for the person's situation and the difficulty they may have in feeling able to discuss all aspects of their offending openly. It is necessary, therefore, that the interviewer does not engage in argument with the person, but rather 'rolls with resistance', so that minimisation, fabrication and denial are not challenged directly, but returned to with gentle, curious questioning later. It is suggested that this questioning is most effective when inconsistencies can be highlighted. This might include highlighting discrepancies between what the person reports in interview and other sources of information, or the person's stated aim and their description of their behaviour, such as where a person says that they do not wish to engage in further offending but report that they frequently use pornography on the internet. Another important part of this strategy is to support and positively re-enforce the person's adaptive coping in order that they might come to believe that they can cope with change in the future.

Current functioning and trigger factors

In the interview it is important to assess the individual's current psycho-social functioning, including antisocial attitudes, social isolation, any negative peer influences, episodes of interpersonal aggression and impulsivity that might be currently be present in the individual's life. These may act as maintaining or trigger factors for offending and should be considered in the assessment of imminent risk in the clinical formulation.

Current attitudes

Once you have established the interviewee's background history and gained an understanding of what happened around the time of the offence, it is important to question them about their current attitude towards their behaviour. Do they still feel justified? Do they feel ashamed? Is there any current evidence of distorted thinking about their offending or their victims? Do they show an awareness of the dynamic risk factors or trigger factors for themselves? Are they able to identify any strategies they have to manage these risks? Are they aware of the patterns of the build-up to their offending behaviour? When judging the insight (or lack of) that the person has at this stage of the interview, it is also a good point to consider the person's responsiveness to possible treatment. The degree of curiosity or concern that the person has about their behaviour may prove to be a useful indicator of their motivation to engage usefully in treatment. Crucially, it is important to ask about the individual's attitudes. Are they justifying how they acted, do they hold distorted ideas about entitlement to take sex from anyone they want, do they view children as sexually available? This set of questions should also consider any changes in attitudes since arrest or deciding to seek help. This can be a useful point in the interview to explain the theory underlying treatments for sexual offending behaviour, that is, that a person's thought process will have a direct effect on their behaviour. Crucially, it is important to assess for the presence of implicit theories about potential victims of crimes, such as women or children (Polaschek and Ward 2002; Ward and Keenan 1999). These attitudes display a core belief that may lead directly to offending behaviour, such as 'women always want to have sex'. When such beliefs can be discovered, they can usefully become a focus in treatment.

Attitudes and barriers towards treatment

Depending on their attitudes towards their risk and readiness to change, individuals may be more or less well disposed to considering treatment. Future management, treatment and more generally 'what happens next' is an important conversation to have towards the end of the interview. Assessment for treatment should include assessing how motivated the person currently is to change, what they would like to be different in their lives and in themselves, and how resistant they are to engaging in a process of change. Many individuals are nervous about what treatment might entail and this is a good opportunity to invite them to ask questions. Some individuals will be in a position of not having a choice as they are being assessed within a criminal justice framework and may be compelled to attend treatment as part of a prison or probation requirement and some will be considering treatment on a voluntary basis. In either case, successful engagement in treatment will be easier if the interviewer maintains the therapeutic stance and empathises with their anxiety and ambivalence about engagement in a process of change. Most individuals are reticent about attending treatment in a group context and may resist this, stating that they would rather engage in individual treatment. It is important in this instance to inform them that group treatment is the most effective form of intervention as demonstrated by the research literature (see the following chapter) and that this is the treatment best-suited to their needs.

It is also useful to discuss what the potential barriers to treatment might be. Often these will revolve around the individual's resistance and ambivalence, but they might also include other factors, such as a possible deterioration in their mental health, increased substance mis-use, difficulties coping with the stress attending treatment induces, practical difficulties of getting time off work to attend treatment, difficulties in telling family members where they are going and other practical or financial difficulties in attending treatment.

Suitability for treatment and potential barriers to engagement

Referrers will usually want to have some idea of the recommendations that would be useful to help the individual change their behaviour in the future. When considering the individual's suitability for treatment their motivation is an important aspect of the assessment. Many people will find it difficult to consider attending a treatment group, and this should be discussed sensitively. It is helpful to explain that it is normal for people to feel anxious when considering engagement in treatment; however, treatment offers the best opportunity for them to learn about their behaviour and prevent further offending that will harm others and potentially lead to further involvement with the criminal justice system.

FORMULATION

Once the assessment has been completed, a formulation should be developed drawing on models that help understand sexual offending behaviour and the individual whom you are assessing. A formulation can be usefully thought of as a story that explains what events and internal factors led the person to behave in the way that they have. Drawing on work of authors in other fields (Carr 1999) a framework for arriving at a formulation is shown in Figure 7.1.

Figure 7.1 aims to help the assessor give relevant weight to the issues and factors that might have a bearing on the individual's behaviour. It offers a format for examining what background variables may have led the individual to be vulnerable to developing a sexually deviant behaviour pattern, possible trigger factors, events in their life that may serve to maintain the problem, factors that might be protective that could be useful in helping the person make change and a format for tying in static and dynamic factors in the consideration of risk. It is hoped that the use of a formulation-based approach offers the assessor the opportunity to form an understanding not only of the individual's risk but also of their vulnerabilities and psychological and mental health needs so that a more rounded and useful set of recommendations can be made that may help to effect a change.

Using the formulation diagram shown in Figure 7.1, several factors could be seen to contribute to Brian's indecent assault (see case examples). It could be hypothesised that Brian's mental health difficulties and poor self-esteem had developed out of his early life experiences and contributed to his developing attitudes which helped him avoid feelings of depression by believing that he was highly attractive to women. These attitudes could, in turn, be thought of as maintaining factors as they perpetuate his behaviour. Similarly, low self-esteem and deviant peers could be thought of as additional maintaining factors. Trigger factors could be seen to be his feelings of depression and his substance mis-use. Protectively, Brian is capable of discussing his feelings and is aware that he has a problem, he has not attempted to deny or minimise his crime and engaged well with the assessor.

All the dynamic factors are present and actuarial measures would rate Brian as a 'medium' risk of re-offending (recidivism rate 1.3% over two years, 18.1% over 19 years). The recommendations in this case could be for Brian to receive extra help for his depression, take measures to help him reduce his drinking, suggest to staff looking after him in the future that his mood state needs to be monitored more closely and also recommend that he undertakes sex offender treatment, as he has shown some curiosity about his behaviour.

CASE EXAMPLE

Brian is a man in his early thirties with a history of community mental health team involvement as he has a diagnosis of paranoid schizophrenia. He has also been treated in the past for depression. He has recently been charged with indecent assault on a female resident in the hostel where he lives. Two women have made allegations of similar behaviour but he has not been charged. He has no other forensic history. The woman was known to him but they were not in a relationship. Brian admitted to the crime and is currently awaiting disposal at court. The court has asked for an opinion on future risk and recommendations regarding treatment. He engaged well in the assessment process.

In interview, Brian reported that he had been severely maltreated as a child and had been locked in his bedroom for long periods when his parents would go out. He said that he had been physically abused many occasions by his drunken father and that his mother would watch these events and sometimes laugh, but not join in. Brian said that he had had few friends growing up and had not done well in school, obtaining three GCSEs. He had worked in a range of temporary jobs in his late teens and early twenties before becoming ill. Following this he has not had a permanent job.

Brian stated that he enjoyed pornography and that this had been a source of sexual release for him for many years. He said that he had a large collection of magazines and DVDs. He stated that he had had a few short-term relationships with women in the community and in hospital and voiced beliefs that women 'all love having sex with me'. He said that he would often socialise with other men from the hostel who talked at length about having casual sexual encounters with women.

Later in the interview Brian admitted to feeling very lonely and upset that he had never had a relationship. He said he had begun to realise that at his age it might be more difficult to establish a relationship and had become depressed again and had sought to cope with this through drinking. He said that he was drunk at the time of the offence and felt as though he wanted to have sex with any woman. He said that he knew that what he was doing was wrong, but was uncertain about the motives of the victim, whom he believed had really wanted to have sex with him.

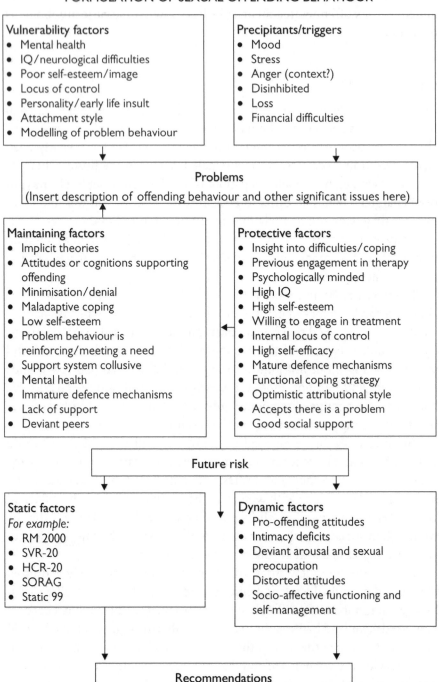

FORMULATION OF SEXUAL OFFENDING BEHAVIOUR

Vulnerability factors
- Mental health
- IQ/neurological difficulties
- Poor self-esteem/image
- Locus of control
- Personality/early life insult
- Attachment style
- Modelling of problem behaviour

Precipitants/triggers
- Mood
- Stress
- Anger (context?)
- Disinhibited
- Loss
- Financial difficulties

Problems
(Insert description of offending behaviour and other significant issues here)

Maintaining factors
- Implicit theories
- Attitudes or cognitions supporting offending
- Minimisation/denial
- Maladaptive coping
- Low self-esteem
- Problem behaviour is reinforcing/meeting a need
- Support system collusive
- Mental health
- Immature defence mechanisms
- Lack of support
- Deviant peers

Protective factors
- Insight into difficulties/coping
- Previous engagement in therapy
- Psychologically minded
- High IQ
- High self-esteem
- Willing to engage in treatment
- Internal locus of control
- High self-efficacy
- Mature defence mechanisms
- Functional coping strategy
- Optimistic attributional style
- Accepts there is a problem
- Good social support

Future risk

Static factors
For example:
- RM 2000
- SVR-20
- HCR-20
- SORAG
- Static 99

Dynamic factors
- Pro-offending attitudes
- Intimacy deficits
- Deviant arousal and sexual preoccupation
- Distorted attitudes
- Socio-affective functioning and self-management

Recommendations

Figure 7.1 Diagram for the formulation of sexual offending behaviour

SUMMARY AND CONCLUSIONS

This chapter has sought to offer the reader a framework in which to structure assessments leading to a formulation of a person's functioning and the motivation for their behaviour. The next chapter seeks to show how this formulation-based approach to assessment leads to helpful treatment interventions which may help individuals make and sustain change.

REFERENCES

American Psychiatric Association (APA) (1994) *Diagnostic and Statistical Manual of Mental Disorders.* (4th ed.). Washington DC: APA.

Beckett, R. C. (1994) 'Assessment of Sex Offenders.' In T. Morrison, M. Erooga and R. C. Beckett (eds) *Sexual Offending Against Children.* London: Routledge.

Carr, A. (1999) *Child and Adolescent Clinical Psychology: A Contextual Approach.* London: Routledge.

Craissati, J. (2004) *Managing High Risk Sex Offenders in the Community: A Psychological Approach.* Hove: Brunner–Routledge.

Home Office (2003) *Criminal Justice Act.* London: HMSO.

Mann, R. (1996) *Motivational Interviewing with Sex Offenders: A Practice Manual.* Hull: NOTA Publication.

Marshall, W. L., Anderson, D. and Fernandez, Y. (1999) *Cognitive-Behavioural Treatment of Sexual Offenders.* Chichester: Wiley.

Miller, W. R. and Rollnick, S. (1991) *Motivational Interviewing.* New York, NY: Guilford Press.

Millon, T. (1994) *Manual for the Millon Clinical Multi-Axial Inventory* (third edition). Minneapolis, Minn.: National Computer Systems.

O'Reilly, G. and Carr, A. (2004) 'Assessment of Juvenile Sex Offenders'. In G. O'Reilly, W. L. Marshall and A. Carr (2004) *Handbook of Clinical Intervention with Young People Who Sexually Abuse.* London: Taylor & Francis.

Pollaschek, D. L. L. and Ward, T. (2002) 'The implicit theories of potential rapists: what do our questionnaires tell us.' *Aggression and Violent Behaviour 7,* 385–406.

Prochaska, J. O. and DiClemente, C. C. (1982) 'Transtheoretical therapy: toward a more integrative model of change.' *Psychotherapy: Theory Research and Practice 19,* 276–288.

Ward, T. and Keenan, T. (1999) 'Child molesters implicit theories.' *Journal of Interpersonal Violence 14,* 821–838.

Ward, T. and Stewart, C. A. (2003) 'The treatment of sex offenders: risk management and good lives.' *Professional Psychology: Research and Practice 34,* 353–360.

Ward, T., Bickley, J., Webster, S. J., Fisher, D., Beech, H. and Eldridge, H. (2004) *The Self-regulation Model of the Offense and Relapse Process. A Manual. Volume I: Assessment.* Victoria, BC: Pacific Psychological Assessment Corporation.

8

Treatment, Relapse Prevention and Building 'Good Lives'

Tim Green

INTRODUCTION

This chapter is in two parts: a brief overview of the evidence base for treatment of sexual offending and a practical description of treatment provision. For the purposes of this chapter the terms 'patient' and 'offender' are used interchangeably, as many offenders are also mental health patients in hospital or community settings. Treatment in sexual offending should follow a formulation of the offender's difficulties (see Chapter 7). The recent development of the 'good lives' self-regulation model (Ward and Fisher 2006; Ward and Stewart 2003; Ward, Yates and Long 2006) directs therapists' concern to the psychological functioning of their patients in a holistic sense, rather than treating their sexual offending behaviour in a vacuum. It is interesting there is no available information in the recidivism literature regarding people who have *not* re-offended. It may be that they have successfully used skills learnt in treatment, or it may be that other factors were protective, such as an ability to establish a career, a relationship or otherwise find meaning, fulfilment and 'goods' in life. It is important to be mindful that patients in sex offender treatment, in particular those with mental disorder, have marked and profound difficulties in their psychological functioning, and these difficulties may have been a significant contributing factor to their deviant behaviour.

Many other behaviours which are maladaptive and can hurt others are approached therapeutically and it is important that sex offending is offered the same status if useful intervention work is to take place. For example, other behaviours used to manage internal conflict and negative emotional states, such as alcoholism or drug abuse, or even legal sex addiction, are seen as manifestations of an individual needing treatment, but sexual offending behaviour is sometimes viewed as something that needs to be treated punitively. This has been reflected in the debate about whether the term 'treatment' is even an appropriate one with this population (Prentky 2006).

This chapter therefore seeks to offer some findings about the effectiveness of established treatments for sexual offending behaviour and recidivism rates; it describes the common themes found in the literature regarding treatment approaches and describes the experiences of the Sex Offender Service (SOS) at the Shaftesbury Clinic in its work with mentally disordered sex offenders. A distinction needs to be made between 'treatment' and 'management' with sex offenders. This chapter focuses primarily on treatment, and future management in the community after treatment is addressed in Chapter 9.

EFFECTIVENESS

Is treatment effective?

Since Martinson (1974) wrote his 'nothing works' paper, much attention has been rightly given to evaluating the effectiveness of offender treatment. One of the problems affecting all effectiveness research on psychological treatments is the time delay between treatment delivery and publication of results. Published literature may be describing treatment from 10 to 15 years ago. Obviously, treatments may have progressed, adapted, changed and improved during the intervening period. Anecdotal information disseminated at conferences may have led to revisions of treatment protocols, local services may have adapted their treatments to meet local demands on resources and so forth. Therefore, results from large-scale research should be read with caution and interpreted carefully.

As mentioned in Chapter 2, there is little published about the relationship between mental disorder and sexual offending, although parallels are drawn with the literature for violent offenders when considering risk. This is a peculiar comparison, as there may be very different pathways that lead an individual to offend either violently or sexually. As this book is focused on mentally disordered offenders, there is consequently very little literature to draw on to describe treatment effectiveness. Little large-scale work on incarcerated mentally disordered offenders has been done and there is no randomised controlled trials (RCT) evidence available. Thus comparisons will need to be drawn with the much larger database describing sex offender treatment effectiveness with prisoners and those on probation. Whilst it is likely that a significant proportion of this group has a mental disorder, most likely personality disorder, it is not the same population which might be treated within the mental health system. So caution must be used in interpreting the data; however, the comparison is still a useful one.

Home Office documents describe recidivism rates for sex offenders and relate these findings to effectiveness of sex offender treatment. In one Home Office document, Falshaw, Friendship and Bates (2003) make the point that sex offender treatment has traditionally aimed to reduce *re-offending*, and this is different to how recidivism is described. These authors suggest that unofficial data regarding sexual offending behaviour (gleaned from anonomised research findings and the police national computer) that does not lead to reconviction suggests that the recidivism rate is 5.3 times higher than the reconviction rate. The salient point for sex offender treatment is that as the reconviction rate is known to be low (Grubin 1998) it is difficult for sex offender treatment programme evaluators to tell if there has been a significant decrease in offending after treatment. Again, caution is required in the interpretation of research findings.

Friendship, Mann and Beech (2003) conducted a large-scale review comparing 647 prisoners who had completed sex offender treatment in prison with 1910 prisoners who had not completed treatment. Statistically significant results were observed when sexual and violent reconviction rates were combined at two-year follow-up. This was not the case for sexual conviction alone, where there was no statistically significant difference. These authors suggest that a number of the violent convictions may have been sexually motivated but were processed by the courts as a violent crime. They conclude that treatments should be more specifically targeted to treatment needs of the individuals, with greater care taken in assessing the treatment requirements of those entering treatment.

Hood *et al.* (2002) studied 192 male sex offenders followed up for four and six years after release. These workers found that less than 10 per cent of their sample had been reconvicted after six years, although those who were reconvicted were the ones thought to be the highest risk by the parole board and were reconvicted of more serious crimes. The authors do not comment on the numbers within their study who had undergone treatment when incarcerated.

In meta-analytic reviews, cognitive behavioural therapy (CBT) programmes to treat sexual offending are thought to have a modest but significant effect in reducing recidivism. The widest scale review available in recent years comes from Hanson *et al.* (2002) who conducted a meta-analysis of 43 studies (*n* = 9454) and found a difference in recidivism between treatment and no-treatment of 12.3 per cent to 16.8 per cent. Zgoba and Simon (2005) separated out the results for child molesters and rapists and found similar rates for treatment effectiveness treatment when compared with a no-treatment group (treated rapists 15% compared to 19.4%; treated child molesters 11.3% compared to 16.1%). Losel and Schmucker (2005) conducted a meta-analysis on 69 controlled outcome studies of sex offender treatment (*n* = 22,181). They found an absolute difference in sexual recidivism between treatment and comparison groups of 6.4 per cent. They also comment on medical treatments (surgical castration and hormonal medication), stating that these treatments showed larger effects than psychological treatments, but also say these results are confounded by methodological and offender variables. Kirsch and Becker (2006) comment on these finding and suggest that treatment can only demonstrate modest reductions in sexual recidivism for two main reasons: first, they point to flaws in the aetiological theory of sex offending, and second, they mention flaws in the theory of treatment delivery, suggesting that the methods used are not specific enough to treat the psychological needs of the offender. These authors also suggest that treatment regimens could be improved by tailoring the therapy on offer more specifically to the needs of those receiving it and that more attention should be paid to developing and understanding of these needs in assessment. Prentky (2006) comments that there is no such thing as 'the' recidivism rate for sex offenders, as they comprise too heterogeneous a group to make a sensible comparison with each other. He similarly recommends that offenders should be thought about as individuals and their risk and treatment needs be thought of accordingly.

What model of treatment is effective?

Brooks-Gordon, Bilby and Wells (2006) report nine randomised controlled trials found in a database and hand search of the literature. In total this covered 567 adults, 52 per cent of whom had offended against children. They found that across these trials CBT reduced re-offending at one year but there was an increase in arrest rates for those who had treatment at 10 years. These authors also point to flaws in other studies, such as failing to follow up for a 10-year period (only one study of the nine followed up for this period). Losel and Schmucker (2005) found a six per cent difference in those who had been treated compared with those who had not. They also found good support for cognitive-behavioural interventions and suggest that those that do not contain any behavioural elements show non-significant outcomes.

Other authors have suggested that there is no good evidence for sex offender treatment showing any benefit, even when conducted under stringent conditions (Rice and Harris 2003), pointing to the short follow-up periods and the small difference in relation to the recidivism rates of those who have offended following a prison sentence. Marshall (2006), in an extensive review of the available empirical evidence and critique of other meta-analyses, points out that the evaluation of sex offender treatment is no easy task and comments on the difficulties of establishing robust RCTs in this area of treatment. He suggests that the effect size for sex offender treatment is similar to that for some other forms of psychological treatment. Furthermore, it may be demonstrated to be superior to some medical treatments for specified conditions, such as coronary bypass surgery, which despite having poor effect size, is clearly still a treatment worth undertaking. He concludes that the treatments with the greatest empirical support for non-recidivism are the ones that have a combination of cognitive-behavioural therapy and relapse prevention.

For some time now research evidence has pointed to group treatment being more effective than individual treatment (Morrison, Erooga and Becket 1994). Group treatment is thought to offer patients an opportunity to learn from each other's experiences, gain a sense of support for their difficulties and need for behavioural change, be able to think as a group to generate creative solutions to problems and develop a broader understanding and also to challenge each other as peers when minimisation and denial occurs.

Seto (2006) helpfully suggests that the difficulties often encountered in the evaluation of treatment effectiveness may be because researchers are attempting to view sex offender treatment effectiveness as a static variable, which, once undertaken, will remain unchanging throughout the rest of the person's life. Clearly this is not a wholly sensible way to consider human behaviour. Seto (2006) suggests that more may be gained by viewing sex offender treatment effectiveness as a dynamic variable, so that treatment may effect some significant change in the individual's being that makes them more resistant to destabilisers and less vulnerable to offending, but at certain times of extreme stress or in certain circumstances offending may re-occur. Seto (2006) also makes the point that no study thus far has sought to establish whether treatment performance over time, requiring at least two measurements, predicts recidivism over and above established static risk factors that comprise validated actuarial risk scales. Such research could lead to treatment performance being included in such scales in the future.

In tandem with these arguments that individuals should have treatment that is responsive to their particular needs, comes research that suggests the most effective types of treatment and treatment delivery. Cognitive-behavioural methods are widely thought to have great utility in the treatment of sexual offending behaviour. Yates (2003) states that the programmes identified as being the most successful focused on targeting attitudes which supported sexual offending, victim empathy, social skills training, deviant sexual arousal and cognitive processes associated with mood states. The emphasis in CBT is that cognitions affect behaviour and that helping the individual to gain an understanding of the thinking process that would lead them to sexually offend offers them an opportunity to develop other cognitions which might help them to avoid relapsing into previous patterns of offending. There is a strong emphasis on skills acquisition so that the individual does not have to rely continually on their entrenched behavioural repertoire which includes offending to manage their mood and internal world.

Some authors have been critical of the relapse prevention model in the treatment of sexual offenders (Laws and Ward 2006). They argue that rather that being a maintenance programme after treatment, relapse prevention has become both the maintenance regimen *and* the treatment itself. They go on to suggest that the evidence for the effectiveness of CBT programmes for sex offending show no good evidence and suggest that shortcomings in relapse prevention (RP) may explain this. Marques (2000) found a lack of evidence for effectiveness of relapse prevention; however, Alexander (1999) found a 7.2 per cent re-arrest rate for those who had engaged in a relapse prevention programme compared with 17.6 per cent for those untreated across almost 11,000 offenders from 79 different sex offender treatment studies.

THEORETICAL MODELS UNDERPINNING TREATMENT

Models of sexual offending have been reviewed in Chapter 1 and will not be repeated in detail here. The main models generally drawn upon in treatment programmes, including the SOS, have been Finkelhor's (1984) four pre-conditions, Wolf's (1985) offence cycle and Ward and Seigert's (2002) pathways model, as well as the 'Good Lives' model (Ward *et al.* 2006). The SOS has endeavoured to remain flexible and use a formulation-based approach that seeks to match the appropriate model to the patient rather than try to make the patient fit the model. This has been an important and useful framework from which to deliver treatment that best meets the needs of patients.

Addressing the cognitions related to sex offending that have shaped a learned pattern of behaviour, directed and maintained by attitudes and beliefs, will be the main component of any cognitive-behavioural therapy. Recently there have been some authors who have sought to develop the extent of the cognitive model to include schema theory (Mann and Shingler 2006). They offer a critique of the cognitive distortion model suggesting that 'excuse-making behaviour' seen in sex offenders is a normal and even healthy part of normal human psychological process and demonising it in sex offenders leads to unrealistic expectations as it is asking them to do something that is counter-intuitive to human beings. Despite this, other authors see the tackling of cognitive distortions as important and see the addition of other aspects of understanding individuals' thought processes as complementary rather than competitive (Marshall 2006).

Two key theoretical models underpinning treatment at the SOS are described in more detail below.

Relapse prevention

Relapse prevention was originally developed by Marlatt (1982) as a self-management plan to help individuals with addictive behaviours to anticipate and cope with high-risk situations over time, which has a high risk of them falling back into patterns of addictive behaviour. This is achieved through cognitive-behavioural interventions taught to the person as well as a plan of behavioural procedures which aim to help to minimise exposure to high-risk situations and other destabilisors.

Within the framework of relapse prevention, the patient identifies high-risk situations which were present in the past before offending, and which are hypothesised to present a risk of re-offending. In these situations it is hypothesised that the individual perceives that he or she has little control and therefore the risk of lapsing into a previous maladaptive behaviour is increased. RP training helps the individual to establish coping resources – that are not maladaptive offending behaviour – to manage when they are in a high-risk situation. This could be taking steps to avoid a situation in which the patient knows they become sexually aroused, such as being alone with children, or finding ways to cope with a situation which occurs unexpectedly, through cognitive means of self-talk or behavioural means of escaping the situation having made an excuse.

Another important aspect to relapse prevention is the awareness of 'seemingly irrelevant decisions'. This term describes situations where the individual 'accidentally' finds themself in a high-risk situation, and which objective review suggests they manipulated circumstances so that they were in the situation that they have arrived at through a process of rationalising their decision-making process. Examples may include people taking a vocational decision to work in a school 'because it was the only job I could get'.

Consideration is also given to lapses and relapses in the RP model. 'Relapse' refers to a return to sexual offending behaviour, 'lapses' are defined as elements in the pre-offence cycle that might lead to a full blown relapse if not checked quickly, such as an increase in deviant fantasy material. The abstinence violation effect descried in the RP literature may then have a significant effect as it facilitates the escalation of a lapse into a relapse. As offenders feel that they have lapsed, they may either become hopeless and feel that they have failed or become excited at having lapsed undetected and return to offending. Therapeutically, clinicians have the goal of helping the patient to identify the situation in which they typically offended in the past and develop means of avoiding or coping with these situations. It is suggested to the patient that they must become adept at self-monitoring, possibly through the use of a diary of their thoughts and fantasies. The 'problem of immediate gratification' is considered, as an awareness develops around the need the patient may have to seek immediate indulgence to satisfy their mood state, and alternative indulgences may be offered in place of offending. Patients are taught that, whilst lapse may happen, the urge that builds up to a lapse may feel very strong at the time but that it will always pass and that distraction can be an effective means of coping with the urge. In the RP model a set of distraction thoughts and behaviours are developed with patients and given to them in writing so that they may refer to it when they are vulnerable to lapse. This is often difficult as the patient may recall the positive feeling associated with previous offending and it may be clinically appropriate to discus minimisation of harm and minimisation of lapse with the patient rather than total abstinence from dangerous situations. A common example of this is the use of legal internet pornography to satiate sexual needs in those who have committed internet child pornography offences. The therapist will discuss these lapses with the patients as slips or mistakes that do not represent a total loss of control, and the patient is encouraged to regain control as soon as a lapse is identified. It is emphasised that sex offending is not an impulsive behaviour and that certain risk factors may be anticipated and identification and management of these risks can be undertaken with planning and awareness on the part of the patient.

'Good lives'

The 'good lives' model is a recent development and is well described in Ward and Stewart (2003) and Ward et al. (2006). This model attempts to move away from an emphasis on the offending of the past and the development of a relapse prevention plan, to an augmented understanding of individuals' functioning. It seeks to develop a new life with the individual in which the focus is on developing 'goods' – positive and rewarding experiences over which the individual feels that they have mastery and control, and which afford them pleasure. The aim is then to maximise these experiences in an individual's life in the hope that they will seek out these experiences as rewarding means of managing their moods rather than engaging in offending.

The 'good lives' model differs from what its authors see as traditional RP treatment as it believes that many offenders may not have problems with maintaining gains after treatment and therefore may not need to have relapse prevention training, although no account is made of how treatment failures are considered. The authors also argue that the RP model is insufficiently sensitive to the heterogeneity of sexual offenders as it assumes a single pathway to offending. Ultimately, a distinction is drawn between the avoidance goals of RP, which seeks only to help the person extricate themselves from risk once they are in the situation, with the approach goals of 'human goods', in which positive aspects of the individual's life which keep them from offending are highlighted as means to avoid experiencing a need to offend as the individual is seeking out a desired state in a non-offending way rather than acting to avoid a negative mood. Ward *et al.* (2006) usefully point out that there has been limited consideration of the individual in treatment in recent years and that considerations of approach goals should be *added* to the evidence base, that clearly favours cognitive-behavioural-orientated treatments. These authors describe their understanding of sexual offending as occurring when: individuals seek to gratify a number of goals through sexual offending and use various strategies to obtain them; there are different trajectories reflecting the fact that these goals are indirectly or directly associated with offending; and treatment therefore needs to equip offenders with the capabilities to achieve their goals based on these differences in goals and strategies in certain environments (Ward *et al.* 2006).

The 'good lives' model is extremely useful to the process of assessment and treatment as it prevents clinician from viewing the individual as a part-object, only examining their offending behaviour rather than the whole person. This model greatly aids the formulation-based approach to understanding the individual's behaviour and offering a tailored treatment that will address their specific needs.

THE PROCESS OF TREATMENT

SOS at the Shaftesbury Clinic

The Shaftesbury Clinic is a medium-secure unit in south London which provides a forensic mental health service to inpatients and outpatients. As described in Chapter 6, the SOS within the clinic undertakes assessments and treatment of inpatients, referrals from other health agencies (e.g. community mental health teams), probation (usually when there is concern about the presence of a mental disorder), social services and self-referrals. Typically, the patients on the treatment programme have some form of mental health problems or personality disorder. Patients in treatment may be either inpatients or outpatients.

The therapeutic team

Treatment of this type should not be delivered by one individual but through a team (as discussed in Chapter 7). It is helpful when considering mentally disordered offenders if this team is multidisciplinary and can offer opinions from several perspectives. Beckett (1994) emphasises how the supervision and support available in the treatment process is as important as the content of the treatment programme. At the SOS it has been found helpful to have three or four therapists working in rotation in the group, so that two will be in the room per session with one observing from behind a one-way mirror and one having a week's break. This system has worked well as it allows for several perspectives on feedback and ensures that no one becomes 'burned out'. It is vital that it is the same therapists who work with the patients throughout the course of the group, as instability of therapists will lead to a poorer therapist–patient alliance and consequently a poorer treatment outcome. It is also important to consider and plan for issues of gender mix of therapists before the group therapy.

Prior considerations

Once assessment and formulation has been completed it will be necessary to discuss attendance for treatment with the patient. Frequently, people are concerned about being in a group as they feel that this is an exposing experience and causes them great anxiety. Concerns often expressed are that they will be humiliated or shamed by others, that they will be attacked or that others on their ward or in the community will find out about their crimes through a lack of confidentiality in the group. It is important to acknowledge these concerns and discuss them with individuals. It is often helpful to acknowledge their ambivalence as a natural anxiety that is shared by many who are entering treatment. It is also important to communicate that all men in the group will be in a similar position and that this will make the experience easier and will encourage confidentiality within the group. Many patients state that they will not be able to cope with a group but would happily do the work on an individual basis. It should be explained that the group treatment is known to be more effective than individual treatment and that this is the treatment that is on offer. A caveat to this is if the assessment has identified that the patient is too vulnerable at the present time to engage in treatment this person should be considered for treatment at a later stage when their mental health or other issues have improved, and the mental health team looking after them should be encouraged to stay in contact with the SOS and alert them to any improvement in the individual's mental state.

It is imperative that the therapeutic team members meet before the group begins to discuss how they will work together. As the team may have members from different disciplines, with inherently different working cultures, it is useful to discuss as a group how to work together, and make differences in approach explicit from the outset. It is also helpful to meet before each group to decide who will do which 'tasks' within that session. Along with this preparation it is important that each member of the treating team is aware of the offending and other issues related to each group member. This will involve access to the assessment report and other sources of information. Treating team clinicians should also ensure that they read feedback from others who are involved in each patient's care.

Psychometric measures

At the Shaftesbury Clinic group members are routinely given psychometric measures from the STEP battery (Beech 1998) as well as a personality measure, the Millon Clinical Multi-axial Inventory (third edition) (Millon 1994). Use of these measures leads the facilitators to an understanding of both how the person thinks in relation to their offending but also how their personality functioning may affect their progress through treatment.

Suitability for treatment

Other authors (Craissati 1998) have suggested that offenders with serious mental illness, psychological disturbance and total deniers may be unsuitable for treatment. Our experience has been that treatment offered to people with serious mental illness and psychological disorder is still beneficial as long as their mental state is stable enough for them to engage in group work, that is, not actively psychotic in a way which interferes with their ability to focus and relate interpersonally. In practice we have not had total deniers within the group but have occasionally offered a series of individual sessions working at the 'hypothetical' level or general criminogenic factors.

Composition of the group

At the Shaftesbury Clinic a one-year programme is run, with mixed inpatients and outpatients, that follows a cognitive-behavioural treatment model adapted to the needs of the patients. Some adaptations that have been incorporated include the use of over-learning (repeating material) so that individuals with mental health difficulties might best access it. In our group, we have tended not to give many homework exercises as this may be too challenging for some of the more mentally unwell members of the group. Efforts have also been made in the group to discuss individual's mental health difficulties and needs, in particular when considering relapse prevention and how individuals seek support from the mental health system to avoid recidivism. The formulation-based approach followed in assessment facilitates this process. In addition to these considerations we have worked with criminological considerations, including having a mix of convicted and unconvicted men in the group. Doing this has the advantage of offering treatment to a broad number of people in need efficiently, but also has the disadvantage of setting up a 'divide' within the group and allowing unconvicted participants to feel that they have done less harm, which offers them an avenue to minimise their actions. Similarly, those who have been convicted of similar behaviour to those in the group who did not receive a conviction may feel a keen sense of injustice that might interfere with effective group functioning.

Treatment content

Following the literature available detailing treatment effectiveness, the programme at the Shaftesbury Clinic follows a cognitive-behavioural framework, incorporating relapse prevention and 'good lives' ideas into treatment. The treatment package covers several modules: 'Hot seat' sessions (offence disclosure); explanation of models of offending; exploring cognitive distortions; victim empathy; interpersonal functioning; the role of fantasy in offending; and relapse prevention and 'good lives'. The methods of treatment include group discussion on the topics with examples being drawn from offenders' accounts of their behaviour. This group discussion format is established early on, as members take it in turns to present their offending for a whole session: why they believe it occurred, who was involved, how they planned it, how they thought about it, what motivated them to do it, what they did to avoid detection, how they were apprehended and so forth.

In the initial session of the group it is important to establish the group rules for therapeutic work. These should be generated by the group with guidance from the facilitators. Absolute confidentiality from group members is clearly paramount, although facilitators need to be clear about the extent of their confidentiality; expressly, that they will be feeding back to other involved in the patient's care, including probation officers and other criminal justice agencies where appropriate, and that they will be writing a report at the end of the programme that will be shared with the patient before being sent to the referrer. It will also have to be made clear that confidentiality will be breached by the facilitators if they believe that harm is in any way imminent, or if new offences are described in sufficient detail so that a victim is identifiable. Other ground rules that typically help a group to function well include having respect for others' opinions, not dominating the discussion, not interrupting others, being sensitive to others, being on time, not meeting outside the group, not attending the group if inebriated and not missing sessions. A rule has been established that if a group member misses two consecutive sessions, without contact to apologise, they may be asked to leave the group if the other group members feel this is the correct course of action. Following the establishment of ground rules it is important that each member of the group states what behaviour has brought them to the group. This is not intended to be a lengthy description, but should be a short statement, such as stating the offence for which they have been convicted or the concerns that their team had that led to them being referred. This is often a painful part of the group process but is necessary in order to establish trust and boundaries and to show that the facilitators will not collude with the offender's desire to minimise and deny their behaviour. It is mandatory that all group members make a statement in the initial session and that it is done early on in the session. This can lead to a discussion about the anxieties offenders have in relation to being in the group and offers an opportunity to discuss the content of future sessions and what will be expected of group members (e.g. that they will discuss their behaviour in some detail) throughout the group process.

The aim of cognitive-behavioural treatment is to give offenders a set of thinking skills that, on the one hand, help them understand how they began offending and, on the other, helps them to develop new thinking skills and behavioural strategies to avoid recidivism. It is hoped that the elements described above are sufficiently comprehensive and offer alternative thoughts which might be used at times of stress and higher risk of re-offending. It is also hoped that this treatment package will appraise participants of how their particular risk builds up, what the thoughts or behaviours are at the beginning of a risky cycle of behaviour, and what are the 'hot thoughts' or specific cognitive distortions they use to allow themselves to offend? What are the high-risk situations that might precipitate offending behaviour? These learned tools are collated into a personalised relapse prevention plan that might include not only thoughts and behaviours to avoid, but also positive 'goods' in the individual's life that they might access at times of low mood instead of resorting to offending behaviour.

Managing denial

Much of the clinical work in the management of denial has been detailed in the preceding chapter, but it is an important consideration for therapeutic work as well as assessment. Classically, in the psychoanalytic literature denial is thought of as a defence against being overwhelmed by anxiety of something that is too frightening for the conscious mind to process. This dynamic may be at play in the treatment of sex offenders, although it may also be the case that patients are simply frightened of being judged by others and wish to keep elements of their behaviour hidden from others. Denial and minimisation are common themes in work with sex offenders. The principles of motivational interviewing may usefully be applied within a group treatment setting and it can be very powerful for patients who are in denial to be challenged by their peers in what should be a safe and supportive environment. Whilst it is important for the therapist to continue to 'roll with resistance', efforts on the part of patients to minimise and deny their behaviour should be gently challenged and questioned in treatment. It is considered inappropriate to bring into the room information that the therapist may know but that the group member has not disclosed; however, judicious questioning by the therapists may help the group member to disclose more over time and to drop their defence of denial and be able to work more constructively. Fernandez (2006) makes several interesting points about avoiding the traditional approach of attempting to 'break' the sexual offender, who is usually assumed to be lying or overly defensive. She suggests instead treading a middle ground that is neither collusive nor damning in order to make the offender feel safe and heard whilst not excused.

Recently, some agencies have established preparatory programmes for sexual offenders to enable some thinking about denial to occur before treatment proper begins (Marshall and Moulden 2006). This programme includes disclosure of their offence and life history. The goal is to demonstrate to participants that treatment can be a positive experience and can help them get past and recover from the initial anxiety about disclosure. The hope is that this will enable speedier and more efficient use of therapy proper, as the individual has been able to drop their denial and engage more fully in therapy with more motivation. This programme is in its infancy and awaits evaluation, although early anecdotal evidence is encouraging.

Multi-agency working

Similar to the process of assessment, communication between all the agencies involved in patients' care is imperative at all times. Throughout treatment it is vital that regular feedback is given to other teams, agencies and other stakeholders that surround the patient. This might include other health service bodies, probation, multi-agency public protection panel and others. At the Shaftesbury Clinic, it has been found that emailing brief feedback to other involved parties after each treatment session has been very helpful in keeping understanding of patients, their risks and their needs forefront in professionals' minds. Additionally, with patients who may be experiencing some difficulty, either of an emotional type or of understanding content, it has been helpful to have another professional outside the SOS (e.g. probation officer, doctor, nurse) to meet regularly with the patient to talk to them about how they are experiencing the group. Although, on the face of it, this may seem to be a labour-intensive process, it has been found that it has greatly enhanced patients' ability to access treatment. This multi-agency approach has the advantages of sex offender therapists not being seen as somehow colluding with the offender and also prevents the sex offender treatment team as being seen as the 'special' team that holds the unique solution to offenders' treatment needs (Craissati 1998).

Formulation-based approach

As discussed in Chapter 7, greater therapeutic success can be predicted if a formulation-based approach, which will seek to understand all the needs of the patient, is used. We have sought to use a formulation approach to ensure that we do not fall into the trap suggested by Laws and Ward (2006) that 'one size does not fit all' when they comment on RP approaches to treatment. In this way, we hope to help the individual gain an understanding of the aetiology of their offending, behaviour, their motivation to engage in offending as a way of meeting a need inside themselves, an understanding of the maintaining factors for their behaviour and the ability to self-monitor and develop strategies to offer themselves alternative, 'good' ways of meeting their needs without offending. In such a way we hope to help the individual deal with the trauma of their illness, the contributory factors that have led them to offend and think with them about building a new and productive non-offending future.

To help offenders with conceptualising and remembering the strategies they have gained in treatment, we have adapted the diagram shown in Figure 8.1 to help patients maintain the gains it is hoped they have made in treatment. We have found it useful for patients to develop this diagram themselves, filling in the their own word in each section, as part of a presentation they give to the rest of the group, so that the other group members and the facilitators can give them suggestion as they make their presentation. The resulting document can then be taken away by the group member to keep with them. Often small index cards are provided that might be kept in a wallet or on the person to facilitate remembering what has been discussed in treatment.

CASE EXAMPLE

Brian received a community rehabilitation order at court with a requirement that he attended treatment. He reported that he was nervous about group treatment as he was worried about others finding out about his offending. He was reassured by the facilitators and managed to come to the group and discuss his offence in his 'hot seat' session well. Over the course of the group Brian made several comments, such as 'Women like having sex all the time,' which were pointed out by the facilitators and other group members to be cognitive distortions and deeply held beliefs about women and sex that could lead him to future offending. Brian admitted to the group that offending often happened for him when he was feeling vulnerable and depressed. He said that he used to drink to cope with low mood and that since he had stopped this he found that offending gave him a good feeling that he was powerful. Discussion about 'good lives' in the group uncovered the fact that Brian was a keen gardener and that he felt a great sense of self-esteem when gardening. He stated that he had not been able to engage in gardening for some time owing to his mental health difficulties.

Brian was able to produce a non-offending future plan that included self-monitoring to identify when he was in a low mood and would be vulnerable to offending. Whilst he did not develop any alternative thoughts to his distorted cognitions, he was able to recognise that these thoughts could

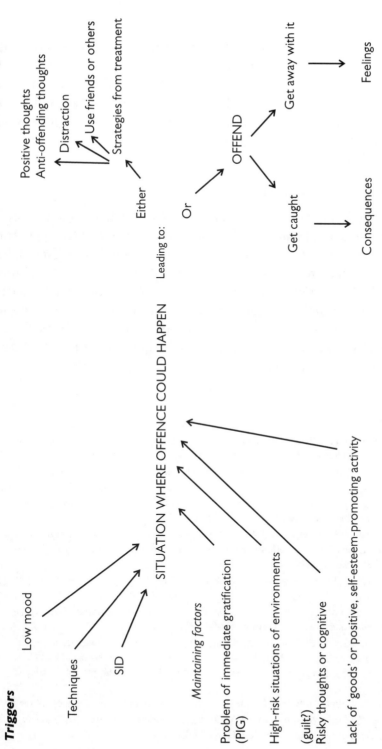

Figure 8.1 A strategy to help offenders remember what they have learnt in treatment

lead to offending and he could choose to distract himself instead. Through consistent liaison with the referring team, a gardening project had been identified for Brian, which he began towards the end of the treatment group. The treating team felt confident that, whilst there were still areas that could benefit from work, Brian had made some good progress and was in a position to manage his risk better.

SUMMARY AND CONCLUSIONS

Interestingly, despite the concern about sexual offending and the efforts to manage risk of re-offending in the community, there is no current guidance from the National Institute for Clinical Excellence (NICE) regarding best practice in the treatment of sexual offending for mentally disorder offenders. Contentious issues remain about therapeutic models and the effectiveness of treatment, but there is, however, clearly some encouraging data supporting treatments. It is hoped that this chapter has offered both an overview of treatment evaluation and some helpful advice and guidance in the provision of treatment.

REFERENCES

Alexander, M. A. (1999) 'Sex offender treatment efficacy revisited.' *Sexual Abuse: A Journal of Research and Treatment 11*, 101–116.

Beckett, R. C. (1994) 'Assessment of Sex Offenders.' In T. Morrison, M. Erooga and R.C. Beckett (eds) *Sexual Offending Against Children*. London: Routledge.

Beech, A. R. (1998) 'The psychometrictypology of child abusers.' *International Journal of Offender Therapy and Comparative Criminology 42*, 319–339.

Brooks-Gordon, B., Bilby, C. and Wells, H. (2006) 'A systematic review of psychological interventions for sexual offenders I: Randomised controlled trials.' *Journal of Forensic Psychiatry and Psychology 17*, 3, 442–466.

Craissati, J. (1998) *Child Sexual Abusers: A Community Treatment Approach*. Hove: Psychology Press Ltd.

Falshaw, L., Friendship, C. and Bates, A. (2003) *Sexual Offenders: Measuring Rreconviction, Reoffending and Recidivism*. London: Home Office: HMSO.

Fernandez, Y. (2006) 'Focusing on the Positive and Avoiding the Negativity in Sexual Offender treatment.' In W. L. Marshall, Y. M. Fernandez, L. E. Marshall and G. A. Serran (eds) *Sexual Offender Treatment: Controversial Issues*. Chichester: John Wiley & Sons.

Finklehor, D. (1984) *Child Sexual Abuse: New Theory and Research*. New York, NY: Free Press.

Friendship, C., Mann, R. and Beech, A. (2003) *The Prison-based Sex Offender Treatment Programme: An Evaluation*. London: Home Office.

Grubin, D. (1998) *Sex Offending Against Children: Understanding the Risk*. London: Home Office.

Hanson, K., Gordon, A., Harris, A., Marques, J., Murphy, W., Quinsey, V. and Seto, M. (2002) 'First report of the collaborative outcome data project on the effectiveness of psychological treatment for sex offenders.' *Sexual Abuse: A Journal of Research and Treatment 14*, 169–194.

Hood, R., Shute, S., Feilzer, M. and Wilcox, A. (2002) *Reconviction Rates of Serious Sex Offenders and Assessments of their Risk*. Home Office Research Findings No. 164. London: Home Office.

Kirsch, L. G. and Becker, J. V. (2006) 'Sexual offending: theory of problem, theory of change and implications for treatment effectiveness.' *Aggression and Violent Behaviour 11*, 208–224.

Laws, D. R. and Ward, T. (2006) 'When One Size Doesn't Fit All: The Reformulation of Relapse Prevention.' In W. L. Marshall, Y. M. Fernandez, L. E. Marshall and G. A. Serran (eds) *Sexual Offender Treatment: Controversial Issues*. Chichester: John Wiley & Sons.

Losel, F. and Schmucker, M. (2005) 'The effectiveness of treatment for sexual offenders: a comprehensive meta-anlaysis.' *Journal of Experimental Criminology 1*, 117–146.

Mann, R. E. and Schingler, J. (2006) 'Schema-driven Cognition in Sexual Offenders: Theory, Assessment and Treatment.' In W. L. Marshall, Y. M. Fernandez, L. E. Marshall and G. A. Serran (eds) *Sexual Offender Treatment: Controversial Issues*. Chichester: John Wiley & Sons.

Marlatt, G. A. (1982) 'Relapse Prevention: A Self-control Programme for the Treatment of Addictive Behaviours.' In R. B. Stewart (ed.) *Adherence, Compliance and Generalization in Behavioral Medicine*. New York, NY: Brunner/Mazel.

Marshall, W. L. (2006) 'Diagnostic Problems with Sex Offenders.' In W. L. Marshall, Y. M. Fernandez, L. E. Marshall and G. A. Serran (eds) *Sexual Offender Treatment: Controversial Issues*. Chichester: John Wiley & Sons.

Marshall, W. L. and Moulden, H. M. (2006) 'Preparatory Programmes for Sexual Offenders.' In W. L. Marshall, Y. M. Fernandez, L. E. Marshall and G. A. Serran (eds) *Sexual Offender Treatment: Controversial Issues*. Chichester: John Wiley & Sons.

Martinson, R. (1974) 'What works? Questions and answers about prison reform.' *Public Interest 35*, 22–54.

Marques, J. K. (2000) 'How to answer the question: "Does sex offending treatment work?".' *Journal of Interpersonal Violence 14*, 437–451.

Millon, T. (1994) *Manual for the Millon Clinical Multi-axial Inventory* (third edition). Minneapolis, Minn.: National Computer Systems.

Morrison, T., Erooga, M. and Beckett, R. C. (1994) *Sexual Offending Against Children: Assessment and Treatment of Male Abusers*. London: Routledge.

Prentky, R. (2006) 'Sex Offender Management: A Critical Appraisal of our Progress.' Paper presented at National Organisation for the Treatment of Abusers, York. September.

Rice, M. and Harris, G. (2003) 'Actuarial assessment of risk among sex offenders.' *Annals of the New York Academy of Sciences 989*, 198–210.

Seto, M. C. (2006) 'Interpreting the treatment performance of sex offenders.' In A. Maltravers (ed.) *Sex Offenders in the Community: Managing and Reducing the Risks*. Uffcolme: Willan Publishing.

Ward, T. and Seigert, C. A. (2002) 'Towards a comprehensive theory of child sexual abuse: a theory knitting perspective.' *Psychology, Crime and Law 9*, 319–351.

Ward, T. and Stewart, C. A. (2003) 'The treatment of sex offenders: risk management and good lives.' *Professional Psychology, Research and Practice 34*, 4, 353–360.

Ward, T. and Fisher, D. (2006) 'New ideas in the treatment of sexual offenders.' In W. L. Marshall, Y. M. Fernandez, L. E. Marshall and G. A. Serran (eds) *Sexual Offender Treatment: Controversial Issues.* Chichester: John Wiley & Sons.

Ward, T., Yates, P. and Long, C. (2006) *The Self-regulation Model of the Offence and Relapse Process: Volume 2: Treatment.* Victoria, BC: Pacific Psychological Assessment Corporation.

Wolf, S. C. (1985) 'A multi-factor model of deviant sexuality.' *Victimology: An International Journal 10*, 359–374.

Yates, P. M. (2003) 'Treatment of adult sexual offenders: a therapeutic cognitive-behavioural model of intervention.' *Journal of Child Sexual Abuse 12*, 3/4, 195–232.

Zgoba, K. M. and Simon, L. M. J. (2005) 'Recidivism rates of sexual offenders up to 7 years later: does treatment matter?' *Criminal Justice Review 30*, 2, 155–173.

9

The Impact of Personality Disorder on Working with Sexual Offenders

Sharon Prince

INTRODUCTION

Research on the prevalence of personality disorder in those who sexually offend has not been extensive. Studies to date, however, indicate that the rate of personality disorder amongst sexual offenders is consistently greater than that which would be expected in the general population (Marshall *et al.* 2006) and the nature of the relationship between personality disorder and sexual offending is complex and often indirect (see Chapter 3 for a more extensive discussion). The types of personality disorder that are most commonly observed amongst sexual offenders are antisocial personality disorder, with rates as high as 40 per cent (Motiuk and Porporino 1992), borderline and narcissistic personality disorder. Given the rates of personality disorder among sexual offenders, we would expect that there might be more information about how to work with this group of offenders, who often pose quite significant and varied challenges. Unfortunately, this information is limited, but publications in recent years have begun to focus more specifically on this issue, and on modifications which could be made to traditional treatment programmes. Some of this work has involved the integration of models and concepts applied in therapy for the non-offending personality disordered population – providing an opportunity for innovative practice.

This chapter will focus on providing an overview of both the 'psychiatric' and a psychological understanding of personality disorder, and on exploring the concepts of schemas and emotional dysregulation as two significant targets for treatment when working with personality-disordered individuals. Lastly, the chapter discusses the challenges faced by professionals, and potential solutions to them, when working with this client group.

DEFINITIONS OF PERSONALITY DISORDER

The term 'personality disorder' is one that often makes practitioners, from whatever setting or professional background, feel anxious because they believe that they do not have the relevant skills or resources to work with this client group. These clients are often difficult to engage, make high demands of both professionals and services, can evoke strong negative feelings and provoke a sense of therapeutic nihilism. It is the challenges of working with this client group, often within the absence of a model of understanding, that induces both this pessimism and anxiety. However, there is a developing evidence base for the treatment of non-offending individuals with personality disorder and an emerging evidence base for the treatment of personality-disordered offenders.

Personality disorder, as defined by the *Diagnostic and Statistical Manual of Mental Disorders*, fourth edition (DSM-IV) (APA 1994) is:

> An enduring pattern of inner experience and behavior that deviates markedly from the expectations of the individual's culture. This pattern is manifested in two or more of the following areas: cognition, affect, interpersonal functioning, and impulse control. The enduring pattern is inflexible and pervasive across a broad range of personal and social situations, leads to clinically significant distress or impairment in social, occupational or other important areas of functioning and is a stable pattern of long-term duration (at least since early adolescence). The enduring pattern is not better accounted for as a manifestation or consequence of another mental disorder or due to direct physiological effects of a substance or general medical condition.

The DSM-IV (APA 1994) defines 10 different types of personality disorder, which may be organised into clusters. The three main clusters are:

- *Cluster A – 'odd, eccentric' type*: paranoid, schizoid, schizotypal personality disorders.

- *Cluster B – 'emotional and dramatic' type*: antisocial, borderline, histrionic, narcissistic personality disorders.

- *Cluster C – 'anxious and fearful' type*: avoidant, dependent, obsessive personality disorders.

There is ongoing debate about the legitimacy of the concept of 'personality disorder' and the validity of the psychiatric categorical approach. A full rehearsal of these concerns is beyond the scope of this chapter; however, from a psychological perspective, the significant overlap between the categories suggests that personality disorder might be more helpfully represented by a dimensional system. This dimensional system would conceptualise personality disorder as representing maladaptive variants of personality traits found in the general population. This deconstruction or unpacking of global constructs (i.e. diagnostic categories) some way contributes to understanding the underlying difficulties experienced by those described as having a personality disorder. Furthermore, from a clinical perspective, there are few links between diagnosis and treatment decisions.

A psychological definition of personality disorder has been defined as 'the failure to achieve adaptive solutions to life tasks' (Livesley *et al.* 1994). These adaptive failures involve one or more of the following (Livesley 2003).

Failure to establish stable and integrated representations of self and others

When asked to describe themselves, individuals with personality disorder will often struggle with the question and provide very little information – 'I don't know who I am or what I want.' This is in marked contrast to individuals with a more integrated sense of self, who are usually able to give a very rich description of their different roles: mother, wife, worker, friend and so on; an account of their relationships with others; hobbies; likes and dislikes. The paucity of information provided by the individual with personality disorder reflects their fragmented sense of self and problems with identity.

Interpersonal dysfunction, as indicated by the failure to develop the capacity for intimacy, to function adaptively as an attachment figure, and/or to establish the capacity for affiliative relationships

Individuals have difficulty establishing mutual and reciprocal relationships. Relationships are often characterised by struggles for dominance and control, which is often manifested in some form of abuse: psychological, physical or sexual.

Failure to function adaptively in the social group, as indicated by the failure to develop the capacity for pro-social behaviour and/or co-operative relationships

Individuals engage in antisocial or criminal behaviour, or both. They can be antagonistic and are frequently in conflict with peers, work colleagues or others. Livesley (2003) continues that these failures or deficits are only indicative of personality disorder when they are enduring and they may be traced to adolescence or early adulthood, and when they are not caused by a pervasive mental disorder.

This definition derives from evolutionary psychology and the idea that personality is essential for the survival of man. Cantor (1990) suggested that a major function of personality is to solve major life tasks, which could be summarised as the need to develop a coherent sense of self or identity and the capacity for effective relationships with others. Adaptive solutions to these tasks were critical to our ancestors but are also relevant within contemporary society. Indeed, the failure to resolve these tasks is indicated by the suicide rate of individuals with personality disorder. In essence, a psychological conceptualisation of personality disorder suggests two related problems: problems with a sense of self or identity, and severe and chronic difficulties with interpersonal relationships.

PERSONALITY DISORDER AND SEXUAL OFFENDING

Some of the psychological problems exhibited by sex offenders are also observed in those diagnosed with personality disorders: antagonism, hostility, impulsivity; lack of empathy; intimacy deficits; social skills deficits and emotional dysregulation, to name but a few (Beech and Ward 2004; Hanson and Harris 2000; Ward and Siegert 2002). Indeed, many of these deficits are identified as significant targets for treatment and also as risk factors in terms of sexual recidivism. Determining the significance of these psychological deficits, in terms of the individual's offending profile, is dependent upon a comprehensive formulation-based assessment, as discussed in Chapter 7. When working with a sexual offender who has a personality disorder, this comprehensive assessment should consider an analysis of both the offending behaviour and also the relationship between this behaviour and the individual's psychological difficulties. It is not sufficient to consider just the individual's 'diagnosis' as this will not usually provide the information required to formulate the individual's offending behaviour and risk.

Personality disorder, schemas and offending

In the last 15 years work has focused on the role of schemas in offending behaviour (Mann and Shingler 2006). Authors working in this field have not directly addressed working with personality-disordered offenders; however, their conceptualisations and interventions parallel the work of those who have developed treatments for individuals with personality disorder, for example, Young, Klosko and Weishaar's (2003) schema therapy and Beck and Freeman's (1990) cognitive therapy. Schemas can be thought of as broad organising principles which make sense of an individual's life experiences; in essence, they are information-processing structures. Schemas which develop as a consequence of abusive experiences or environments may be termed 'maladaptive' and are considered to be at the core of personality difficulties (Young *et al.* 2003). Young and colleagues (2003) define maladaptive schemas as broad, pervasive themes regarding ourselves and our relationships to others, which are developed during childhood and are dysfunctional to a significant degree. Schemas contain beliefs, attitudes, assumptions and rules which shape an individual's responses and behaviours in the world.

The term 'schema' is analogous to the notion of 'implicit theory', proposed by Ward and Keenan (1999), in the sex offender literature. Schemas related specifically to sexual offending have been identified as hostile masculinity (Malamuth, Heavy and Linz 1993), suspicious of women (Malamuth and Brown 1994) and sexual entitlement, suggested by Mann and Shingler (2006), from the work of Hanson, Gizzarelli and Scott (1994). Other hypothesised schemas related to sexual offending have been proposed and readers are directed to Mann and Shingler (2006) and Ward and Keenan (1999) for further elaboration.

Sex offenders with a personality disorder could be thought of as holding some of these offence-related schemas, but also more general maladaptive schemas found within the non-offending personality-disordered population. Indeed, these more 'general' maladaptive schemas could also significantly influence the individual's offending behaviour as well as contributing to their overall level of impaired functioning. Young *et al.* (2003) describe 18 'general' maladaptive schemas.

In the example of a child molester diagnosed with borderline personality disorder, individuals with this diagnosis hold schemas about mistrust or abuse, abandonment, defectiveness or shame and emotional deprivation. Young *et al.* (2003) categorise these schemas as encompassing a theme of 'disconnection and rejection', whereby the individual is unable to form secure, satisfying attachments and believes that their needs for safety, love, nurturance and stability will not be met. These schemas can result in the interpretation of an event in a threatening way and consequently elicit distorted cognitions or thoughts. For example, if the defectiveness or shame schema is activated by perceived rejection, this could elicit the belief, 'I am no good, I'm disgusting' with an associated affect of shame. Attempts to manage this and other aversive feelings through engaging in sexually deviant fantasies or other behaviours could contribute towards offending. Therefore, it is important to identify not only offence-related but other clinically relevant schemas that may be significant in the individual's offence chain.

A similar model of understanding could be applied to a sex offender with antisocial personality disorder, although these individuals are less likely to be seen in a community treatment setting. The predominant schemas characterising individuals with antisocial personality disorder are focused on entitlement or grandiosity and insufficient self-control and discipline; again, categories proposed by Young and colleagues (2003) (but not explicitly in relation to this diagnostic category). These schemas are encompassed within a theme of 'impaired limits' which is defined by the individual's difficulty respecting the rights of others, co-operating and keeping commitments. Antisocial individuals are described as selfish, spoiled and narcissistic, and view others as either exploitative or vulnerable. Associated beliefs among these individuals might be, 'People are there to be taken' and 'I need to look out for myself'. In the event that a schema is triggered the associated affect, for example anger, revenge or excitement, could result in a behavioural response that again, forms part of the offence chain.

Mann and Shingler (2006) describe a recent study in which Mann identified four schemas related to sexual offending. It is reported that Mann acknowledged the role of schema-related cognitions in offence chains, but concluded that they were not major motivators for offending, 'other factors, such as, (sexually deviant interests) were more clearly observed immediately prior to the decision to offend' (Mann and Shingler 2006, p. 179). However, even if the role of schemas is a distal rather than a proximal factor in offending, thoughts associated with the schema, in conjunction with other risk factors related to offending, increase the likelihood of sexually assaultative behaviour.

Identification of schemas can be difficult as they usually operate outside conscious awareness; however, they can be inferred from attitudes and beliefs that individuals might have about themselves, others and the world. The *Young Schema Questionnaire* (Young and Brown 1990, 2001) is a self-report measure and consists of a long (205 items) and a short (75 items) form. The long form assesses all the maladaptive schemas as proposed by Young. The task for the clinician is to look for patterns among the endorsed items and explore their meaning with the client. Mann and Shingler (2006) propose the use of 'life maps' or 'life histories' as a useful tool for identifying recurring thinking patterns, which can provide information about underlying schemas. Marshall *et al.* (2006) also adopt a similar autobiographical procedure for eliciting schemas.

Treatment usually involves, first, educating the individual about the concept of schemas, and then supporting them to recognise how their varied dysfunctional thoughts may be considered to be subsumed within underlying schemas. Second, more traditional cognitive restructuring work, including developing challenges or alternatives to the schema. The aim of the intervention is not to change the schema, as these are extremely stable, but to help individuals develop self-awareness and reduce the impact of the schema through strategies learnt in treatment.

Personality disorder, emotional dysregulation and offending

Emotional dysregulation is a difficulty commonly experienced by individuals with a diagnosis of personality disorder. Problems with affect regulation are assumed to arise from an interaction between the individual's biological predisposition and a childhood environment characterised by abuse or neglect, or both (Linehan 1993; Livesley 2003). The individual is perceived to have difficulties in being able to identify, label and manage their own emotional responses and tolerate distress. There is considerable evidence that emotional dysregulation has an adverse impact upon many areas of functioning, including the development of a stable identity (Linehan 1993), interpersonal relationships (Calkins 2004; Linehan 1993) cognition and behaviour. Indeed, problems with emotional regulation can be considered to impact upon general self-regulation. The destabilising effects of emotional dyscontrol are most apparent in individuals with borderline and antisocial traits.

Various researchers in the field of sexual offending have demonstrated the influence of negative affect on sexually deviant behaviour (Hanson and Harris 2000; Proulx, McKibben and Lusignan 1996). However, Hanson and Bussiere (1998) found that it is not the overall level of distress that matters when predicting recidivism, but the strategies used by offenders to regulate their affect which is significant. Ward and Hudson's (2000) self-regulatory model of the relapse process, proposes a number of different pathways to offending. In this model dysfunctional self-regulation in a number of domains, including affect, are associated with an increase in the likelihood of relapse.

Given the significance of negative mood in the relapse process and the likelihood that sex offenders with personality disorder will have chronic difficulties with managing emotions, interventions with this group should focus specifically on treating deficits in emotional control – 'developing adequate self-regulatory processes and control over the expression of emotions should diminish the tendency to sexually offend' (Marshall *et al.* 2006, p. 33). A further reason for focusing on mood management in this group, is to try and reduce the attrition rate due to individuals feeling over-whelmed by their emotional experiences during treatment.

Cognitive-behavioural treatment of emotional dysregulation usually involves the following.

- Helping the individual identify and label emotions. This can be taught through the use of handouts, for example, providing clients with a vocabulary for describing both their positive and negative emotional experiences. This psycho-educational approach should also be combined with an exploration of affect changes that occur within treatment sessions. Helping clients articulate emotions; identify triggers to changes in affect; and exploring how their emotional experiences can be thought about and managed, is considered an essential aspect of effective therapy.

- Education about the role and function of emotions. Clients with a personality disorder often believe that feelings, especially negative feelings, are bad and will often try to avoid them. Teaching about the benefits of both positive and negative emotions and the role that they have in social interaction and communication, builds tolerance.

- Affect and distress tolerance. Individuals often believe that if they allow themselves to fully experience negative affect, such as anger or sadness, that these feelings may never dissipate or that something terrible might happen. A useful therapeutic approach would be to focus on modifying cognitions associated with emotional arousal for example, the belief that 'these feelings will never go away' could be replaced with the more adaptive, 'these feelings are terrible but they have occurred before and do not last long' or 'if I get too angry then I will end up killing myself' to 'feelings cannot kill me, I can be angry and be OK'. Clients need to experience painful emotions without dissociating or escalating them, this can be learnt through a variety of cognitive and behavioural strategies.

- Affect regulation. Individuals can develop self management skills, including distraction – refocusing of attention from the emotional trigger; decreasing physiological arousal associated with the emotion, for example slowed breathing or relaxation; encouraging adaptive help-seeking behaviour; inhibiting maladaptive mood-dependent behaviours.

It is noteworthy that many of the treatment programmes in high-secure settings for dangerous individuals with severe personality disorder, focus on the identification and tolerance of affect before offence-related work. The rationale underlying this approach reflects the observation that treatment drop-out is associated with individuals feeling overwhelmed by their emotional experiences and the understanding that the development of affective empathy requires a good range of emotional awareness within ourselves.

Psychopathy and sexual offending

Much attention has been given to psychopathy as a personality construct associated with both violent and sexual offending (see Blackburn 1993; Coid 1993; Hare 1996). However, the predominant contemporary model of understanding within the forensic arena is that of Hare's (1991, 2003) description of psychopathy. It is important to highlight that this construct comes under significant criticism for both its validity and clinical utility. Hare has described the psychopath as having significant difficulties in three areas of functioning: the interpersonal, affective and behavioural domains. Interpersonally, the individual is grandiose, egocentric, manipulative, dominant, exploitative and cold-hearted; affectively, they display shallow and labile emotions, are unable to form long-lasting personal bonds, are devoid of principles or goals and lack empathy and genuine remorse or guilt; behaviourally their lifestyle is impulsive, unstable and sensation-seeking; they readily violate social norms and fail to fulfil social obligations. The construct is assessed by use of the Psychopathy Checklist – Revised (PCL-R), which combines a semi-structured interview with a thorough analysis of an individual's criminal or clinical records, or both. This evaluation indicates the degree of psychopathic traits shown by an individual along a spectrum from low or medium through to high and very high.

Research has indicated that individuals with high or very high levels of psychopathic traits are notoriously difficult to treat, as they have personality characteristics which render them resistant to treatment and disruptive within group therapy. Indeed, there has been a general view that psychopathic sex offenders are untreatable (Meloy 1995; Reid and Gacono 2000) or possibly made worse by treatment (Prendergast 1991; Rice, Harris and Cormier 1992). Concern that the treatment of psychopaths could be harmful because treatment programmes enable them to develop skills that they can use to further manipulate and exploit others has been challenged by recent research.

A meta-analytic review by Salekin (2002) of treatments involving psychopaths, indicated that there were treatment effects in this group of patients. The most effective treatments were multimodal involving group and individual therapy; psychoanalytic and cognitive behavioural therapies and the inclusion of family members. Treatment was also intensive and long term. However, given the methodological limitations of this review, a cautionary note is attached to the findings and further research is required. In a narrative review of psychopathy and treatment, D'Silva, Duggan and McCarthy (2004) concluded that there were insufficient robust data to support the view that treating psychopaths makes them worse. In addition, research by Barbaree, Langton and Peacock (2006) indicated that their treatment programme did not increase the re-offence rate of psychopathic clients.

In terms of working therapeutically with psychopaths, Marshall et al. (2006), in a description of their treatment programme, stated that they include individuals who score above 20 (a moderate score) on the PCL-R. They explain that they have no more than two individuals with this score in their groups, believing that this militates against the disruptive interpersonal dynamics that they might have on the group. They also state they respond to co-operation and progress by all clients with immediate self-rewards, to which psychopaths respond extremely well. Interestingly, however, it seems that to date, the treatment programme of Marshall *et al.* (2006) has had few individuals who could be described as meeting the original criteria for a Hare definition of psychopathy, that is, a score above 30 (i.e. very high).

CHALLENGES FACED WHEN WORKING WITH THIS CLIENT GROUP

Developing a working relationship

One of the significant indicators of personality disorder, as previously outlined, is severe and chronic difficulties with interpersonal relationships, and we would expect these difficulties to be manifested in the professional–client relationship. Norton and Hinshelwood (1996, p. 723) state

> the trademark of SPD [severe personality disorder] patients is an impairment of their interpersonal and social functioning. This makes it difficult to engage many of them in treatment since the clinical encounter with them is frequently marked by negative feelings, both in them but also in the staff involved in treatment.

For example, individuals diagnosed with borderline personality disorder are known for their intense emotional reactions in treatment sessions and can be overly demanding or dependent, whereas those with antisocial personality disorder are often experienced as dismissive, intimidating and threatening, and are resistant to treatment. Professionals often feel disconcerted by the powerful emotions evoked within sessions and the difficult interpersonal dynamics. In order to function as competent and effective practitioners, it is important to have an understanding of the reasons underlying these intense emotional reactions and interpersonal challenges.

Individuals with personality disorder have internal working models of relationships, which have been shaped by their early caregiving experiences, which in the main have been characterised by abuse or neglect, or both. These inner working models influence and shape other relationships.

Consequently, an individual may perceive others as being abusive or untrustworthy and could hold the belief that 'others cannot be trusted, people will hurt me' or 'I need to attack first or risk being a victim'; beliefs and expectations which could affect the development of a therapeutic relationship. Sometimes these patterns of relating by the client are not always conscious and in the psychodynamic literature this phenomenon is referred to as 'transference' – that is, the client relating to the practitioner on the basis of previous relationships.

Given these interpersonal challenges, developing a collaborative working relationship with an individual with personality disorder is a complex process and can take some time, requiring skill and effort on the part of the worker. The emphasis on collaboration and the role of the therapist within the intervention is also highlighted by practitioners working within sex offender programmes (Beech and Hamilton-Giachritis 2005; Mann and Shingler 2006; Marshall *et al.* 2006). Indeed, confrontational and aggressive styles are no longer being viewed as effective and there is an emphasis within the literature upon warmth, empathy, being direct and rewarding.

The notions of negotiation and collaboration around treatment goals may seem a strange notion in the treatment of sexual offenders, where usually the client will have goals that the therapist does not share. However, a truly collaborative relationship is extremely motivating and enhances commitment to the therapeutic process. Collaboration involves searching for mutually agreed therapeutic goals, the practitioner indicating that their client has the potential to change and being open about the therapeutic process, including the content of treatment and possible outcomes. Essentially, the practitioner should be as transparent as possible about treatment and goals, should establish and maintain a validating treatment process, build motivation for change and communicate their commitment to helping the individual to lead a more fulfilling life.

Motivation is a significant issue when working with sex offenders, especially when the majority are not usually seeking help and treatment is mandated. When working with individuals with personality disorder issues motivation can be an even greater block to treatment. A 'lack' of motivation in individuals with personality disorder should be considered as part of the pathology (Livesley 2003) and not a criterion for exclusion from treatment (unless perhaps the individual is a total denier of their offending behaviour). Building and maintaining motivation for change should be an element of any intervention drawing upon motivational interviewing techniques (Miller and Rollnick 2002).

Personality-disordered clients often express strong emotions in the session, as previously discussed. Part of the therapeutic process is to facilitate discussion of these feelings in order to develop an understanding of what thoughts or images triggered the emotional response and how individuals can increase their self-management skills. Strong emotional responses within the practitioner, for example anger, hopelessness, empathic feelings of depression or attraction, should be attended to and not dismissed. These strong feelings are often referred to as 'countertransference' in the psychodynamic literature, and could be considered as providing invaluable information about clients' internal worlds, their early relationships and attachment styles (Adshead 2004; Strasburger 1986). Practitioners have to be open to reflecting upon these feelings and obtaining supervision or consultation to make sense of their experiences. The capacity for reflection and openness to supervision militates against behaving in a manner which undermines the therapeutic process.

In organisations where professionals work with disturbed individuals, defensive processes and structures can often be adopted to manage unacknowledged anxiety, for example social distancing between staff and patients, detachment, ritualistic task performance and resistance to change (Menzies-Lyth 1988). Although Menzies-Lyth's study was conducted in a general hospital setting, institutional defences can be inferred from many practices within settings that work with mentally disordered offenders, and which can have a deleterious effect on the establishment and maintenance of the therapeutic relationship. In a community setting, this might include speaking about clients in perjorative terms or acting in ways which do not respect the individual's dignity. In an attempt to manage the anxieties and challenges inherent in the work individuals and teams should consider supervision or consultation as being an essential, rather than desirable requirement of the work.

Practitioners within the field of personality disorder have identified that the interpersonal skills of the practitioner may be crucial in maintaining the individual in treatment (Bateman and Tyrer 2004). A number of attributes held by effective workers include being open to working with individuals with personality disorder, non-perjorative but appropriately boundaried, able to confront client's behaviours, open and able to seek advice and support, and reflective and able to withstand the emotional impact of the work. Institutions should also provide structures that support the work of professionals working with this client group. This would include managers being clear about the expectations that they have of staff in terms of their roles and responsibilities, and coherently defining the purpose of the organisation and associated tasks. Priority should also be given to both management and clinical supervision, and continuing professional development, if workers are to maintain their motivation, job satisfaction and reduce the likelihood of burn-out.

Treatment 'versus' public protection

A further challenge in the work with this client group is the difficulty defining the primary task; do we want to treat, punish or lock away? (Lavender 2002). Recent policy guidance for individuals with personality disorder (DoH 2003), proposed a framework which indicated that services needed to address three areas of functioning: mental health need; offending behaviour and risk; and social functioning. It may be inferred, therefore, that workers in this field, no matter what their context, have a very complex task given the multiple needs of the personality-disordered sex offender. Indeed, the notion of treatment is not as 'straightforward' as policy guidance might lead us to believe; for example, what constitutes a good treatment outcome? Is it the alleviation of distress, the reduction of risk or the promotion of an individual's quality of life? Moreover, it would seem that the value given to the outcome depends on the organisation and the expectations of those within and outside of the system.

The dual role of practitioners working with mentally disordered offenders, that is, public protection and treatment, are not necessarily complementary and can often come into conflict. However, practitioners can find a synthesis to these roles if from the outset they are clear, with themselves and clients, about the boundaries and limits of therapy, such as the limits of confidentiality. Discussion about this and other potential requirements, which conflict with the 'traditional' boundaries of the therapist and client relationship, should be discussed openly. This approach is consistent with the development of a collaborative relationship.

SUMMARY AND CONCLUSIONS

This chapter has focused on what could be considered to be the most significant issues to hold in mind when working with this particular client group, whether they are in individual or group treatment. Individuals diagnosed with personality disorder are a heterogeneous group with multiple and complex needs. Adopting a psychological framework to make sense of the complexities and needs of individuals with personality disorder who sexually offend allows the practitioner to hold on to therapeutic optimism, instead of the pessimism and nihilistic beliefs that are so often associated with these individuals. It is essential that this work is supported appropriately: practitioners require access to regular supervision, consultation and training, and clients should receive appropriate support and treatment from mental health services if their mental health problems are to be prevented from undermining community treatment.

REFERENCES

Adshead, G. (2004) 'Three Degrees of Security; Attachment and Forensic Institutions.' In F. Pfafflin and G. Adshead (eds) *A Matter of Security: The Application of Attachment Theory to Forensic Psychiatry and Psychotherapy*. London: Jessica Kingsley Publishers.

American Psychiatric Association (APA). (1994) *Diagnostic and Statistical Manual of Mental Disorders*, 4th edition. Washington, DC: APA.

Barbaree, H. E., Langton, C. and Peacock, E. (2006) 'Sexual Offender Treatment for Psychopaths: Is It Harmful?' In W. L. Marshall, Y. M. Fernandez, L. E. Marshall and G. A. Serran (eds) *Sexual Offender Treatment: Controversial Issues*. Chichester: John Wiley & Sons.

Bateman, A. W. and Tyrer, P. (2004) 'Services for personality disorder: organisation for inclusion.' *Advances in Psychiatric Treatment 10*, 425–433.

Beck, A. T. and Freeman, A. (1990) *Cognitive Therapy of Personality Disorders*. New York, NY: Guilford Press.

Beech, A. R. and Hamilton-Giachritsis, C. E. (2005) 'Relationship between therapeutic climate and treatment outcome in group-based sexual offender treatment programs.' *Sexual Abuse: A Journal of Research and Treatment 17*, 127–140.

Beech, A. R. and Ward, T. (2004) 'The integration of etiology and risk in sexual offenders: a theoretical framework.' *Aggression and Violent Behaviour 10*, 31–63.

Blackburn, R. (1993) *The Psychology of Criminal Conduct: Theory, Research and Practice*. Chichester: John Wiley & Sons.

Calkins, S. D. (2004) 'Early Attachment Processes and the Development of Self-Regulation.' In R. F. Baumeister and K. D. Vohs (eds) *Handbook of Self-Regulation: Research, Theory and Applications*. New York, NY: Guilford Press.

Cantor, N. (1990) 'From thought to behaviour: "having" and "doing" in the study of personality and cognition.' *American Psychologist 45*, 735–750.

Coid, J. (1993) 'Current Concepts and Classifications of Psychopathic Disorder.' In P. Tyrer and G. Stein (eds) *Personality Disorder Reviewed*. London Royal College of Psychiatrists: Gaskell Press.

Department of Health (DoH). (2003) *Personality Disorder: No longer a Diagnosis of Exclusion.* Policy Implementation Guidance for the Development of Services for People with Personality Disorder. London: DoH.

D'Silva, K., Duggan, C. and McCarthy, L. (2004) 'Does treatment really make psychopaths worse? A review of the evidence.' *Journal of Personality Disorders 18*, 163–177.

Hanson, R. K. and Bussiere, M. T. (1988) 'Predicting relapse: a meta-analysis of sexual offender recidivism studies.' *Journal of Consulting and Clinical Psychology 66*, 348–362.

Hanson, R. K., Gizzarelli, R. and Scott, H. (1994) 'The attitudes of incest offenders: sexual entitlement and acceptance of sex with children.' *Criminal Justice and Behaviour 21*, 187–202.

Hanson, R. K. and Harris, A. (2000) *The Sex Offender Needs Assessment Rating (SONAR): A Method for Measuring Change in Risk Levels,* User Report 1998–01. Ontario: Department of the Solicitor General.

Hare, R. D. (1991) *Manual for the Hare Psychopathy Checklist – Revised.* Toronto: Multi-Health Systems.

Hare, R. D. (1996) 'Psychopathy and antisocial personality disorder: a case of diagnostic confusion.' *Psychiatric Times 13*, 39–40.

Hare, R. D. (2003) *Hare Psychopathy Checklist – Revised (PCL-R)* 2nd edition Technical Manual. Toronto: Multi-Health Systems.

Lavender, A. (2002) 'Developing services for people with dangerous and severe personality disorders.' *Criminal Behaviour and Mental Health 12*, S46–S53.

Linehan, M. M. (1993) *Cognitive-Behavioral Treatment of Borderline Personality Disorder.* New York, NY: Guilford Press.

Livesley, W. J. (2003) *Practical Management of Personality Disorder.* London: Guilford Press.

Livesley, W. J., Schroeder, M. L., Jackson. D. N. and Lang, K. L. (1994) 'Categorical distinctions in the study of personality disorder: implications for classification.' *Journal of Abnormal Psychology 103*, 6–17.

Malamuth, N. M., Heavy, C. L and Linz, D. (1993) 'Predicting Men's Antisocial Behaviour Against Women: The Interaction Model of Sexual Aggression.' In G. C. N. Hall, R. Hirschmann, J. R. Graham and M. S. Zaragoza (eds) *Sexual Aggression: Issues in Etiology, Assessment and Treatment.* Washington, DC: Taylor & Francis.

Malamuth, N. M. and Brown, L. M. (1994) 'Sexually aggressive men's perceptions of womens' communications: testing three explanations.' *Journal of Personality and Social Psychology 67*, 699–712.

Mann, R. E. and Shingler, J. (2006) 'Schema-Driven Cognition in Sexual Offenders. Theory, Assessment and Treatment.' In W. L. Marshall, Y. M. Fernandez, L. E. Marshall and G. A. Serran (eds) *Sexual Offender Treatment. Controversial Issues.* Chichester: John Wiley & Sons.

Marshall, W. L., Marshall, L. E., Serran, G. A. and Fernandez, Y. M. (2006) *Treating Sexual Offenders. An Integrated Approach.* London: Routledge.

Meloy, R. (1995) 'Antisocial Personality Disorder.' In G. Gabbard (ed.) *Treatment of Psychiatric Disorders* (2nd edition). Washington, DC: American Psychiatric Press.

Menzies-Lyth, I. (1988) *Containing Anxiety in Institutions.* London: Free Association Books.

Miller, W. R. and Rollnick, S. (eds). (2002) *Motivational Interviewing: Preparing People to Change Addictive Behavior.* New York, NY: Guilford Press.

Motiuk, L. and Porporino, F. (1992) *The Prevalence, Nature, and Severity of Mental Health Problems among Federal Male Inmates in Canadian Penitentiaries*. Report no. 24. Ottawa: Correctional Services of Canada.

Norton, K. and Hinshelwood, R. D. (1996) 'Severe personality disorder. Treatment issues and selection for in-patient psychotherapy.' *British Journal of Psychiatry 168*, 723–731.

Prendergast, W. E. (1991) *Treating Sex Offenders in Correctional Institutions and Outpatient Clinics: A Guide to Clinical Practice*. New York, NY: The Haworth Press.

Proulx, J., McKibben, A. and Lusignan, R. (1996) 'Relationships between affective components and sexual behaviours in sexual aggressors.' *Sexual Abuse: A Journal of Research and Treatment 8*, 279–290.

Reid, W. J. and Gacono, C. (2000) 'Treatment of antisocial personality, psychopathy, and other characterologic antisocial syndromes.' *Behavioral Sciences and the Law 18*, 647–662.

Rice, M. E., Harris, G. T. and Cormier, C. (1992) 'Evaluation of a maximum security therapeutic community for psychopaths and other mentally disordered offenders.' *Law and Human Behaviour 16*, 399–412.

Salekin, R.T. (2002) 'Psychopathy and therapeutic pessimism: clinical lore or clinical reality?' *Clinical Psychology Review 22*, 79–112.

Strasburger, L. H. (1986) 'The Treatment of Antisocial Syndromes: The Therapist's Feelings.' In W. Reid, D. Dorr, J. I. Walker and J. W. Bonner III (eds) *Unmasking the Psychopath*. London: Norton and Company.

Ward, T. and Hudson, S. M. (2000) 'A Self-regulation Model of Relapse Prevention.' In D. R. Laws, S. M. Hudson and T. Ward (eds) *Remaking Relapse Prevention with Sex Offenders: a Sourcebook*. Thousand Oaks, CA: Sage Publications.

Ward, T. and Keenan, T. (1999) 'Child molesters' implicit theories.' *Journal of Interpersonal Violence 14*, 821–838.

Ward, T. and Siegert, R. J. (2002) 'Toward a comprehensive theory of child sexual abuse: a theory knitting perspective.' *Psychology Crime and Law 9*, 319–351.

Young, J. E. and Brown, G. (1990) *Young Schema Questionnaire*. New York, NY: Cognitive Therapy Center of New York.

Young, J. E. and Brown, G. (2001) *Young Schema Questionnaire: Special Edition*. New York, NY: Schema Therapy Institute.

Young, J. E., Klosko, J. S. and Weishaar, M. E. (2003) *Schema Therapy. A Practitioner's Guide*. New York, NY: Guilford Press.

10

Multi-agency or Multidisciplinary Working with Sexual Offenders

Sarah Galloway and Adina Seupersad

INTRODUCTION

The literature uses various terms to describe multi-agency or multidisciplinary working and this chapter will begin by defining the various terms used. The rationales for working in the varying team configurations are discussed, along with the achievements and challenges of joint working. The Sex Offender Service (SOS) at the Shaftesbury Clinic consists of a truly multidisciplinary team. Individual professionals from within that team also liaise and work jointly with other mental health teams and professional agencies, providing both a multidisciplinary and a multi-agency approach in managing sex offenders. Inevitably, by the nature of different disciplines or teams coming together, the potential for tensions may exist, and it is important to be aware of and address the factors which can contribute to this.

For some professionals working with sexual offenders may not be an attractive or popular clinical area. Sexual offenders are often demonised resulting in some staff making 'defensive' decisions (Matravers 2003). The work may provoke unpleasant personal feelings or staff may feel unskilled, and Chapter 13 discusses these issues in more detail. The introduction of multi-agency public protection panels (see Chapter 5) has also strengthened and structured the multi-agency management of sexual offenders. For both personal and professional reasons, therefore, this is not an area of work in which individual professionals should be working in isolation.

DEFINING THE TERMS

The UK government discusses, at various points, that professionals should work as a team and there should be joint working and collaboration, but it has not set a definition for these terms. Leathard (1994) identified over 50 possible meanings of the concept of a 'team'. The terminology is problematic; meanings are culturally and contextually determined and dependent upon the perspective of the author (McCallin 2004). There are many interpretations of interdisciplinary working. The concept is relatively new, poorly understood and has multiple definitions (Leathard 2003). What is clear is the interpretations of interdisciplinary working vary and there is no common understanding (Miller, Ross and Freeman 1999).

Farrell, Schmitt and Heinemann (2001) defined a multidisciplinary healthcare team as a group of colleagues from two or more disciplines who co-ordinate their expertise in providing care for patients. This definition is shared by Marshall *et al.* (1979), who stated that in the UK the terms 'interdisciplinary' and 'multidisciplinary' are viewed as referring to a team of individuals, with different training backgrounds, who share common objectives but make a different but complementary contribution. Although for some 'inter' means working between two groups only, multidisciplinary or multiprofessional are preferable terms to denote a wider team of professionals. For some 'interprofessional' is the key term that refers to interaction between the professionals involved, albeit from different backgrounds, but who have the same joint goals in working together. In contrast, 'intraprofessional' refers to different specialist groups, for example, multi-agency public protection panels. Furthermore, interpretations differ as 'interprofessional' can mean different things to different groups of people, even among professionals who speak different languages which influence their mode, thought and identity (Pietroni 1992).

From the above definitions, 'multidisciplinary teamwork' refers to the coming together and contribution of academically different disciplines. 'Multidisciplinary' and 'interprofessional' are terms often used to express the coming together of a wider range of health and welfare professionals. However, compared with multidisciplinary working, interprofessional working not only involves different professionals who co-ordinate care, but is a more intense relationship which involves a process of evaluation and the development of care plans. Gibbons (1999) describes interprofessional working as a deeper level of collaboration in which processes such as evaluation and the development of care plans are done jointly with professionals from different disciplines putting their knowledge together in an independent manner.

It is therefore essential for teams to be clear what their aims and objectives are from the beginning. Van Eyke and Baum (2002) state that successful collaboration is based on agencies' mutual need to work together, and working collaboratively must be perceived as reaping greater benefits than working in isolation. Teamwork is an essential component of interprofessional working. A team could be described as a set of players on one side in a game such as football, that is, the attributes of the team, with each having individual skills and distinct functions. There is evidence that working in teams enhances the organisation's effectiveness (Kallerberg and Moody 1994).

RATIONALE FOR MULTI-AGENCY OR DISCIPLINARY WORK

Pressure for change has grown following a number of high-profile cases, such as the inquiries into the care and treatment of Christopher Clunis (North East Thames and South East Thames Regional Health Authority 1994), Victoria Climbié (DoH 2003) and John Barrett (NHS London 2006), which share a number of areas. Some of the criticisms within the reports include a lack of communication between health and social services and other relevant agencies, the absence of a seamless service and joined-up care, an absence of teamwork or fragmented teams, poor communication, absence of medical profession and medical dominance. This was further supported by the Bristol Royal Infirmary Inquiry (2001), which found a flawed system of care with poor teamwork between professionals and too much power in too few hands.

There is evidence within the literature to both support and refute the concept of interprofessional working. Hudson (2007) had a pessimistic view of interprofessional working and, in contrast, Cook, Gerrish and Clarke (2001) were supportive, whereas Irvine et al. (2002) viewed interprofessional working as the most effective method of delivering care. The latter paper identified features such as commonality of values, accountability, commonality of location and culture whereby all members of the organisation are said to share in a commonality of cases. Successful working relied upon the pressing focus upon the resolution of a case rather than pursuing separate professional contributions.

This notion is of particular importance in a clinical setting, whereby the needs of the clients are met by a variety of agencies, including health, social care, voluntary and the criminal justice services. The growth in complex cases has led to an increase in the likelihood of case commonality and, in a recent study, 42 per cent of a social services' client population was shared with the community health trust (Keene and Xuefang 2005).

From the evidence it could be suggested that the potential advantages outweigh the disadvantages. Payne (2000, p. 51) recommends a joint working policy for multidisciplinary working and described this as: 'a group of people, each of whom possesses particular expertise each of whom is responsible for making individual decisions who together hold a common purpose who meet together to communicate, consolidate, and collaborate knowledge from which plans are made, actions determined and future decisions influenced'.

THE CHALLENGES OF WORKING WITH OTHERS

Brooker and Whyte (2000) undertook a 12-month research study into multidisciplinary working in a secure psychiatric environment. Their findings indicated that professions and the teams were interacting with each other, but the extent to which they interacted remained unclear. Multi- and interdisciplinary tensions were the most frequently cited source of difficulties and pressure across all professional groups and at all levels of security and these authors found that within teams there were also different interpretations of multidisciplinary team-working.

Team behaviours can pose a challenge to interprofessional working, and identifying and analysing such behaviour could help with the integration of teams. Millar, Ross and Freeman (1999) described three distinct behaviours as barriers. The first behaviour was described as the 'fragmented approach', with no shared vision or philosophy of care, rare team meetings, poor communication, decision-making made by a single professional, an absence of understanding of each other's role and professionals being very protective of their boundaries, knowledge and skills. The second type of behaviour was described as 'peripheral and core working', where there is a presence of a core team, a shared vision and philosophy, but group meetings rarely held.

Although such care groups tend to be better-informed than those working within the fragmented approach, communication is mixed and role under-standing is seen as superficial, with absence of any role flexibility. The third type of behaviour was described as 'integrated working', with a shared phi-losophy and vision, with users at the centre, all team members being expected to contribute to problem-solving; information and knowledge is freely shared and there is collective responsibility. The advantages of this behaviour are continuity and consistency of care, lack of ambiguity and effective decision-making processes through the sharing of information which draws upon a wider source of ideas.

As well as difficulties arising *between* team members, a number of authors have identified the potential for difficulties in working relationships to arise between different *agencies*. For example, co-ordination between mental health and social services has been identified in the past as being notori-ously poor (Eaton 1998; Owens 1998), and Hardy, Turrell and Wistow (1992) identified five areas which may act as barriers to joint working and planning across these agencies: structure, legitimacy, procedural, finance and professional issues.

More personal qualities, such as values, beliefs, disciplinary attitudes and socialisation, also affect working relationships, and can be equally destabilis-ing where disagreements arise. In relation to this, Bellack and O'Neil (2000) have called for closer scrutiny of our values and beliefs about diversity within working relationships, and the importance of respecting the individual con-tributions of team members has also been emphasised (Payne 2000).

GOOD PRACTICE IN MULTIDISCIPLINARY WORKING

Several authors have studied good practice in multidisciplinary working and identified features of both the practices of the team and of the organisa-tion which contribute to efficient and effective team-working. Some of these are outlined below.

Specific team task behaviours

Several aspects of team working have been identified as essential to good practice, for example, good co-ordination, organisation, decision-making and problem-solving skills. Good practice includes 'adapting to change, participating in change, managing the self and managing others' (Pethybridge 2004). Teams work well when members are socially competent, willing to share information, negotiate decisions and solve problems. In order to communicate well and be committed, individuals need a certain level of self-knowledge and confidence in their own professional role and skills, and should respect that of others.

Communication

The ability to communicate effectively is an imperative antecedent to collaboration between team members (Thompson *et al.* 2002). As well as day-to-day decision-making and clinical care, good communication is essential for examining progress, clarifying expectations, cross-fertilising ideas and gaining consensus on problems raised and making mid-course corrections as necessary (Putz and Shinn 2002). Effective communication will enhance the quality of care for patients and improve the effective use of resources, by, for example, avoiding duplication of work (Southill, Mackay and Webb 1995).

Addressing power differentials

Power plays a significant influence in collaborative work across clinical settings. The varied interests of professionals may potentially generate tensions and conflicts. One identified problem with team-working is the effect of perceived differences in status upon harmonious relationships (Hudson 2002), and when some team members are perceived to be of higher seniority than others, effective networking relationship may be impeded. Jones (2005) refers to this as 'turf battles' between professionals, which could be resolved by the distribution of power and decision-making, as far as possible. Collaboration is non-hierarchical in nature and assumes that power is based on knowledge and expertise rather than on role and function. Le Gris *et al.* (2000) suggested that in collaborative groups, those people who possess expertise in the given area must make decisions.

Organisational culture

Good practice in organisations depends upon the culture, which represents the shared values, beliefs and language of the people in the organisation. The culture sets the limits and direction of organisational behaviour (Huq and Martin 2000). Thylefors, Dawson and Jones (1987) noted that high levels of team efficiency were related to a supportive atmosphere, together with well-distributed activity among the team. A sense of common purpose is also one of the key qualities observed by Payne (2000).

Skill mix and individual qualities

Payne (2000) also notes that every team requires a combination of skills and expertise and in well-functioning teams there will be members who are recognised for a particular strength or quality. Polkinthorne (1998) argues that interdisciplinary work requires a certain degree of intellectual fortitude, for different professionals to be prepared to learn from each other, show mutual tolerance and acceptance. Working closely with colleagues from diverse disciplines, who have a different knowledge base, philosophy, mind-set and even language, can be challenging. Flexibility of thought, open-mindedness and critical thinking is essential. Finally, Holland (2004) suggests that for interprofessional working to be successful, team members must recognise that coming together means learning together. Learning to let go of disciplinary defensiveness is essential for multidisciplinary team-working. This will encourage colleagues to feel free to share knowledge so that the collective effectiveness is greater than that which could be achieved by any one individual alone (Chan 2003). This was also recognised by Gibbons (1999), who produced guidelines for psychiatric working in multidisciplinary teams and suggested that consultation, collaboration and supervision were central areas in which professionals ought to receive training.

MULTIDISCIPLINARY WORKING WITH SEX OFFENDERS

The report, *Managing Sex Offenders in the Community* (HM Inspectorate of Probation/HM Inspectorate of Constabulaires 2005), highlighted a number of areas of concern following inspection of the implementation of the multi-agency public protection panel and interactions between the police and the National Probation Service. The report called for a strengthening of relationships between the multi-agency public protection panel and other agencies, improvement in the management of high-risk cases, improved liasion and a joint training programme. In addition, it suggested that the police provided trained specialist officers and changed their practice to move away from personal expertise to research-based approaches.

There are many advantages in bringing together teams to manage sex offenders in the community. Much of the work focuses on risk assessment and management, and Morgan and Hemming (1999) have outlined three interventions in relation to this.

- *Preventative risk management* (including attention to the working relationship, education and early warning signs of relapse).

- *Management of escalating situations* (including de-escalating techniques, rapid responses and crisis intervention).

- *Post-incident supportive management* (including positive support for victims and a culture of learning rather than instant retribution through blaming).

The SOS has found that bringing together different professionals, who each have areas of expertise, can provide a number of benefits to both clients and professionals. For professionals it can provide an opportunity to learn from others and acquire new skills, such as risk assessment and management, treatment approaches and professional development. For clients it ensures that all aspects of their care are delivered by those best-placed to provide it.

The SOS frequently provides time-limited, focused treatments and interventions to individuals whose care is primarily managed by another mental health team or agency (such as probation or social services). Often, joint work is carried out (such as risk assessments), and decision making and problem-solving are addressed in a multidisciplinary and multi-agency context. In order for this approach to work successfully, it is important for it to be explicit about who is responsible for each part.

CASE EXAMPLES

Chapter 8 has already described the relapse prevention approach to managing future potential risk of sexual offending. The following case examples illustrate how this approach can be applied in a multidisciplinary or multi-agency setting, and highlight formal and informal frameworks of support. Many clients will describe having interventions 'done' to them or enforced upon them. The approach used with the following case examples adopts a collaborative approach.

CASE EXAMPLE 1

Mr C was referred to the SOS by the reverend of his local church. Mr C is a longstanding member of the church and has attended for over 18 years. He is a 35-year-old, single man, who lives alone in a bedsit.

The church became concerned about Mr C following two allegations of sexually inappropriate behaviour towards children. The reverend was approached by parents of an eight-year-old boy who claimed Mr C had spoken to him in a sexual manner. The reverend and the church's Child Protection Officer spoke to Mr C about appropriate sexual boundaries and behaviour with children and believed the matter had been resolved.

Almost immediately, another parent informed the reverend that an incident had occurred several months previously in which Mr C had persuaded his eight-year-old daughter to play in the church garden and had removed her T-shirt before she ran away. Mr C had convinced the girl 'not to tell anyone' and it is unclear what his intentions were had the girl stayed.

The reverend had contacted social services about these events but it was not felt that a response could be made as there was no familial abuse, and the reverend did not receive any response from his request for help from the Public Protection Unit.

The church's Child Protection Officer and the reverend devised the following contract or plan for Mr C:

- Not to talk or mix with the children.

- He was not allowed to be in the same room as and was not to talk to or stand next to a child.

- He was not to sit or stand next to a child during church service. He had to move if a child sat next to him.

- Under no circumstances should Mr C accompany a child to the toilet/garden/secluded area. If a child asks for help he should immediately get another adult.

The reverend became aware of our service after discussions with his local GP and Mr C was promptly referred to the SOS.

Part of the work between the SOS and the church was to examine how realistic some of the contract was (i.e. not being in the same room as a child), who was going to monitor this and what would be the sanctions if this was broken. It was also important to acknowledge the tremendous efforts the church had made to prioritise child safety and also seek help for Mr C. Church members were willing to be part of Mr C's future support framework (Figure 10.1).

Mr C initially minimised his inappropriate behaviour and viewed his actions as minor indiscretions. To aid Mr C to develop an understanding

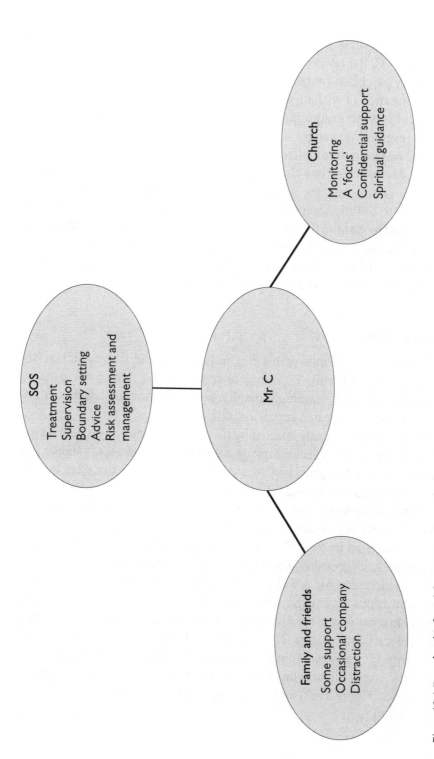

Figure 10.1 Formal and informal frameworks of support

SOS

Treatment
Supervision
Boundary setting
Advice
Risk assessment and
management

Church

Monitoring
A 'focus'
Confidential support
Spiritual guidance

Mr C

Family and friends

Some support
Occasional company
Distraction

into the seriousness of the situation, several meetings were convened between Mr C, the reverend, the church Child Protection Officer and the community psychiatric nurse from the SOS. The reverend found himself in a difficult situation of wishing to remain supportive to Mr C but also wanting to protect his wider congregation, and Mr C had some difficulty accepting that the reverend was angry with him.

Mr C was keen to complete the relapse prevention framework, partly for his own development but also to 'please' the reverend. Mr C felt that in some way completing the work with the SOS would 'redeem' him and enable him to be fully accepted back into the congregation. Nonetheless, he worked hard to identify future risk situations, potential routes to relapse and effective coping strategies (Figure 10.2). The relapse prevention framework was completed by Mr C together with the community psychiatric nurse from the SOS, and it was then shared with the church.

CASE EXAMPLE 2

Mr A is a 25-year-old man with a diagnosis of paranoid schizophrenia. His childhood was difficult, including rejection by his biological parents, resulting in adoption, learning difficulties and behavioural problems. Mr A was the victim of repeated sexual assaults while in foster care.

Mr A was subsequently rejected by his adoptive family as his illness progressed. In a psychotic episode Mr A approached a lone female of a similar age requesting she accompany him to a disco. She declined the offer but he followed her into an alley and sexually assaulted her by touching her breasts. He informed her he wanted to have sex with her. As he pushed her to the ground, her screams alerted a passer-by and Mr A ran away. A few days later Mr A was arrested by the police as he matched the victim's description and was positively identified by the victim in an identification parade.

It was clear that Mr A was mentally unwell and he was admitted to an acute admissions psychiatric ward, whereby his behaviour became highly sexually inappropriate, openly masturbating and making sexual comments to female staff and patients. The SOS assessed Mr A and agreed to become involved in his care, providing individual treatment with the community psychiatric nurse, identifying areas of risk, formal and informal support frameworks (Figure 10.3) and compiling a relapse prevention framework (Figure 10.4).

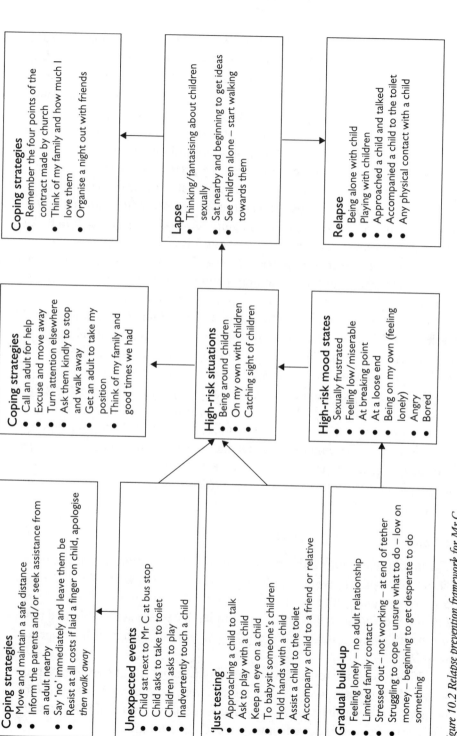

Coping strategies
- Remember the four points of the contract made by church
- Think of my family and how much I love them
- Organise a night out with friends

Coping strategies
- Call an adult for help
- Excuse and move away
- Turn attention elsewhere
- Ask them kindly to stop and walk away
- Get an adult to take my position
- Think of my family and good times we had

Coping strategies
- Move and maintain a safe distance
- Inform the parents and/or seek assistance from an adult nearby
- Say 'no' immediately and leave them be
- Resist at all costs if laid a finger on child, apologise *then walk away*

Lapse
- Thinking/fantasising about children sexually
- Sat nearby and beginning to get ideas
- See children alone – start walking towards them

Relapse
- Being alone with child
- Playing with children
- Approached a child and talked
- Accompanied a child to the toilet
- Any physical contact with a child

High-risk situations
- Being around children
- On my own with children
- Catching sight of children

High-risk mood states
- Sexually frustrated
- Feeling low/miserable
- At breaking point
- At a loose end
- Being on my own (feeling lonely)
- Angry
- Bored

Unexpected events
- Child sat next to Mr C at bus stop
- Child asks to take to toilet
- Children asks to play
- Inadvertently touch a child

'Just testing'
- Approaching a child to talk
- Ask to play with a child
- Keep an eye on a child
- To babysit someone's children
- Hold hands with a child
- Assist a child to the toilet
- Accompany a child to a friend or relative

Gradual build-up
- Feeling lonely – no adult relationship
- Limited family contact
- Stressed out – not working – at end of tether
- Struggling to cope – unsure what to do – low on money – beginning to get desperate to do something

Figure 10.2 Relapse prevention framework for Mr C

It is appropriate to say that both Mr A and the community mental health team found that some difficulties emerged during treatment regarding sexual offending and future risk management. Mr A was deeply embarrassed by his actions, which often prevented him from discussing the index offence. The community psychiatric nurse and social worker in the community mental health team felt unskilled and anxious, requiring increased correspondence providing support and guidance.

Mr A was able to complete the relapse prevention framework over a period of 12 weeks with the community psychiatric nurse from the SOS. Mr A agreed to share the relapse prevention framework with his team, and it was made available to the team on a computer disk to enable them to make changes as necessary in the future, viewing his risk as a dynamic concept. The community psychiatric nurse from the SOS met with the community psychiatric nurse from the community mental health team twice to discuss the work and to pass on the work from the SOS to the team.

The case was closed by the SOS, but after 18 months Mr A was referred back to the SOS as he had been exhibiting sexually disinhibited behaviour to female residents at his hostel. The SOS met with the community mental health team and the hostel staff and it became clear that Mr A was using large amounts of cannabis and displaying early warning signs of relapse. Most significantly, Mr A felt he had some right to behave in this way and displayed some concerning attitudes towards women, which needed to be identified and addressed. With a multidisciplinary approach and support and a re-focus on risk management Mr A was able to remain in the community, maintain his hostel placement and not commit any further offences.

SUMMARY AND CONCLUSIONS

The literature highlights the many different interpretations of multi-agency or multidisciplinary working: often teams are working with role ambiguity, power struggles, cultural differences and different philosophies of care. Equally, we have seen that positive examples of care are achievable, and how the multi-agency public protection panel has strengthened inter-agency working.

What is required for successful working is respect for the value each professional group brings and embracing different ways of working instead of professional defensiveness. More work is required, especially as cases are often complex and require many agencies' collaboration.

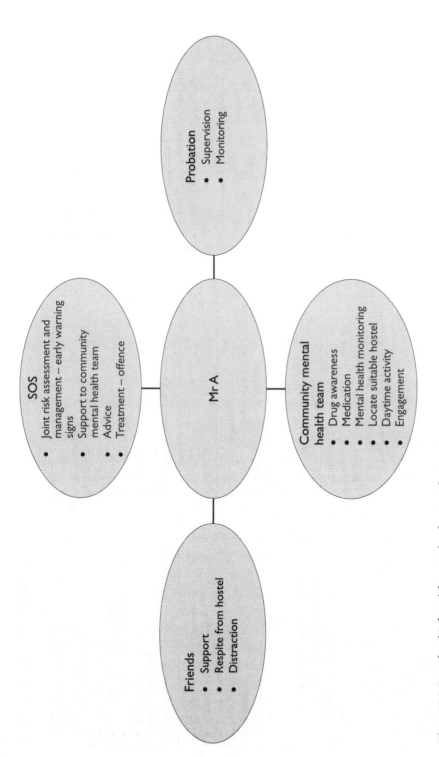

Figure 10.3 Formal and informal frameworks of support for Mr A

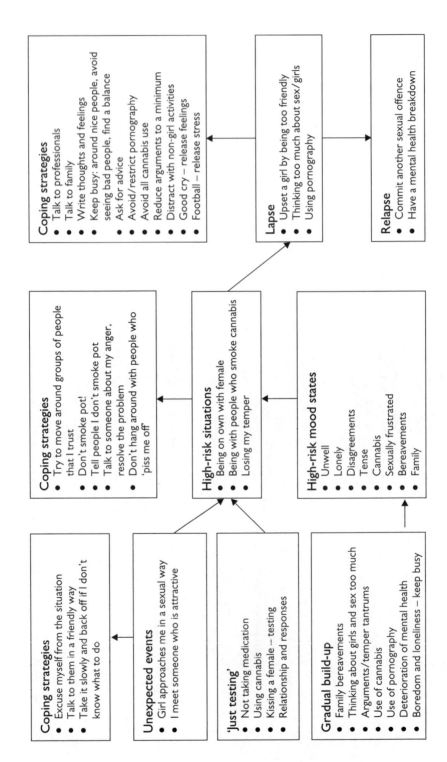

Coping strategies
- Talk to professionals
- Talk to family
- Write thoughts and feelings
- Keep busy: around nice people, avoid seeing bad people, find a balance
- Ask for advice
- Avoid/restrict pornography
- Avoid all cannabis use
- Reduce arguments to a minimum
- Distract with non-girl activities
- Good cry – release feelings
- Football – release stress

Lapse
- Upset a girl by being too friendly
- Thinking too much about sex/girls
- Using pornography

Relapse
- Commit another sexual offence
- Have a mental health breakdown

Coping strategies
- Try to move around groups of people that I trust
- Don't smoke pot!
- Tell people I don't smoke pot
- Talk to someone about my anger, resolve the problem
- Don't hang around with people who 'piss me off'

High-risk situations
- Being on own with female
- Being with people who smoke cannabis
- Losing my temper

High-risk mood states
- Unwell
- Lonely
- Disagreements
- Tense
- Cannabis
- Sexually frustrated
- Bereavements
- Family

Coping strategies
- Excuse myself from the situation
- Talk to them in a friendly way
- Take it slowly and back off if I don't know what to do

Unexpected events
- Girl approaches me in a sexual way
- I meet someone who is attractive

'Just testing'
- Not taking medication
- Using cannabis
- Kissing a female – testing
- Relationship and responses

Gradual build-up
- Family bereavements
- Thinking about girls and sex too much
- Arguments/temper tantrums
- Use of cannabis
- Use of pornography
- Deterioration of mental health
- Boredom and loneliness – keep busy

Figure 10.4 Relapse prevention framework for Mr A

REFERENCES

Bellack, J. P. and O'Neil, E. H. (2000) 'Recreating nursing practice for a new century: recommendations and implications of the PEW health professions commissions' final report. *Nursing and Health Care Perspectives 21*, 1, 14–21.

Bristol Royal Infirmary Inquiry. (2001) *The Inquiry into the Management of the Care of Children Receiving Complex Heart Surgery at the Bristol Royal Infirmary.* Bristol: Royal Infirmary.

Brooker, C. and Whyte, L. (2000) *Multidisciplinary Working in a Secure Psychiatric Environment.* Sheffield: University of Sheffield and Hallam University.

Chan, C. A. (2003) 'Examining the relationship between individual, team and organisational learning in an Australian hospital.' *Learn Health Social Care 2*, 223–235.

Cook, G., Gerrish, K. and Clarke, C. (2001) 'Decision making in teams: issues arising from two UK evaluations.' *Journal of Interprofessional Care 15*, 141–151.

Department of Health (DoH). (2003) *The Victoria Climbié Inquiry.* London: HMSO.

Eaton, L. (1998) 'Arranged marriages.' *Health Service Journal 108*, (5627), 24–26.

Farrell, M., Schmitt, M. and Heinemann, G. (2001) 'Informal roles and the states of interdisciplinary team development.' *Journal of Interprofessional Care 15*, 30, 281–295.

Gibbons, K. (1999) 'Teamwork in primary care: an evaluation of the contribution of integrated nursing teams.' *Health and Social Care Community 7*, 367–375.

Hardy, B.,Turrell, A. and Wistow, G. (eds). (1992) *Innovations in Community Care Management.* Aldershot: Avebury.

Her Majesties Inspectorate of Probation/Her Majesties Inspectorate of Constabularies. (2005) *Managing Sex Offenders in the Community – Joint Inspection on Sex Offenders.* Available at www.inspectorates.homeoffice.gov.uk/hmiprobation/inspect_reports/thematic-inspect ions1.html/sothematic.pdf, accessed on 19 March 2008.

Holland, K. (2004) 'Interprofessional working and learning for integrated health and social care services.' *Nurse Education Practice 4*, 228–229.

Hudson, B. (2002) 'Interprofessionality in health and social care: "The Achilles heel of partnership".' *Journal of Interprofessional Care 16*, 1, 7–17.

Hudson, B. (2007) 'Pessimism and optimism in interprofessional working: the Sedgefield integrated team.' *Journal of Interprofessional Care*, 1, 3–15.

Huq, Z. and Martin, T. N. (2000) 'Workforce cultural factors in TQM/CQI implementation in hospitals.' *Health Care Management Review 25*, 80–93.

Irvine, R., Kerridge, L., McPhee and Freaman, S. (2002) 'Interprofessional care and ethics: consensus or clash of cultures?' *Journal of Interprofessional Care 16*, 199– 210.

Jones, M. (2005) 'Cultural Power in Organisations. The Dynamics of Interprofessional Teams.' In G. Whiteford and C. V. Wright (eds) *Occupation and Control in Practice.* Sydney: Elsevier.

Keene, J. and Xuefang, L. (2005) 'A study of a total social service population and its inter-agency shared care population.' *British Journal of Social Work 35*, 1145–1161.

Kallerberg, A. and Moody, J. (1994) 'Human resource management and organisational performance.' *American Behavioral Science 37*, 948–962.

Leathard, A. (1994) *Going Interprofessional: Working Together for Health and Welfare.* London: Routledge.

Leathard, A. (2003) *Interprofessional Collaboration from Policy to Practice in Health and Social Care.* New York, NY: Brunner–Routledge.

Le Gris, J., Weir, R., Browne, G., Gofni, A., Stewart, L. and Easton, S. (2000) 'Developing a model for collaborative research: the complexities and challenges of implementation.' *International Journal of Nursing Studies 37*, 65–79.

Marshall, M., Preston, M., Scott, E. and Wincott, P. (eds). (1979) *Teamwork For and Against: An Appraisal of Multidisciplinary Practice.* London: British Association of Social Workers.

Matravers, A. (ed.) (2003) *Sex Offenders in the Community: Managing and reducing risks.* Uffculme: Willan Publishing.

McCallin, A. (2004) 'Interdisciplinary practice – a matter of team work: an integrated literature review.' *Journal of Clinical Nursing 8*, 6–14.

Miller, C., Ross, N. and Freeman, M. (1999) *Shared Learning and Clinical Teamwork: New Directions in Education for Multiprofessional Practice.* Researching Professional Education. London: ENB Research Report Series for Nursing, Midwifery and Health Visiting.

Morgan, S. and Hemming, M. (1999) 'Balancing care and control: risk management and compulsory community treatment.' *Mental Handicap and Learning Disability Care 3*, 1, 19–21.

NHS London. (2006) *The Independent Inquiry into the Care and Treatment of John Barrett.* London: South West London Strategic Health Authority.

North East Thames and South East Thames Regional Health Authority. (1994) *The Report of the Inquiry into the Care and Treatment of Christopher Clunis.* London: HMSO.

Owens, D. (1998) 'Joint Working: Dual carriageway.' *Health Service Journal 108*, 5672, 29.

Payne, M. (2000) *Teamwork in Multiprofessional Care.* Basingstoke: Macmillan.

Pethybridge, J. (2004) 'How team influences discharge plan from hospital: a study of our multi-disciplinary teams in an acute hospital in England.' *Journal of Interprofessional Care 18*, 1, 29–41.

Pietroni, P. (1992) 'Towards reflective practice – the language of health and social care.' *Journal of Interprofessional Care 1*, Spring, 7–16.

Polkinthorne, J. (1998) *Belief in God in an Age of Science.* New Haven, CT: Yale University Press.

Putz, B. E. and Shinn, L. J. (2002) 'Strategic patrnerships.' *Journal of Nursing Administration 32*, 182–184.

Southill, K., Mackay, L. and Webb, C. (1995) *Interprofessional Relations in Health Care.* London: Edward Arnold.

Thompson, D., Socolar, R., Brown, L. and Haggerty, J. (2002) 'Interagency collaboration in Seven North Carolina Counties.' *Journal of Public Health Management and Practice 8*, 5, 55–64.

Thylefors, B., Dawson, C. R. and Jones, B. R. (1987) 'A simple system for the assessement of trachoma and its complications.' *World Health Organization Bulletin 65*, 477–483.

Van Eyk, H. and Baum, F. (2002) 'Learning about interagency collaboration: trialling collaborative projects between hospitals and community health services.' *Health and Social Care in the Community 10*, 262–269.

11

Non-abusing Parents and their Role in Risk Management

Sarah Galloway and Natalie Hogg

The first I knew that something was wrong was when the police came knocking on my door at 6.30 a.m. with a search warrant. (Ms P)

The social worker made it clear within 10 minutes of meeting me that she viewed me as 'unable to protect' until she could prove otherwise. (Ms O)

INTRODUCTION

The non-abusing parent's responsibilities are multifaceted; as a parent and a partner she is required to protect her children, monitor the abuser's behaviour and contribute to the management of his risk as part of this process of protection. Many men who have offended or carried out sexually inappropriate behaviour against a child remain in the family home or at least continue to have contact with their children. Others start a family or join a new family where there are children. This chapter uses the term 'abusers' to describe both men with convictions and those with problematic behaviour, instead of 'offender' as not all men have convictions. Therefore, along with consideration of the risk posed by the abuser, consideration of the non-abusing parent's ability to protect her children is an integral part of the management of risk within the wider system surrounding the abuser. Although, with one exception, our service has been asked to assess female non-abusing parents, we acknowledge that men can also be in this role. However, given that our experience is almost exclusively in working with females, the focus for this chapter will be on the female non-abusing parent.

This chapter aims to explore the significant role that the non-abusing parent plays in the child protection framework. It will address the complex issues that arise around the assessment of the non-abusing parent's ability to protect, and details a psycho-educative intervention that addresses risk management. The chapter will also comment on the complexities of interactions between non-abusing parents and the different agencies which become involved in supporting them. Case examples will be used to illustrate the process of assessment and intervention with this client group.

LITERATURE REGARDING NON-ABUSING PARENTS

Often, the focus of risk assessment remains preoccupied with the abuser himself; however, an abuser's risk should not be assessed in isolation when he is embedded within a family structure where there are potential victims (Craissati 2004). Craissati (2004) describes a child protection triangle which identifies three factors that must be considered in the protection of a child from abuse. These are: the offender's risk characteristics; the child as a potential victim; and the mother as a non-abusing parent.

Despite the crucial role that women play in child protection within a multitude of situations, the literature largely focuses on non-offending mothers of abused children, and even this group is rarely studied in its own right (Nakhle Tamraz 1996). Nakhle Tamraz (1996) comprehensively reviewed the literature on non-abusing mothers of sexually abused children and found that much of the information that exists is opinion-based, and obtained through clinical insights, fragmented observation and reconstructed data. Meanwhile, the research-based literature on non-abusing mothers has poor theoretical foundations and is over-reliant on case studies. There are also numerous methodological flaws, including a failure to use instruments with psychometric properties and sampling that depended solely on clinical referrals. Also, data are often obtained by interviews and mostly focus on maternal reactions to disclosure. Nakhle Tamraz (1996) draws the conclusion that neither the opinion-based nor the research-based literature has consolidated an integrated perspective on non-offending mothers.

The research literature regarding the non-abusing parent predominantly focuses on mothers of children who have been abused. However, in reality, a partner may be called on to undertake the protective role for their child or for the abuser's child, even if this child has not been a victim of the abuse. There are a number of reasons why a woman may be assessed for her ability to protect her child when the child has not been a victim. Such cases arise when the abuser has abused other children, either during or before the start of their relationship, or if the abuser has been accessing child pornography. Craissati (2004) argues that it is reasonable to assume that the issues are largely similar in both cases; however, the impact of disclosure may be diluted if the victim is not the non-abusing mother's own child. There is a need within a clinical setting to consider the complexity of the role that the non-abusing parent can have in the family of an offender and, in particular, the complex role she holds by being mother, partner and protector.

ASSESSMENT

The ability and willingness of a mother to protect her child from further abuse is more important than the severity or the frequency of abuse in predicting whether the child is removed by social services (Pellegrin and Wagner 1990). Social services rely on non-abusing parents as external inhibitors (Smith 1994). Therefore, assessing a non-abusing parent's ability to protect should be a priority for resources. Smith (1994) argues that any assessment work should be done with the non-abusing parent on her own and separate from the alleged offender.

Smith (1994) has outlined 10 key areas that should be addressed during an assessment of mothers of sexually abused children. We have adapted these areas of assessment where necessary so that they can be applied to parents who are protecting children in situations where it is not their own children who have been the victims of the abuser (italic type is used where relevant). The areas outlines for assessment are:

1. The non-abusing parent's position regarding the child's disclosure *or their position regarding the disclosure of abuse of another child.*

2. The non-abusing parent's feelings towards the child (*their own or another child*) following disclosure.

3. The non-abusing parent's role in the disclosing process.

4. The non-abusing parent's position regarding who is responsible for the abuse.

5. The non-abusing parent's perceived options for protection.

6. The non-abusing parent's co-operation with statutory rights.

7. The non-abusing parent's relationship history.

8. The non-abusing parent's openness about sexual abuse in their family, community and support network.

9. The non-abusing parent's own abuse history.

10. The non-abusing parent's vulnerabilities, such as disability.

Smith (1994) argues that how a non-abusing parent functions in these areas may be shown on a continuum between 'optimal' and 'dismal' ends of functioning. In some areas the mother may move between different ends of functioning and consequently her ability to protect will also change. It is therefore important to consider these areas as dynamic factors where change is likely to affect the individual's ability to protect. For example, before a court hearing a non-abusing partner may believe her partner is innocent. However, she may also say that should he be found guilty she would review her position thus changing her motivation to protect.

Prognostic indicators

Smith (1994) and Craissati (2004) recommend an assessment of the non-abusing parent's relationship history, vulnerabilities, abuse history and experience of sexual abuse in their own family owing to their importance as prognostic indicators of her ability to protect her children in the future.

According to Craissati (2004) poor prognostic indicators for a non-abusing parent's ability to protect are:

- a childhood history of severe and repeated sexual or physical abuse

- a relationship with her own mother which was characterised by extreme rejection and emotional deprivation

- repeated pattern of relationships with men who are abusive sexually and/or physically abusive towards the woman or her children

- previous concerns of neglect and abuse towards her own children
- mental health difficulties, including personality disorder or substance abuse.

The women referred to our service are assessed on these factors and the frequency of identification of poor prognostic indicators for these women is outlined in Figure 11.1.

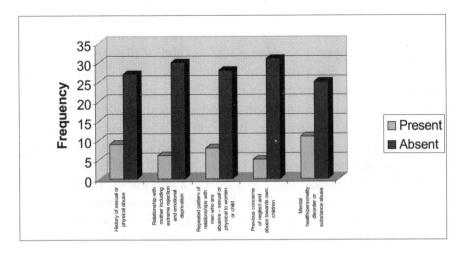

Figure 11.1 Prognostic indicators of protection (Craissati 2004) taken from clinical data

Understanding the abusive behaviour

It is important to establish a non-abusing parent's reaction to a disclosure of offending, regardless of whether or not it is the child who has made the disclosure, or whether it is incest or another offence that has taken place. It is important to establish both her attitudinal and emotional reaction to the disclosure both at the time of the disclosure and as time has progressed. According to Bentovim (1991) it is essential to assess the stance of the mother and to establish how sympathetic she is towards the victim and whether she scapegoats or blames the victim. It is also helpful to establish her understanding of how she believes her reactions have been viewed by agencies involved since the disclosure.

Although clinical opinions often intimate that the non-abusing partner is aware of the sexual abuse, research data show that non-abusing mothers are generally unaware of the abuse and present with high levels of distress following disclosure (Nakhle Tamraz 1995; Mapp 1998). Nakhle Tamraz (1995) argues that after a disclosure of abuse the non-abusing parent will often be viewed as having transgressed her cultural responsibilities of fulfilling her marital and mothering functions, leading to her feeling criticised and blamed by others. Women can often be expected to terminate their relationship with the abuser and are deemed unable to protect the children if the abuser continues to remain in the family (Farmer and Owen 1998).

According to Hooper (1992), maternal reactions to the disclosure of incest can vary considerably. They can experience a sense of loss, a lack of trust in a reliable partner, in their mothering ability, their femininity and their control over life events. According to Bolen and Lamb (2004), following a disclosure, one-third of non-offending guardians respond with vacillation in support and these non-offending guardians are at greater risk for having their children removed. Bolen and Lamb (2004) argue that this perceived vacillation is, in fact, ambivalence and reflects the struggle between the guardian's allegiances to both the child and the abuser. They also argue that while guardians may vacillate in terms of their beliefs about the abuse, behaviourally they may still be able to provide support to their child. Equally, belief that the abuse occurred does not necessarily equate to provision of a safe environment, and a study by Bolen, Lamb and Gradante (2002) showed that guardian's belief that abuse occurred was a better indicator of emotional support than providing for the basic safety of the child.

Plans for protection

Another important area for assessment is to establish how much importance the non-abusing parent places on the protection of their child, and what measures they intend to put in place to do so. It is also important to establish how well the partner engages with statutory authorities and to what extent she takes a clear role in continuing to support disclosure to appropriate authorities.

Our experience of working with non-abusing parents is that it is often difficult for partners initially to devise strategies for protection. This appears to be because it requires them to reflect on areas that they have previously not had to consider, or have taken for granted. An inability to generate protection strategies is not necessarily of concern, particularly if the non-abusing parent is receptive to the suggestion of measures that need to be put in place to protect the child. If the parent is not capable of developing a protection plan, or of carrying out a plan that is developed with them, it is important to re-assess the level of risk to the child given that this important protective factor is not in place (Smith 1994).

CLINICAL EXPERIENCES OF WORKING WITH THE NON-ABUSING PARENT IN THE SEX OFFENDER SERVICE

Referrals

Referrals to our Sex Offender Service (SOS) for assessment of a non-abusing parent's ability to protect their children from an abusing partner have increased since the development of the service in 1993 (see Chapter 6). Increasingly, agencies are recognising that an understanding of the non-abusing parent's ability to protect is of equal relevance as the abuser's risk of re-offending when considering the safety of children. Currently the SOS is deemed the most appropriate agency to undertake such assessments because it has extensive knowledge both of patterns of offending and risk management throughout the system.

This section draws upon relevant literature as well as clinical data of referrals of non-abusing parents collected from a nine-year period from 1998 to 2007. The SOS received 48 referrals over this nine-year period. Of these referrals 25 per cent ($n = 12$) did not attend, distributed evenly over this period. The referrals were generated from a number of agencies, Social Services (83%), solicitors (6%), court reports (6%), psychiatrists (2.5%) and unknown (2.5%). The women referred to the service were from a diverse group from a range of different socio-economic backgrounds and ranged in age from 22 to 56 years. All the women were either mothers to be, mothers themselves and four were grandmothers.

They were from the following ethnic groups: White-British (74%); White-other (8%); Black-Caribbean (6%); Black-British (2%); Asian (2%); Asian-Indian (2%) and unknown (6%).

The data found the women's marital status was: married (31%); cohabiting (29%); single (19%); unknown (11%); with a partner (6%); and separated (4%). Some of the women were employed (23%), including a variety of occupations, (62.5%) were unemployed and 14.5 per cent unknown.

From our clinical data 10 per cent ($n = 5$) of women have formed relationships with men who offended in previous relationships, including
offences such as rape, buggery, indecent assault and internet offences.

Suspicious minds

During assessments conducted by the SOS, the women often described a
difficult initial encounter with Social Services and felt that they had been
treated with suspicion. Some felt that they had been viewed as a possible
secondary offender. Others felt criticised for not having been aware that the
abuse was taking place. Some women who have started a relationship with
abusers who had abused in the past felt angry that Social Services were both
interfering in their relationship and examining their parenting skills which
had previously never been called into question. These concerns of being
judged by social workers and other professionals may, to some extent, be
accurate perceptions, reflecting an assessment process where professionals
are called upon to make certain judgements about the non-abusing parent's
behaviour and attitudes. However, non-abusing parents may also be
sensitive to criticism owing to their own belief that they should have known
about the abuse. It is also important to note that some women are at the
'dismal' end of functioning in terms of protection (Smith 1994). However,
there is a risk of making the assumption that all women are at this end of
functioning when many may, in fact, be at the 'optimal' end of the
continuum.

Many women felt that they had been 'let down' by Social Services and
that they had been 'pre-judged'. They strongly believed that they had been
treated as though they had also been an offender. They felt an overwhelm-
ing feeling of confusion as they had strong feelings towards both partners
and children, but felt they needed to take sides.

It is only in the last decade that we have accepted that female offending
occurs, but this continues to be absent from serious study (Denov 2004).
Occasionally, the SOS receives referrals for a woman's ability to protect,
which, in turn, highlight concerns about their own risk to children.
Although not within the scope of this chapter, research does show that
women also commit sexual offences (Kelly, Regan and Burton 1991;
Saradjian and Hanks 1996). The SOS has received six referrals that have
highlighted problematic behaviours, including offering indecent photographs of children for sale, indecent assault on a child, indecent assault on a
female peer as a teenager and inappropriate sexual boundaries.

Assessment

The service assesses both individuals separately to maximise the potential for both abuser and non-abusing parent to speak openly during the assessment process.

Where possible, the SOS endeavours at some point in the assessment process to meet the abuser and his partner together. This meeting is arranged in order to observe their interactions and to understand how, as a couple, they narrate their experiences and understanding of the abusing parent's behaviour and the need for risk management.

Often, the partner may not know the victim personally, and it is important to establish whether or not they feel any empathy for the victim and how seriously they take their partner's offending. It is important to establish whether the non-abusing parent has a clear understanding of the circumstances in which the offence occurred, and to establish her attitude towards the offending. This is particularly important in terms of determining whom she identifies as being responsible for the abuse. Figure 11.2 outlines the reported reactions of women assessed by the SOS to the disclosure of abuse as a continuum and highlights the varying responses.

Protected and terminated relationship

Protected, confronted partner

Protected, but felt blamed

Historical offences, so a 'dilution' of the protective response

Some protection, 'minimised' or queried seriousness of allegations

Denied allegations

Chose partner over child

Colluded or set up abuse

Participated in the abuse

Figure 11.2 A continuum of non-abusing parents' reactions to the disclosure of abuse (taken from clinical data).

A PSYCHO-EDUCATIVE GROUP FOR NON-ABUSING PARENTS

According to Bentovim (1991) there is a need for parents who are in a non-abusing role to have a greater authority over the children and the offender. It is also important for them to have strong supportive networks. Through the assessment process it frequently becomes clear that non-abusing parents are in need of a space to share their stories and to develop skills and knowledge to enable them to protect their children and to understand their partner's offending. This has been described in the literature by Calder (2001). Some of the women talk of isolation and a lack of support. Many lack a thorough understanding of how the abuser has come to offend. They also have difficulty in coming to terms with their new role as protector and the increasing awareness that this responsibility will continue throughout their children's early years until adulthood and may potentially extend to grandchildren as well.

Bentovim (1991) argues that specific work needs to be undertaken with mothers to help them develop a sense of assertive protectiveness of their child. The SOS has addressed this need by providing a psycho-educative group, which is focused on developing knowledge and awareness of offending and the skills to manage risk.

The SOS has developed a group programme which takes place over eight weeks. This group is not focused on parenting, but is, rather, an opportunity for non-abusing parents to think about protection of their children and how they move forwards as partners of abusers, or if separated from these abusers, how they move on safely to other relationships. According to Smith (1994) non-abusing partners should have knowledge of both general and specific risk in relation to the protection of their children and this is the primary objective of the group programme.

The following areas are addressed in the group with a view to developing the participants' awareness of the process of abuse, awareness of risk and risk management.

Stereotypes about men who abuse and distorted thinking

During this module, the heterogeneity of men who offend is highlighted. It is important for the non-abusing partner to understand that there is not one specific type of person who will abuse children, and they need to be guided by attitudes and behaviours rather than unhelpful stereotypes. The non-abusing parent will often have difficulty viewing her partner or ex-partner as the 'type' of person who would abuse others, and, indeed, will struggle with how her relationship with an abusive man fits with her view of herself. Therefore it is important to identify how men carry out abusive behaviour in the context of distorted thinking and behaviour, rather than relying on unfounded stereotypes as a guide.

Planned behaviour and models of offending

There is a diverse range of processes by which men come to abuse, and no single model is applicable to all individuals. However, our clinical experience of assessments suggests that many of the women's partners have been aware at some level that their behaviour was wrong, and the Finkelhor Model (Finkelhor 1984; see Chapter 1) is helpful as a framework with which to understand how this occurred. An understanding of how their partners planned to abuse and the pattern of their sexually abusive behaviour can allow the non-abusing parent to understand the process by which their partners have come to offend and facilitate them in identifying ways in which they can be alert to similar behaviour in the future. This can often be a significant moment for the non-abusing parent, especially for those who were in a relationship with their partners at the time of their offending. It can help them to realise the ways in which they were subverted and misled in order to facilitate their partner's offending. This is also an opportunity for the non-abusing parent to highlight gaps or an omission in her understanding of her partner's offending. It can highlight the extent to which their partners have not been clear with them about how they came to abuse and identify key areas for further discussion with their partners in order to be sure that they have the full understanding of the risk. The facilitators will usually be aware of the abuser's pattern of offending and risk factors because of the assessment process. It is important that, when doing this work, facilitators do not disclose confidential information but allow the non-abusing parent herself to identify what information she needs to know.

Communicating with the child about the abusing parent's past behaviour and future risk

Often, the non-abusing parent has concerns about how to talk to their child about their partner's offending. It is important for them to be honest with the child and to discuss the pertinent issues with their children at a level which they understand. Often, if the non-abusing parent is managing contact between child and abuser, they will have to explain to the child why the abuser no longer lives with them and why they are monitoring this contact so carefully. The non-abusing parent can often feel blamed by the children for preventing the abusing parent from being in the family home.

Sexual boundaries

This module addresses sexual boundaries within the family. Some of the non-abusing parents will have been in environments where there will have been a lack of safe sexual boundaries owing to the behaviour of the offending partner. Others may not have given consideration to the importance of such boundaries, or may not have experienced adequate modelling of boundaries when they were children. Encouraging the non-abusive parents to think about the sexual boundaries that need to be in place in their family, and how they will maintain such boundaries, is an important part of the protective process.

Risk management

With a detailed understanding of potential patterns of offending, and an understanding of the specific issues relating to their situation, women can begin to think of 'alert lists' which will warn them of increased risk. The group sessions place emphasis on the non-abusing parent's understanding of her partner's offending in order to alert her to future concerning behaviour. The non-abusing parents group also allows each group member to develop an 'escape route'. This is a clear plan that each of the women will follow in the event of serious concerns for their children. Often, the anxiety that the women feel about protecting their children while continuing their relationship is better managed when they have an understanding of how they focus their attention, and the appropriate areas that require monitoring. This can give the non-abusing parents a sense of empowerment over their situation which they may not previously have had.

GROUP EVALUATION

Group members often use the space to discuss their anxieties and distress at their experiences. This, coupled with the provision of practical skills and knowledge, gives them a sense of empowerment and an ability to manage the risk in their complicated family system. Qualitative pre- and post-assessments demonstrate clear improvements in group members' knowledge of risk and strategies for risk management. Some of the personal goals for members of the group include being able to talk to their children about what had happened, meeting a new partner and knowing how to ensure the safety of their child in specific situations. At the end of the group the members reported that these goals had been met. Overall, they reported being able to manage their roles as both partner, mother and protector more efficiently.

Following separate interventions with offenders and partners there may be potential for couples work during the next phase of rehabilitation (Bentovim 1991). For work with couples to take place it is important that the non-abusing parent knows about the abuse, and that both individuals understand and appreciate each other's views and feelings relating to the offending. It can also be helpful to help the couple to look at issues of sexuality between them at this stage.

PROBLEMS WITH ENGAGEMENT

Inevitably, there are those women who are reluctant to engage in an assessment and/or treatment. There are a number of factors in our experience which influence whether or not a non-abusing parent is willing to engage with our service. These include:

- inflexible work commitments
- an inability to withstand the emotional strain of talking about their experiences
- reluctance to engage with another service when often they are already overwhelmed with the number of professionals or agencies involved
- the absence of a conviction, which can raise questions about the necessity of their attendance
- concerns about the stigma and meaning of attending appointments provided by the SOS
- changes in child protection arrangements, such as de-registration on the Child Protection Register.

Where possible it may be helpful to speak to the non-abusing partners by telephone initially, which can reassure them about how the appointment will be structured and discuss any concerns they may have. It is also important to be flexible in providing appointments. It is often the encouragement and support of social workers that enables the non-abusing parents to attend. However, it is important to acknowledge that, despite the social worker trying to provide as much support as possible, often the non-abusing parents will view this as pressure to attend against their will. In such instances it is important to acknowledge this difficulty and encourage the non-abusing parent to consider the benefits in being open and honest in the appointment.

CASE EXAMPLES

The case examples will draw upon two differing clinical cases the authors were involved with. The first is a family where grooming occurred within it and raises questions about the role of the non-abusing parent. In the second, the non-abusing parent was completely unaware that her husband was using child pornography and the referral was primarily based on her reaction to the situation.

CASE EXAMPLE 1

Mrs E separated from her husband of 20 years and father of their daughter as a result of the domestic violence in their relationship.

Shortly after the separation the daughter disclosed to a teacher that her father had been behaving in a sexually inappropriate manner towards her. Their case was referred to Social Services by the school and Mrs E and her daughter were interviewed by the police.

Mr E had heavily encouraged Mrs E to work night-shifts in order to spend time alone with his daughter, and to gradually exclude her from a parenting role with her daughter. He was able to create this role over several years making him the primary care-giver and pushing Mrs E further away, both physically and emotionally, from her daughter. It must also be acknowledged that she willingly adopted this position without questioning the impact it had on the relationship with her daughter.

It was alleged that as Mrs E's daughter entered puberty Mr E began behaving in a sexually inappropriate manner towards her. His behaviour included showing his daughter pornographic videos as a means of 'sex education' and asking her to masturbate or touch him under the auspices of teaching her about male genitalia.

Social Services referred Mr and Mrs E to the SOS for an assessment of the risk Mr E posed to his daughter and an assessment of Mrs E's ability to protect her daughter.

Mrs E was assessed using the key areas recommended by Craissati (2004) and Smith (1994) which highlighted new concerns about her ability to protect for the following reasons.

- Mrs E could not elicit any protective strategies she might employ or any relevant behaviours that would trigger concern.

- Mr E was easily able to manipulate Mrs E and she was unable to form her own sexual boundaries.

- Mrs E had a lack of understanding of sexually appropriate behaviour and boundaries.

- Although Mrs E accompanied her daughter to the police station for an interview, she did not fully believe her daughter's account and even attributed some of the blame towards the daughter for 'egging him on'.

The SOS made the following recommendations.

- Mrs E to attend the partners group, focusing on strengthening non-abusing skills.

- Mrs E and her daughter to be referred to family therapy in order to strengthen their relationship and move forward as a family unit.

The police did not proceed with the case and Mr E has no cautions or convictions. It is also interesting to note that he has not pursued contact with his daughter.

Mrs E completed the partners group 18 months after her initial assessment by the service. It was noticeable that she made progress in the following areas.

- Mrs E could identify appropriate sexual boundaries in her relationships, and with regards to her daughter

- She could identify behaviours such as grooming and also identify potential high-risk situations.

Mrs E has been discharged from the SOS and continues attending family therapy with her daughter. Her case remains open with Social Services, which now has minimal contact, and her daughter has been deregistered.

Mrs E is actively seeking a new relationship.

CASE EXAMPLE 2

Ms P was referred by Social Services for an assessment of her ability to protect her four-year-old daughter, following her partner's caution and sex offender registration for accessing and downloading child pornography.

The main factor which warranted the referral was Ms P's reaction to her partner's arrest, which was described by Social Services as 'hysterical'. It was felt that she minimised the risk posed to her daughter. Ms P became aware of her partner's interest in child pornography when the police arrived at 6.30 a.m. one morning to execute a search warrant. Her partner's details were traced via an international police operation targeting internet offenders.

Initially, Ms P refused to believe her partner's involvement, believing that the sites had been accessed 'accidentally' or that fraudulent use of his credit card had occurred.

Ms P came from a stable background and had none of the poor prognostic indicators as previously described. However, she was not complying with Social Services as she found their involvement 'too intrusive' and avoided assessment because 'the more people who know, the greater the chance of family and friends finding out'.

Ms P was assessed by the SOS, which recommended that she attend the partner's group in order to:

- strengthen her current knowledge of protective factors

- understand sexual offending behaviour, relapse prevention and risk management, and be able to relate this to her situation

- receive support because Ms P felt alone and was reluctant to discuss her circumstances with her family

- Ms P and her partner were referred for couple therapy, as she reported their relationship had deteriorated since his arrest.

It was particularly important for Ms P to receive support and increase her knowledge about sexual offending, as her partner could or would not give her a detailed explanation for his behaviour.

During the assessment Ms P did present with a tendency to minimise her partner's behaviour, and she was keen to stress that the images also included adults. It was clear that she felt torn between her partner and daughter, and loved them both.

The assessment and the group work demonstrated that Ms P was clearly confused and shocked with her situation, leading Social Services to believe that she would be unable to protect her daughter. However, Ms P's behaviour, in both the assessment and in the group sessions, indicated that, clearly, she was capable of protecting her daughter adequately.

Ms P found the stressors of models of offending particularly difficult, especially thinking about men committing contact offences, which reinforced her position of minimising her circumstances when compared to other group members.

Ms P was discharged from the SOS on completion of the programme and remained in contact with Social Services. She formed a close relationship with her new social worker and increasingly saw the value in this support.

CONCLUSION

This chapter outlines the process of assessment and intervention with the non-abusing parent. It highlights the importance of the non-abusing parent's protective role and the complexity of their position following a disclosure of abuse. The chapter highlights areas for assessment and key areas for psycho-educative intervention. It also discusses the difficulties in working with individuals who are reluctant to engage with services and who are unwilling to consider the risks posed by their partner to their children.

The women referred for 'ability to protect' assessments are from a diverse and varied walks of life. They are not necessarily all mothers of abused children, and many take on a protective role in unusual circumstances. Some women's background histories are unremarkable while others are part of complicated and damaged families. Their parenting skills, behaviours and attitudes are scrutinised from the outset of contact with services, which can place them under a great deal of stress. A comprehensive assessment can help to establish the areas of protection with which the non-abusing parents struggle with as well as their strengths and resources for coping. Our assessments are often the first opportunities women have to discuss their situations. Psycho-educative groups are crucial in providing the non-abusing parent with the necessary information in order for them to take on the role of protection and allow services working with the family to hand over the responsibility and again empower the parent to care for her child. Group interventions also provide a supportive nature and facilitate learning and sharing of experience between members. This can be very rewarding for group members who have often lost social support because of the stigma that is placed on them after their partner's abusive behaviour.

REFERENCES

Bentovim, A. (1991) 'Clinical Work with Families in which Sexual Abuse has Occurred.' In C. R. Hollin and K. Howells (eds) *Clinical Approaches to Sex Offenders and Their Victims.* Chichester: John Wiley & Sons.

Bolen, R. M. and Lamb, L. J. (2004) 'Ambivalence of nonoffending guardians after child sexual abuse disclosure.' *Journal of Interpersonal Violence 19*, 2, 185–211.

Bolen, R. M., Lamb, L. J. and Gradante, J. (2002) 'The needs-based assessment of parental (guardian) support: a test of its validty and reliability.' *Child Abuse and Neglect 26*, 10, 1081–1099.

Calder, M. C. (2001) *Mothers of Sexually Abused Children: A Framework for Assessment, Understanding and Support.* Lyme Regis: Russell House Publishing.

Crassati, J. (2004) *Managing High Risk Sex Offenders in the Community: A Psychological Approach.* Hove: Brunner–Routledge.

Denov, M. S. (2004) *Perspectives on Female Sex Offending.* Hampshire: Ashgate.

Farmer, E. and Owen, M. (1998) 'Gender and the child protection process.' *British Journal of Social Work 28*, 4, 545–564.

Finkelhor, D. (1984) *Child Sexual Abuse: New Theory and Research.* New York, NY: Free Press.

Hooper, C.A. (1992) *Mothers Surviving Child Sexual Abuse.* London: Routledge.

Kelly, L., Regan, L. and Burton, S. (1991) *An Exploratory Study of the Prevalence of Sexual Abuse in a Sample of 16–21 Year Olds.* London: CSAU, North London Polytechnic.

Mapp, S. (1998) 'Family Survival.' *Community Care.* 5–11, Feb 26–7.

Nakhle Tamraz, D. (1996) 'Nonoffending mothers of sexually abused children: comparison of opinions and research.' *Journal of Child Sexual Abuse 5*, 4, 75–104.

Nakhle Tamraz, D. (1995) Nonoffending Mothers of Preschool or School-aged Father–Daughter Incest Victims: Abuse and Battering. Unpublished doctoral dissertation. New York, NY: York University, School of Education, Department of Applied Psychology.

Pellegrin, A. and Wagner, W.G. (1990) 'Child sexual abuse: factors affecting victims' removal from home.' *Child Abuse and Neglect 14*, 1, 53–60.

Saradjian, J. and Hanks, H. G. I. (1996) *Women Who Sexually Abuse Children*. Chichester: John Wiley & Sons.

Smith, G. (1994) 'Parent, Partner, Protector: Conflicting Role Demands for Mothers of Sexually Abused Children.' In T. Morrison, M. Erooga and R. Beckett (eds) *Sexual Offending Against Children: Assessment and Treatment of Male Abusers*. London: Routledge.

12

Systemic Interventions with Sexual Offending

Alison Beck

INTRODUCTION

Family or systemic therapy is not widely utilised when working with adults who have offended, although it is more common in work with younger people who have committed crimes, or who are at risk of doing so. An abundance of ideas, therapeutic techniques and practical solutions are lost as a result. This chapter aims to provoke the reader's curiosity to find out more about how systemic ways of working can assist with the protection of victims and prevention of sexual offences perpetrated by people of all ages.

WHAT TREATMENTS WORK?

The evidence base for the effectiveness of systemic interventions aimed at reducing sexual offending is scant; however, it is also the case that even the most widely used cognitive-behavioural therapeutic approaches have no high-quality randomised studies to commend them (Kenworthy *et al.* 2003; White *et al.* 1998) and, furthermore, the evidence that does exist suggests that cognitive-behavioural therapy approaches only make modest contributions to reduced recidivism at around six per cent (Lösel and Schmucker 2005). In their review of the evidence base, Crighton and Towl (2007, p. 36) conclude 'there is a strong imperative to develop and implement treatments with sex offenders' and in relation to all treatments, including cognitive-behavioural therapy, they note that 'treatments remain very clearly experimental and need to be treated as such'.

SYSTEMIC WORK WITH PEOPLE WHO HAVE COMMITTED SEXUAL OFFENCES

There are few published papers dealing explicitly with systemic work with people who have committed sexual offences. By way of illustration three examples of pioneering literature are now highlighted. Smith (1995) adopts a structural family therapy approach (one of the approaches that is not described in detail in this chapter) and explores gender-mediated hierarchy in families where sexual abuse is an issue. Smith (1995) highlights some of the difficulties restructuring families where the non-abusing parent, usually the woman, is put in the hierarchically superior position to protect the children. These difficulties arise from the fact that female superiority runs counter to generally accepted notions of traditional family structure. Smith (1995) makes recommendations for family restructuring at several different levels – within the parental dyad, the marital subsystem and the family as a whole – working towards the ideal of equal but different roles within families.

Earle, Dillon and Jecmen (1998) adopt a model of recovery from sexual addiction and describe individually tailored treatments aimed at nurturing 'authentic intimacy' to overcome alienation from self, others and God. These authors argue that 'authentic intimacy – genuine, real, close, familiar, affectionate and deep understanding of place and subject – is a primary goal of therapy with the sex offender. For the offender, knowing him- or herself authentically and intimately is a prerequisite in the process of truly connecting to others in an authentic and intimate manner'.

Vivian-Byrne (2002) advocates that the emphasis on manualised treatments has lost sight of the need to pay more attention to individual differences as well as patterns of offending, which may be evident between group participants and re-enacted in the group therapeutic encounter, in particular around themes such as power, control and gender issues. The focus on the re-enactment of patterns of behaving is in line with a systemic focus on process rather than content.

EXPERIMENTING WITH SYSTEMIC IDEAS

This chapter describes how systemic approaches may benefit experimental treatments with people who have committed sexual offences and their families. This is illustrated with practical examples. One obvious cautionary note, however, is that we cannot hope to do justice to the wealth of systemic literature and this chapter is merely a taster. Some of the key themes which are important in systemic work are outlined.

Shifting to relationships

There is a fundamental shift in emphasis in systemic practice from the individual to the relational which is both obvious and subtle. Most clinicians, not just those who are influenced by systemic thinking, would consider it essential to work with both the individual who presents with problems (such as sexual offending) and with those around them in order to foster sustained change. However, in systemic practice, relational emphasis involves more than the inclusion of others in the therapeutic endeavour. One important difference in systemic practice is that the problem (in so far as it is focused upon at all) is seen as being located in stuck patterns of relating rather than within an individual. There are a number of important implications which follow from this:

- the person presenting with the problem is not *identified* with it; that is, they do not become the problem and are not encouraged to see themselves as the problem

- change is brought about not by changing the person but by changing the patterns of relating

- everyone within the relational network has potential for changing patterns of relating.

When working with people who have committed sexual offences these three implications pose significant challenges to established practice that are now addressed.

The person is not the problem

Responsibility for the crime

When a person has been convicted of a sexual offence he or she is, in a legal and moral sense, responsible for the act. They will be referred to as a 'sex offender' and identified with the crime. The individual may also come to see themself as a sex offender (perhaps seeking out similar others) – or they may react against that identification and deny or minimise the offence – and they may do both. The identification of people with sex offences is useful for a number of purposes: to ensure that people are appropriately punished for crimes; to ensure that they are properly tracked; and that the risks associated with their behaviour are sensibly managed and so on. However, identification of the person with the crime may not always be helpful therapeutically.

Aim of therapy

The therapist aims to change the behaviour and thus is interested in the question: 'Why has this pattern of behaving become stuck and how can I help to unstick it?' Clearly, sexual offending is one of a number of ways of relating to other people which are potentially open to that individual. Furthermore, it is a pattern of behaviour that must change. However, for many people who commit sexual crimes, change does not feel like an option they can, or want, to achieve. They have become *identified* with the problem and are cut off from other possibilities as a result. They have become 'stuck' in relation to change.

Systemic theory does not preclude working with an individual alone, especially when their intra-psychic relationships (internal dialogue) have becomes stuck and are promoting patterns of high-risk behaviour. However, it is preferable to also work with the system around the individual as this introduces more possibilities for change. The therapist seeks to assist the client in rallying all possible resources, both external and internal to the individual, to release the grip of stuck pro-offending patterns of beliefs, thoughts and feelings. The therapist who emphasises that it is the behaviour and not the person that is the problem can stand shoulder to shoulder with the client and look together at: the problem; the relationship of the problem to the client's system; the system's relationship with change; and potential ways of releasing a stuck system.

Changing patterns of relating

Perturbing the system

Change is brought about not by changing a person but by changing the patterns of relating in the system. Maturana and Varela (1987) argue that therapists cannot instruct clients in how to resolve their problems and rely on the fact that the client will follow those instructions. It is only possible to perturb the client's system, it is not possible to direct it to change in a predictable manner. This may be putting the case at its extreme, and psychological therapists have a range of techniques (e.g. cognitive-behavioural therapy, family therapy and dialectical behaviour therapy) for helping to improve the predictability of the response from the client's system. However, the point is that the client is part of an extremely complex interconnected system to which the therapist does not have direct access. The therapeutic task is to consider how to interact with the client in a way that maximises the chances of bringing about successful change, in this case changing sexual offending behaviour.

Co-creating new patterns of relating

Clients invite us to act into stories that they share with us in the hope that we will act in such a way as to help them relieve their suffering and change their situation. Whatever therapists believe about their own abilities to bring about change, according to dialogic theorists all therapists are limited in their ability to assist their clients – they can do nothing more than add to the client's story through the therapeutic conversation (the 'conversation' may include enactments, role-plays, behavioural experiments and other therapeutic techniques). The only fact the therapist can rely upon is that their instructions will enter the linguistic arena of the client. Social constructionists argue that the truth is not discovered but rather *constructed* in language by communities of people in conversation (both internal dialogues and external ones). There is no single 'right answer' or underlying truth, so, for example, the solution to a problem may have as many answers as there are people in conversation. As therapists we are therefore involved in a unique and creative endeavour with our clients: the art of working with them to deconstruct the current stories they hold about their situations which promote sexual offending, and the co-creation of new stories that do not promote offending and which, in turn, influence their beliefs, rules, transactional patterns and relationships with problem-maintaining contextual variables.

Feedback loop

When considering how to interact with the client in a way that maximises their chances of bringing about successful change, the most important part of the therapeutic process is the feedback loop from patient to therapist. The therapist needs to consider: how is this client indicating to me whether I am being helpful or not?

Predictors of successful outcome

This can pose a considerable challenge to therapists working with people who have committed sexual offences. The client may be unable to acknowledge that the offence occurred, or admit to important details of it. Most experienced practitioners will be aware of the work of Miller, Duncan and Hubble (1997) and Hubble, Duncan and Miller (1999), which highlights that the therapist can be most influential in the therapeutic process by strengthening the therapeutic alliance. The authors outline work that suggests that the effectiveness of therapies resides not in the many variables that ostensibly distinguish one approach from another but, rather, in the factors they share in common (derived from work by Lambert and Ogles 2004). Four factors have been found to be predictive of effective treatment outcome:

1. Extra-therapeutic factors (i.e. the things clients bring into the therapy room and which influence their lives outside of therapy, namely their personal resources) (40%).

2. Treatment alliance (even protocol-driven behaviour therapy is more effective if the therapists are well-liked and have good rapport with clients) (30%).

3. The therapist's technical approach, such as cognitive-behavioural therapy or family therapy and so forth (15%).

4. Placebo effect (or patient hope and belief in the effectiveness of treatment) (15%).

The question is not, therefore, which therapeutic approach the therapist should adopt since a successful therapeutic alliance, defined as broad agreement on goals and approaches established early in therapy, is twice as predictive of success as any technique or therapeutic approach. This research suggests that, when faced with a seeming choice between technique and relationship, a therapist is better off focusing on strengthening the therapeutic relationship in order to overcome barriers to change.

Client-led therapy

When working with the client who is unable to acknowledge the crime, or details of it, the therapist has the advantage of the wisdom and experience of the client and their familiarity with the systems around them to guide their interactions. This may also strengthen the therapeutic alliance. Changing the way we relate to clients can change the way they relate to themselves and to those around them. It can perturb the system sufficiently to bring about lasting change.

CASE EXAMPLE

Julian was a 27-year-old man who had been convicted of sexual assault of his neighbour's children (a 10-year-old boy and an eight-year-old girl) whilst babysitting. He presented as a highly anxious and paranoid individual who did not easily form relationships with other adults. He reported having had sexual fantasies about these children for many years. He said that he was afraid that someone would find out about his thoughts and he had never mentioned his fantasies to anyone except the children. Julian also stated that he was aware that their mother was a single parent and struggling to raise two boisterous youngsters. He offered to help her. At the time of the assessment he would not accept that his offer of help was related to his sexual fantasies about the children.

Julian was asked: 'Do you think the mother thinks that your sexual fantasies are related to your offer of help? Do you think that other adults around you think that your sexual fantasies are related to your offer of help? If they think that these two things are related, what stops you from believing that they are?'

The *purpose* of these relational questions was to strengthen Julian's relational position with other adults and help him to refer to what other adults would think (where in the past he had used children as his reference); and to enable Julian to guide the therapist in understanding the thoughts which disinhibit his offending.

Julian replied that he did not like to think of himself as someone who was purely motivated by personal gratification and he was able to discuss many areas in which he believed he had behaved altruistically. Julian identified that he would like to work on his anxiety at forming relationships with other adults.

What the therapist brings

Of course, therapists also bring their own relational context with them into the therapeutic encounter. In working with a client who is unable to acknowledge the crime, or details of it, the experienced therapist has the advantage of learning from previous work with similar clients. Most therapists will be aware that speaking openly and honestly is a particular challenge for people who have committed sexual offences and they will adjust their behaviour towards the client accordingly (see example below). In this way the therapist and the client perform a 'dance' as they find a fit with one another.

At the outset of therapy a therapist might say 'I have learnt from people in the same situation as you are now that it is extremely difficult to speak openly about the things you have done and thought, and it is even difficult to say these things to yourself, so I wonder if it would be alright with you, if we can proceed on the basis that we will expect the things you say, think and feel to change. I will expect you to be able to tell me more about the things you have done as we get to know each other and as we think together about what the possibilities are for change.' The *purpose* of these questions is to: demonstrate that therapist listens to and learns from clients; introduce the client to the possibility of change; and explain that new ways of thinking, feeling and behaving are co-created by client and therapist.

Making meaning

The measure of a good fit occurs when the therapist and client are able to co-create ways of releasing a stuck system which are meaningful to them both. It may be tempting for inexperienced therapists, overwhelmed with the task of trying to 'make meaning' with an extremely hard to engage client group, to be content with finding the therapy meaningful themselves and persist with a prescriptive format. It may be tempting to pay insufficient attention to feedback from the client about whether the therapeutic encounter is leading to meaningful change to patterns of relating (and, in particular, the offending behaviour).

Challenge of listening

Therapy is about co-evolving empathic relationships with each other. Alda (2006) said that 'listening is allowing yourself to be changed by the other'. This poses a particular challenge for therapists working with people who have committed sexual offences. On the one hand, a client can guide the therapist by indicating whether meaning has been made; on the other, there are real concerns of public safety: does the therapist empathise so much with the client that sight has been lost of the crime and the risks of future offending? These dangers are real and cannot be avoided by simple recourse to *either* listening to the client *or* focusing on public safety. To be effective and responsible therapists must hold both positions: listening to the client and being aware of the dangers of becoming blind to the risks posed by the client's behaviour and unable to prioritise public safety. For this reason, as discussed in Chapters 7 and 8, it is essential that all therapists are properly accredited mental health professionals, with training in working with this client group and that they receive regular supervision and support from experienced supervisors.

Self-reflexivity

Therapists also need to be self-reflexive practitioners. The therapist is part of the therapeutic system and needs to focus on personal processes; the way in which she or he responds to feedback from the client and their family or wider system, and on the way she or he responds as a result of personal experience. Self-reflexivity is the capacity to maintain a level of self-awareness during interactions *and* to use feedback from that reflection to enrich work with clients. Working with people who have committed sexual crimes, among whom there will be individuals who may pose a risk to the therapist or their family (e.g. people who have developed sexual fixations or engage in stalking behaviours), therapists are encouraged to protect themselves and keep personal information private. However, as also discussed in the next chapter, the personal cannot *not* enter the therapeutic context, whether the therapist wishes it or not. Therapy is a personal experience and that is part of the therapeutic endeavour. The self-reflexive practitioner seeks to acknowledge what she or he brings and to use it to assist the client.

My reflections

Therapy is a personal experience. I was working with a man charged (and later convicted) of the kidnap and rape of a school girl (Sophie). I have a daughter of a similar age. As he described to me how he believed that she seduced him I found myself becoming increasingly frightened and angry. He said he was attracted by her young slim body which he felt she 'flaunted'. He said that she told him she was having problems with her parents and he felt that she was asking him, therefore, to offer to pick her up from school and take her to his house, so that she would not have to face her mother.

Being aware of my own feelings I asked: 'How do you think Sophie's mother felt when her daughter was picked up from school by a stranger?' He replied 'She probably felt awful but she should've listened to Sophie, like I did, so she didn't need people like me.' Perceiving that he seemed to blame the mother, and wanting to help him reconsider this, I asked: 'Do you feel Sophie's mother is partly to blame for what happened because she was not there for Sophie?' He replied 'Maybe she could have done more to stop it.' I continued, 'Do you think it is unusual for parents and their teenage children to have problems with each other?' He replied, 'No, I suppose not. I guess I could've taken her to her mother's house and helped them work it out.'

The *purpose* of these questions is to: be aware of my responses; to explore how I can use what I bring to the therapy to help the client; to find a fit with the client; and to co-create new meaningful ways of thinking, feeling and behaving.

Circularity and feedback

The shift in emphasis from the individual to the relational involves a shift to looking at systems. Many psychological therapies, like cognitive-behavioural therapy, emphasise causal explanations that are both positive and linear. For example, billiard ball X moved towards pocket A because billiard ball Y hit it at angle Z. Systemic practitioners often adopt a cybernetic explanation which focuses on feedback loops and is circular. A cybernetic explanation is always negative, in that is it asks, 'Why didn't the alternative possibilities occur?' So, if a monkey strikes a typewriter apparently at random but in fact writes meaningful prose, cybernetic theory would look for restraints, either inside the monkey or inside the typewriter: perhaps the monkey could not strike inappropriate letters; perhaps the type bars could not move if improperly struck; perhaps incorrect letters could not survive on the paper. Somewhere there must have been a circuit which could identify error and eliminate it. Therefore, in shifting to a systemic model, practitioners are encouraged to consider: how are the interconnected parts of the system maintaining this problem (sexual offending) in a circular fashion; and what is restraining change?

Potential for change in the relational network

The notion that everyone within the relational network has potential for changing patterns of relating has potential for troublesome misunderstanding when working with people who have committed sexual offences. The intention would *not* be to transfer responsibility for an offence from the person convicted to other people within the system, nor to the system as a whole. The person convicted of the sexual offence remains responsible for the crime in a legal and moral sense. However, there is an important sense, recognised by most therapeutic approaches, that potential for changing patterns of relating is not located solely with the person presenting with sexual offending. For example, Finkelhor and Asdigian (1996) highlight three factors which place children at particular risk of sexual victimisation; namely, *vulnerability* (physical and psychological), *gratificability* (e.g. female gender for some perpetrators) and *antagonism* (behaviours or ethnic or group identities which may spark hostility or resentment in the perpetrator). This model is clearly relational and, whilst responsibility for the crime remains with the perpetrator, there are factors about other people involved in the perpetrators system (in this instance the victim) that are relevant.

Therapist responsibility

At the point that the therapist enters the therapeutic encounter, she or he also enters the relational network and has potential for changing patterns of relating, including sexual offending: if this were not the case there would be no call for therapy as it would change nothing. This does not make the therapist responsible for change. Remember, if Maturana and Varela (1987) are correct, the therapist does not have direct access to the client's system and may only perturb it. The responsibility of the therapist lies in the delivery of high-quality therapy informed by evidence and properly supervised. The therapist is responsible for their line of questioning – as every question asked relegates another to the realm of the unasked. Therapists must use their authority and expertise to protect victims, to co-evolve new ways of relating which will ease the suffering of individuals within the system beginning with the most vulnerable and to increase the choices clients have for behaving in different ways.

Transgenerational patterns

Family systems theorists conceptualise the family as an emotional unit, a network of interlocking relationships which need to be seen within a multigenerational historical context. Increasing choices for clients often requires exploration of how patterns of relating came to be established within families. This work aims to highlight what is restraining change within the family system and what potential there is to release a stuck system.

CASE EXAMPLE

Yolande is married to, and currently living apart from, Bartholomew, who was convicted of the sexual assault of his eldest daughter, Joylyn, by another marriage. The couple have three female children and Yolande was assessed in terms of her ability to protect them. Bartholomew was recently released from a long prison sentence for the crime, which both he and Yolande deny. Yolande has had no contact with Joylyn since Bartholomew was convicted, although prior to the charges being brought they were close. Yolande comes from a broken home. She was extremely distressed when her parents split up as her father had little contact with her thereafter and her mother was barely able to cope. Yolande was beaten by her mother and sought refuge from these beatings in her relationship with Bartholomew, which began when she was 16 years old. Yolande feels that her mother did not tell her the truth about her relationship with Yolande's father. She said 'Women are liars' and she believes that Joylyn lied about the sexual assault so that she could go to live with her mother in America. She said that Joylyn's mother probably also lied to Joylyn, promising that she would have a better life and more material things if she came to America.

I interviewed Yolande and Bartholomew together:

AB: 'If Joylyn were here with us what would she say to me about why she felt that she needed to bring such serious charges just to get to America?'.

Y: 'She probably didn't know how else to get there.'

AB: 'Why would she want to hurt her father and you like this?'

Y: 'I don't know, I would like to ask her that.'

AB: 'What do you think she would say?'

Y: 'I don't think she would want to hurt me, but may be she felt trapped by Bartholomew, perhaps she was a bit afraid of him.'

AB: 'What was Joylyn's relationship with her father like?'

Y: 'She did what she was told. He was very strict. He wanted to protect her from boys because she's at that age you know.'

AB: 'In your family of origin is that how parents and children behaved with one another?'

B: 'In Yolande's family she was always told what to do and she did it but her mother was never satisfied, that's why I had to get her out of there.'

The *purpose* of these questions is to: bring other people into the therapy, in particular the victim whose voice is often unheard; to gather information (news of something different) and therefore open up new possibilities or choices for behaving; and to make transgenerational connections.

Difference

Bateson (1972, p. 173) explained that 'all knowledge of external events is derived from the relationship between them...to achieve a more accurate perception, a human being will always resort to change in the relationship between himself and the external object. If he is inspecting a rough spot on some surface by means of touch he moves his finger over the spot...what we perceive easily is difference and change – and difference is a relationship.' Selvini *et al.* (1980) argued that what the therapist is looking for is more information and 'information is difference'. It follows from these ideas that to glean information the therapist needs to highlight differences by inviting family members to describe the relationship between other family members. For example, it is more useful to ask Yolande about Bartholomew's relationship with Joylyn than to ask Bartholomew, as she is more likely to introduce different choices for the pattern of that relationship than Bartholomew would do.

In looking for the leverage to make meaningful change, therapists are looking for what Bateson (1972) called 'the difference that makes the difference'. Some differences may be too large to seem like meaningful choices and others may be too small to make a noticeable difference. A therapist may not find a way to completely unstick some systems: I did not find a way with Bartholomew and Yolande to help them acknowledge that the offence had occurred, and Yolande was therefore not considered able to protect her daughters. However, Yolande was able to make some useful connections. For example, she felt that because of the way her family of origin had functioned, she was left feeling unconfident and ugly. Bartholomew gave her the confidence that she had lacked before she met him, he made her feel special and beautiful, and she felt safe with him. She also said that this made it difficult for her to think about what Joylyn might say to her if she were to meet her again. Perhaps in the future something else will perturb this system and these preliminary connections may prove to have been the difference that made the difference.

SUMMARY AND CONCLUSIONS

Systemic practice requires a shift in emphasis from the individual to the relational. Sexual offending is, by definition, relational and therefore well-suited to this way of working. However, there are practice challenges associated with this paradigm shift because the problem (in so far as it is focused upon at all) is seen as located in stuck patterns of relating rather than within an individual. The person presenting *with* the problem is not seen *as* the problem, although in a legal and moral sense they remain responsible for the crime. Furthermore, because the problem is seen as stuck patterns of relating then change is brought about not by changing the person but by changing the patterns of relating. Therefore everyone within the relational network, including the therapist, has potential for changing patterns of relating.

There are many aspects of family therapy and systemic thinking which have not been explored in this chapter. Furthermore, published systemic work with people who have committed sexual offences is extremely limited. There is plenty of room for growth and experimentation to unlock stuck patterns of thinking and behaving in every therapeutic system, including that of sexual offenders and their families, and it is hoped that this chapter has stimulated practitioners to give more thought to this area.

REFERENCES

Alda, A. (2006) *Reader's Digest.* November.

Bateson, G. (1972) *Steps to an Ecology of Mind: Collected Essays in Anthropology, Psychiatry, Evolution, and Epistemology.* Chicago, IL: University of Chicago Press.

Crighton, D. and Towl, G. (2007) 'Experimental interventions with sex offenders: a brief review of their efficacy.' *Evidence Based Mental Health 10,* 35–37.

Earle, R. H., Dillon, D. and Jecmen, D. (1998) 'Systemic approach to the treatment of sex offenders.' *Sexual Addiction and Compulsivity 5,* 49–61.

Finkelhor, D. and Asdigian, N. (1996) 'Risk factors for youth victimization: beyond a lifestyles/routine activities approach.' *Violence and Victims 11,* 1, 3–19.

Hubble, M. A., Duncan, B. L. and Miller, S. D. (1999) *The Heart and Soul of Change: What Works in Therapy.* Washington, DC: American Psychological Association.

Kenworthy, T., Adams, C. E., Bilby, C., Brooks-Gordon, B. (2003) 'Psychological interventions for those who have sexually offended or are at risk of offending.' *Cochrane Database Systemic Review 4,* CD004858.

Lambert, M. J. and Ogles, B. M. (2004) 'The Efficacy and Effectiveness of Psychotherapy.' In M. J. Lambert (ed) *Handbook of Psychotherapy Change.* New York, NY: John Wiley & Sons.

Lösel, F. and Schmucker, M. (2005) 'The effectiveness of treatment for sexual offenders: a comprehensive meta-analysis.' *Journal of Experimental Criminology 1,* 117–146.

Maturana, H. and Varela, F. (1987) *The Tree of Knowledge: The Biological Roots of Human Understanding.* Boston, MA: Shambhala.

Miller, S. D., Duncan, B. L. and Hubble, M. A. (1997) *Escape from Babel: Toward a Unifying Language for Psychotherapy Practice.* New York, NY: Norton.

Selvini, M. P., Boscolo, L., Cecchin, G. and Prata, G. (1980) 'Hypothesizing-Circularity-Neutrality: Three Guidelines for the Conductor of the Session'. *Family Process 19,* 1, 3–12.

Smith, G. (1995) 'Hierarchy in Families where Sexual Abuse is an Issue.' In C. Burck and B. Speed (eds) *Gender, Power and Relationships.* London and New York, NY: Routledge.

Vivian-Byrne, S. E. (2002) 'Using context and difference in sex offender treatment: an integrated systemic approach.' *Journal of Sexual Aggression 8,* 3, 59–73.

White, P., Bradley, C., Ferriter, M., Hatzipetrou, L. A. (1998) 'Managements for people with disorders of sexual preference and for convicted sexual offenders.' *Cochrane Database Systemic Review 4,* CD000251.

13

The Impact on Professionals of Working with Sex Offenders

Sharon K. C. Leicht

INTRODUCTION

Therapists who work with sex offenders are affected by their work. The personal impact of working with sex offenders has been examined through personal accounts and research studies on the therapists who provide assessments and therapy to perpetrators of sexual abuse. Most of the literature has described the work as mentally, physically and emotionally demanding. The recognition that therapists must process the emotion-evoking information they are exposed to in their work environment is fairly recent (Bengis 1997; Ellerby 1997; Erooga 1994; Kearns 1995; Lane 1986; Leicht 2003; Peaslee 1995; Scheela 2001). In this chapter, research into the impact of this type of work on the therapists will be discussed, together with the range of coping strategies used to deal with this. Positive aspects of the work will also be highlighted.

THE PROCESS

Several authors have provided introspective accounts of their own experience of working with sex offenders (Bengis 1997; Freeman-Longo 1997; Giovannoni 1997; Weiss 1998). Even though these therapists come from diverse professional backgrounds (psychology, social work, counselling, nursing and criminology) they all identified changes in their perspectives. Researchers have also investigated therapists' subjective experiences and the impact on them of working with sex offenders (DeCarvalho Petry 2005; Farrenkopf 1992; Jackson, Holzman and Barnard 1997; Lea, Auburn and Kibblewhite 1999; Leicht, Holttum and Sperlinger, in preparation; Rich 1997; Scheela 2001). This has led to a greater understanding of both the process of working with sex offenders for professionals, and their experiences and reactions.

Farrenkopf (1992) surveyed 24 experienced mental health therapists working with sex offenders about the personal impact of this work. From the results, Farrenkopf (1992) proposed a 'Phases of Impact' model whereby therapists identified several progressive adjustment phases in their work with sex offenders. The initial phase centred on feelings of shock, bewilderment and vulnerability, which coincided with encountering the sex offender at a personal level. This phase was followed by a period of professional mission, including hopes for effectiveness, non-judgmental work ethics and empathy for clients. The third phase involved repressed emotions, including anger, resentment and cynicism, often leading to a final phase of either disenchantment or adaptation.

In order to explore the positive and negative experiences of working with sex offenders, Scheela (2001) conducted a qualitative study on 17 mental health therapists employed in an outpatient sexual abuse treatment programme. These therapists described what Scheela (2001, p. 761) identified as a 'remodelling process'. This process involved six non-linear stages: falling apart; taking on; tearing out; rebuilding; doing the upkeep; and moving on. 'Falling apart' could occur during the period when the therapists first provided treatment and were exposed to the stories of abuse, or when there were treatment failures, or when someone re-offended, or when faced with lawsuits. The authors noted that this could also occur during positive developments, that is, 'when offenders did particularly good work and when families were reconciled and reunited', although they do not expand this further. 'Taking on' involved the therapist gaining additional knowledge and experience, and/or learning not to take on responsibilities that belonged to the offender. 'Tearing out' was the process of the therapists dispensing with old attitudes and values and some of their own personal issues. 'Rebuilding' was the adoption of new attitudes and ways of working with the offender. 'Doing the upkeep' involved maintenance and increase of knowledge about sexual abuse and sex offending, self-care and identification of coping strategies. 'Moving on' comprised making changes to treatment programmes over time and/or taking a break from the work. Scheela's (2001) model shares many factors in common with the Farrenkopf's (1992) model. However, the processes in Scheela's (2001) model were described as non-linear and not necessarily progressive, whereas Farrenkopf's (1992) model is a progressive four-phase adjustment process.

Elements of both models were found in Leicht's (2003) qualitative study of four male and four female clinical psychologists (whose experience of working with sex offenders ranged from two years to 25 years). All the psychologists experienced some form of negative response to their clients, although to differing degrees. Most identified a range of emotions which usually began with disgust or repulsion then moved on to fascination or curiosity before eventually arriving at some level of understanding of their client. The majority described having experienced manipulation and deception by the client and an awareness of the potential to develop a collusive relationship with the client. Some reported grappling with the victim–perpetrator dichotomy. Five psychologists emphasised the need to find an acceptable way of working with this client group. Some emphasised the importance of assessment in developing a therapeutic alliance whilst others stressed the need to separate the person from the offence in order to establish a positive therapeutic relationship. Half of the psychologists acknowledged that at times they had questioned the value of their work, while, on other occasions, they believed their work could help offenders change their behaviour and/or prevent future offences. Similarly, using a semi-structured interview with nine male therapists treating sex offenders, DeCarvalho Petry (2005) found that although the therapists experienced disgust about their clients' acts of aggression and other countertransference reactions, they were able to move beyond their negative reactions and to empathise with their clients.

The Farrenkopf (1992) and Scheela (2001) models and the research of Leicht (2003) and DeCarvalho Petry (2005) reflected many of the experiences and reactions reported by other researchers. These experiences and reactions were frequently discussed in terms of countertransference, vicarious traumatisation and burn-out (with the recognition that these phenomena are often considered to overlap), stigmatisation and coping strategies. Each of these issues is addressed below.

EXPERIENCES AND REACTIONS

Countertransference

Sex offenders are known to evoke powerful emotions in therapists (Kearns 1995; Weiss 1998). Farrenkopf (1992) and Scheela (2001) identified the presence of these powerful emotions within each phase of their models. Several authors have discussed the importance of acknowledging all aspects of countertransference in working with sex offenders (Erooga 1994; Gerber 1995; Lane 1986; Lion 1999; Mitchell and Melikian 1995; Mothersole 2000; Weiss 1998). For the purpose of this discussion, the term 'countertransference reactions' is defined as including all the therapist's conscious and unconscious responses to the client (Erooga 1994; Mitchell and Melikian 1995; Strasburger 2001). If unrecognised, countertransference reactions can create problems for the therapist and can affect the therapeutic process (Mitchell and Melikian 1995), in particular with sex offenders (Mothersole 2000).

In his work with patients diagnosed with antisocial personality disorder, Strasburger (2001) identified several countertransference responses which may be experienced by clinicians. These included rejection of the client and the rageful wish to destroy. Furthermore, Erooga (1994) and Gerber (1995) advocated that countertransference must include the difficult issue of sexual arousal that results in attraction within the therapeutic setting. Therapists working with sex offenders, who learn about the sadistic acts and fantasies of their patients, may subsequently need to confront their own sadistic fantasies and impulses (Mitchell and Melikian 1995). Ellerby Gutkin Smith and Atkinson (1993, cited in Ellerby 1997) found that both male and female clinicians experienced sexual thoughts, fantasies and feelings about offenders. In the survey by Jackson *et al.* (1997) of 98 therapists working with sex offenders, 51 per cent reported that their clients' detailed descriptions of offending behaviour triggered their own sexual fantasies. In describing the 'twilight world' of the treatment providers, Bengis (1997, p. 31) discussed how exposure to the perpetrator behaviour might change therapists' perceptions of their own sexual fantasies, impulses and urges, and cause them to wonder if they would be capable of committing the same sexual acts.

Weiss (1998, p. 173) described his experience of countertransference reactions when treating criminals as 'swinging between two poles'. At one end was the experience of curiosity, fascination and attraction. At the other end was annoyance, disgust and aversion. He also maintained that these dynamics were particularly poignant when working with sex offenders because they typically tended to arouse aversion, repulsion and disgust in therapists. He further reported that therapists frequently found themselves titillated, attracted and experiencing voyeuristic excitement as the patient described the sexual offence. Mothersole (2000, p. 50) also discussed the problems that could stem from voyeuristic motivation. There was seen to be a risk of the clinician 'focusing just a little too much on the gory details' because of 'a vicarious thrill from the detail and the outrageousness' of the client's sexual or violent actions. Winer (2001, p. 620) also considered the role of fascination experienced by the therapist when discussing therapists' reactions to patients who had committed evil acts. He expressed the view that evil fascinated therapists even though they were apparently incapable of locating evil in their patients. He further maintained that, the 'serious passivity of our therapeutic stances, partly driven by the fear of being judgemental, by the fear of retaliating and by the use of our vocation to deny our aggressiveness, leaves us longing for stimulation'. Unable to be evil themselves, therapists 'might feel enlivened by being in the presence of evil'.

Weiss (1998) acknowledged that feeling attraction for, or envy of, socially deviant immoral behaviour could be disconcerting for therapists but suggested a different consequence. Weiss (1998) suggested that many mental health workers avoided this disconcerting attraction by either rejecting and hating the offenders or by avoiding any information on their crimes. Mitchell and Melikian (1995) also suggested that holding fantasies about a client might generate difficulties for therapists but they saw them arising from conflict with the therapists' self-concept and/or identity as nurturing, helping professionals. Furthermore, sadistic and/or aggressive feelings may be particularly difficult for female therapists to acknowledge if there is a conflict with a self-image of being accepting and maternal.

Therapists may also identify with either victim or aggressor in various phases of sex offender treatment (Lane 1986; Ryan and Lane 1997). Temple (1996) discussed the possibility of the therapist unconsciously becoming the masochistic victim of a bullying or sadistic situation within the thera-peutic relationship. This involves a client with a sadistic attitude towards the therapist and the therapist either accepting the masochistic role of victim or retaliating by behaving sadistically towards the client. Mitchell and Melikian (1995, p. 89) also suggest that a therapist might want to punish the offender in response to feeling hurt or violated by the offences having been described 'often coldly or in an excited, aroused way'. These authors further recognised that the therapist might want to 'judge and execute a price for the suffering the client has inflicted on others' and cautioned against becoming 'judge or executioner' when making recommendations in court reports or in child protection cases. They also warned against therapists projecting their own anger onto clients so that assessments of dangerousness became inappropriately elevated.

Vicarious traumatisation

Vicarious traumatisation has been identified as perhaps one of the more serious potential effects for therapists who have worked with sex offenders. Vicarious traumatisation has been described as a process by which therapists treating survivors of trauma are vulnerable to alterations in their own cognitive schema generally concerning safety, trust, power, esteem and intimacy (McCann and Pearlman 1990). Such changes are seen to result in adaptation in emotional, cognitive, biological, behavioural and interpersonal areas of the therapists' lives (Rich 1997). These negative effects occur as a result of listening empathically over time while clients share graphic details of their victimization details. Crothers (1995) found that therapists exposed to traumatic stimuli through their interactions with clients experienced symptoms that were similar to those reported in post-traumatic stress disorder. These symptoms were recurrent intrusive dreams, flashbacks, avoidance of the stressful stimuli, emotional numbing, detachment and exaggerated fears that the problem would happen to them. Enhanced feelings of vulnerability in healthcare workers indirectly exposed to traumatic stimuli was also reported by Hedge (2002).

Therapists may well experience secondary post-traumatic stress disorder while working with sex offenders (Kearns 1995; Rich 1997). For the purpose of this discussion the terms 'secondary post-traumatic stress disorder' and 'vicarious traumatisation' will be treated as being interchangeable. Abel (1983) suggested that exploring detailed accounts of violent rape fantasies and horrific acts could imbue the therapist with awareness of a world of pervasive violence, and this has been supported by research indicating that working with sex offenders had led to therapists' feeling less safe in the world and experiencing less trust in the intentions of other people (Bengis 1997; Ellerby 1997; Farrenkopf 1992; Freeman-Longo 1997; Jackson et al. 1997; Lane 1986; Leicht et al. in preparation; Rich 1997; Scheela 2001). Therapists in two studies (Farrenkopf 1992; Leicht et al. in preparation) saw potential abusers everywhere, while Scheela (2001) and

Leicht *et al.* (in preparation) reported that all of the therapists in their studies had developed stricter personal and professional boundaries. Therapists have also identified that they felt more vulnerable to violence against themselves and their families and had increased their vigilance and safety precautions as a result (Bengis 1997; Jackson *et al.* 1997; Leicht 2003; Rich 1997; Scheela 2001).

An increase in vigilance and safety precautions was also identified among therapists by Farrenkopf (1992) and Ellerby *et al.* (1993, cited in Ellerby 1997), with both reporting that female therapists in particular expressed a sense of increased suspiciousness and vulnerability. In Ellerby *et al.* (1993, cited in Ellerby 1997), 42 per cent of the female clinicians described feeling sexualised by the offender. In the study by Scheela (2001) the female therapists discussed safety precautions taken for themselves, including installing security systems, having unlisted phone numbers and addresses, carrying pepper spray or weapons, whereas the male therapists focused more on their sense of vulnerability in relation to the safety of their families.

The negative effect of constantly worrying about offenders re-offending and more children or adults being abused was reported in the studies of Scheela (2001) and Leicht (2003). Both male and female therapists have reported becoming more protective of their own children through fear for their safety and becoming extremely aware of how other people interact with their children (Ellerby 1997; Leicht 2003). In Jackson *et al.* (1997), 59 per cent of the therapists were reported as having heightened anxiety about the safety of their children or grandchildren while some studies have found therapist-parents who became obsessed by efforts to teach their children how to remain safe (Lane 1986; Leicht 2003).

Several studies have reported changes in how male and female therapists behaved around children (Bird-Edmunds 1997; Erooga 1994; Freeman-Longo 1997; Jackson *et al.* 1997; Lane 1986; Leicht *et al.* in preparation; Rich 1997; Scheela 2001). Therapists reported discomfort in caring for and/or touching, either their own or other people's children, through concern that this might be perceived as sexual abuse (Bird-Edmunds 1997; Freeman-Longo 1997; Leicht *et al.* in preparation; Scheela 2001). Both male therapists (Scheela 2001; Leicht *et al.* in preparation) and female therapists (Leicht *et al.* in preparation) have reported increased awareness of their own behaviours and becoming less comfortable with any form of touch because of a fear that the behaviour might be misconstrued as abuse or a fear that they might be sued.

Emotional hardening, as a consequence of hearing about sexual abuse, was another common negative effect reported by therapists who treated sex offenders (Bird-Edmunds 1997; Farrenkopf 1992). Scheela's (2001) study reported this impact in terms of therapists becoming more detached.

Reported alterations to therapists' sex lives have also been linked with vicarious traumatisation (Rich 1997; Leicht 2003). Bird-Edmunds (1997) surveyed 276 providers of treatment to sex offender clients and Rich (1997) surveyed 135 therapists working with sex offenders. Results from both groups revealed that the providers or therapists experienced intrusive images of abuse and alterations in their fantasy and sex lives. Many of the therapists working with sex offenders in the survey by Jackson *et al.* (1997) experienced visual imagery about sexual violence. This imagery was found to be painful, disturbing, repulsive, arousing or some combination thereof. Similar experiences were reported in the individual accounts of Bengis (1997) and Freeman-Longo (1997) and in other studies (Erooga 1994; Farrenkopf 1992; Garrison 1992; Jackson *et al.* 1997; Leicht 2003). Farrenkopf (1992) reported that several therapists disclosed that they avoided love-making on the day they consulted in prisons. Both male and female therapists have been reported as experiencing a reduced interest in sex and a reduction in sexual behaviour (Jackson *et al.* 1997; Ellerby *et al.* 1993, cited in Ellerby 1997). In the study reported by Ellerby *et al.* (1993, cited in Ellerby 1997), male and female clinicians indicated that, as a direct result of exposure to deviant sexuality at work, they had avoided sexual contact, been distracted during sexual contact and prematurely ended sexual contact.

As a direct result of the work with sex offenders, clinicians expressed concern about some of their own past, and possibly abusive, behaviours (Ellerby 1997; Freeman-Longo 1997; Scheela 2001). Freeman-Longo (1997) discussed his sense of gender shame in terms of being the same gender as the majority of sex offenders. Similarly, Farrenkopf (1992) and Leicht *et al.* (in preparation) found that some male therapists were aware of an increased sense of 'collective guilt' over male abusive behaviour (Erooga 1994, p. 220).

Steed and Bicknell (2001) studied 21 male and 46 female sex offender therapists. They concluded that secondary post-traumatic stress was present in their respondents. Their added finding was that therapists with between two and four years' experience were least vulnerable to manifestations of secondary post-traumatic stress. They concluded that most avoidance (as measured by the Impact of Events Scale – Revised, Weiss and Marmar

1995) was experienced by therapists with the least and most experience. However, therapists who were working for between nine and 12 years were most at risk for compassion fatigue, burn-out, intrusion and hyper-arousal.

Burn-out

In discussing secondary post-traumatic stress and burn-out, Kearns (1995) and Abel (1983) warned that therapists working with sex offenders needed to be aware of the potential for burn-out and take the necessary steps to guard against it. Maslach and Jackson (1982) define burn-out as a multidimensional process with the following central constructs: emotional exhaustion; depersonalisation; and a reduced sense of personal accomplishment that can render individuals unable to carry out their work effectively. Erooga (1994) related some of these constructs to the experiences of therapists when they were directly exposed to the way offenders use control and manipulation to manage their world. Erooga (1994) suggested some therapists' experiences might include feelings of being discounted, being ineffectual, anger, helplessness, being powerful, being persecutory or powerlessness.

Another area of tension is that between the dual role of a therapist and that of an agent of social control. This has been identified as a source of considerable stress (Bird-Edmunds 1997; Ellerby 1997; Freemon-Longo 1997; Leicht 2003) and burn-out (Bird-Edmunds 1997). The paradoxical issues associated with a client who is both victim and perpetrator have also been identified as providing a potentially stressful ethical dilemma for therapists (Glaser 2003; Kearns 1995). Therapists have spoken about the difficulty of being mandated to report previously unreported abuse while, paradoxically, trying to encourage offenders to admit abuse as an important aspect of the therapeutic process (Scheela 2001). Other associated issues that have been acknowledged as contributing to stress among therapists have included self-blame for recidivism of sexual abusers, through the linkage of responsibility for risk assessments and the perceived responsibility to protect the community (Glaser 2003; Leicht et al. in preparation). Scheela (2001) found that, as well as being worried about acts of reprisal (from offenders, victims, family members or people who did not appreciate therapists who work with offenders) the therapists were concerned about being sued.

Despite the potential link between the conflicts noted above and burn-out, in a survey of 278 treatment providers Bird-Edmunds (1997) found no direct causal relationship between providing therapy to sex–abuse perpetrators and burn-out. However, the survey results were seen to indicate that therapists working with perpetrators experienced symptoms and reactions which had been linked with stress and burn-out in other studies. The burn-out-related symptoms reported by Bird-Edmunds (1997) which have also been reported by others included fatigue (Farrenkopf 1992), depression (Farrenkopf 1992; Rich 1997), sleep disturbance (Ellerby 1997; Jackson *et al.* 1997), irritability (Bird-Edmunds 1997) and anger and frustration (Farrenkopf 1992). Farrenkopf (1992) also listed dulling of emotions, decreased sense of humour and high stress. Bird-Edmunds (1997) noted that therapists with a history of personal sexual abuse might be at higher risk of burn-out than other therapists.

Stigmatisation

Societal reaction to the treatment of sex offenders has been reported as a further source of dissonance for therapists working with such clients (Freeman-Longo 1997; Jackson *et al.* 1997; Leicht *et al.* in preparation; Scheela 2001). Such stigmatisation has been linked with stress (Freeman--Longo 1997; Leicht *et al.* in preparation) and burn-out (Freeman-Longo 1997) in those providing treatment for sex abusers. Some therapists reported difficulty working with the sex offender population because colleagues and the public either had misunderstood or had taken a negative view of the reasons for doing this work (Aubrey and Dougher 1990; Jackson *et al.* 1997; Lane 1986; Lee 1993; Leicht *et al.* in preparation). Lea, Auburn, and Kibblewhite (1999, p. 114) reported that those who worked with sex offenders were vulnerable to 'attracting a courtesy stigma' because they were perceived by others 'to have sympathy for sex offenders' while Lane (1986) and Leicht (2003) reported a perception that such therapists were protective advocates of sex offenders (Lane 1986; Leicht 2003).

Therapists have reported a perception that people adopted a 'kill the messenger' mentality (Scheela 2001, p. 757) so that the therapists were also seen as 'the enemy' if they spoke in opposition to societal attitudes and/or advocated for offender treatment and the capacity to change (Leicht 2003; Scheela 2001). A survey of clinicians by Ellerby *et al.* (1993, cited in Ellerby, 1997) revealed that 68 per cent reported discomfort with telling people that they worked with sex offenders, 71 per cent considered they needed to justify their work and 90 per cent reported incidences of negative responses from other people about their specialisation. Freeman-Longo (1997, p. 7) reported that, from time to time, negative reactions were even received from staff at the same mental health centre who did not work with sex offenders.

He described being 'shunned by other mental health professionals' for working with sexual abusers and being labelled a sex offender because he treated this client group. In the study by Leicht *et al.* (in preparation) the therapists reported a sense of 'aloneness' and 'alienation' owing to their work being devalued, condemned and/or criticised by colleagues, family, friends and society.

Lea *et al.* (1999) also discussed the professional–personal dilemma experienced by therapists who work with sex offenders. These authors proposed that the dilemma arose because personal attitudes were formed within the broader social context and the public domain (where attitudes of intolerance and prejudice about sex offenders were implicitly set up as the norm) while professional attitudes were formed in an academic environment (where attitudes are assumed to be objectively based). Consequently, for therapists working with sex offenders, there was a fundamental tension between engagement with the public norm, stigmatising sex offenders and engagement with sex offenders in a professional manner.

COPING STRATEGIES

Therapists across a number of studies have identified various coping strategies that have been used to deal with the impact of their work with sex offenders. When they were not in direct contact with the sex offender client, these therapists tended to use a problem-solving approach to coping (Lazarus and Folkman 1984). These approaches included training (Farrenkopf 1992), diversification of work (Farrenkopf 1992; Scheela 2001), separation of work from personal life (Jackson *et al.* 1997; Leicht 2003; Rich 1997; Scheela 2001), hobbies (Jackson *et al.* 1997; Rich 1997; Scheela 2001), use of humour (Rich 1997; Scheela 2001) and self-care (Freeman-Longo 1997; Rich 1997; Scheela 2001). Scheela's (2001) study also reported that many therapists discussed deliberately avoiding movies, books, magazines or television programmes that portrayed sexual abuse.

When in direct contact with the sex offender client, therapists employed an emotion-focused approach to coping (Lazarus and Folkman 1984). This approach involved the use of strategies whereby therapists reframed their attitude both about the nature of the work and about the offenders. These strategies included perceiving the offender as separate from the offending behaviour (Giovannoni 1997; Leicht *et al.* in preparation), perceiving the offender primarily as the victim of abuse (Mitchell and Melikian 1995;

Leicht *et al.* in preparation; Scheela 2001), and attempting to understand the motivation to sexually offend (Lea *et al.* 1999).

Perceiving the sex offender as separate from the sex-offending behaviour has been identified as an effective coping strategy because it allowed a more caring, non-judgemental relationship with the offender and lowered therapist stress levels (Giovannoni 1997; Leicht 2003). Hearing about sex offenders' own victimisation as a child has also been reported as helping therapists to see the sexual abuse as an act separate from the person (Scheela 2001; Leicht 2003). Mitchell and Melikian (1995) suggested that when a therapist perceived a client primarily as a victim, it helped the therapist maintain empathy through minimisation of the offence and therapists have acknowledged that seeing the offender as a victim had allowed them to develop a more positive relationship with that client (Leicht 2003). Furthermore, Mitchell and Melikian (1995) suggest that, as the therapeutic relationship developed, clinicians would experience increasing difficulty in resisting the rationalisations presented by offenders to explain their sexually abusive behaviour. It was suggested that these responses reflected a defensive reaction which enabled the therapists to manage any aggressive, rageful or hateful reactions developing towards the offender. The therapists were seen to effect this management either by treating the client with great gentleness or by avoiding questions or confrontation about the offender's life where such questioning or confrontation might result in the therapist becoming angry with the client.

Winer (2001, p. 615) places a different interpretation on this particular coping strategy by linking it to therapists refusing to conceptualise the offender as evil. By separating the person from the crime and imagining that the offender's motives may be explained, or made meaningful, through an understanding of past experiences, the therapists 'hear no evil'. This avoidance is not just attributed to the therapist's need to find 'meaning' but is also linked to the therapist's need for attachment or connection with the client. This need for attachment or connection is postulated to make it harder for the therapist to be horrified by particular acts committed by clients. A further basis for avoidance of a conceptualisation of clients as evil, is argued to be that evil implies untreatability. Acceptance of such a conclusion would leave a therapist helpless, so coping strategies have to be adopted to resolve an otherwise intolerable situation.

The specific issue of the effective treatment of sex offenders is beyond the scope of this chapter, and has been addressed in Chapter 8. However, it is important to note that a link has been found between effective treatment and the dilemmas for therapists, which has been outlined above. In both Mitchell and Melikian (1995) and Peaslee (1995), effective treatment is considered unlikely unless the therapist has been able to see the client as both an offender and a victim. A simultaneous promotion of acceptance of responsibility for the perpetration of abuse and empathetic explanation of the dynamic issues of abuse is perceived as a necessary condition for effective treatment.

Appraisal of the threat of any stressor can be buffered by the availability and extent of a social support system, the individual's perceived degree of control over the situation, and the coping style employed (Hedge 2002). Some styles of coping have already been discussed. In terms of the impact of the individual's perceived control over the situation Scheela (2001) found that making decisions as a team was seen by therapists as a positive coping strategy. The positive outcome was seen to derive from a sharing of responsibility for management of the sex offender, no single person shouldering blame when problems arose, and therapists learning not to take personally any behaviour of an offender, in particular failure to complete treatment.

Although therapists have identified support from family, friends or representatives from the criminal justice system as helpful (Jackson et al. 1997), the most prevalent coping strategy identified has been to receive adequate supervision and support (Farrenkopf 1992; Jackson et al. 1997; Rich 1997). From their survey of 272 therapists working with sex offenders, Van Deusen and Way (2006) recommended that support from co-workers and supervisors may be important in reducing vicarious trauma, particularly in new clinicians.

A study of 683 therapists providing treatment for sex offenders found that those who reported having limited opportunity to participate in clinical supervision and consultation were more likely to report higher levels of distress and burn-out, whereas those who reported greater opportunity to consult tended to report a greater sense of personal accomplishment in their work (Ellerby 1998, cited by Ennis and Horne 2003). Furthermore, feedback from focus groups in that study indicated that these supports were viewed as beneficial because they offered the opportunity to ventilate emotions, provided an arena in which to receive clinical guidance and direction, and provided a means of confirmation and validation of work undertaken. General support for these results was found by Ennis and Horne (2003, p. 154) in a survey of 59 mental health professionals who worked with sex offenders, although less time spent in supervision was not found to be predictive of increased psychological distress and the majority were described as 'coping quite well with the negative aspects of their work'. Ennis and Horne (2003) suggested that the presence of supportive peers, with whom therapists could process their work-related stressors, appeared to be a valuable alternative to formal supervision. Where a therapist was isolated from both supervisory and peer support, it was suggested that active membership in local or national organisations for those providing treatment to sex offenders might provide an important alternative source of support.

When discussing clinical supervision and forensic work, Mothersole (2000) emphasised the need for clinical supervision for therapists who work with sex offenders so that issues of countertransference and other professional boundary concerns were properly addressed. However, while acknowledging that some personal work-related issues could be dealt with through clinical supervision, he also argued that it was important to avoid turning supervision into a form of personal therapy. He suggested that problematic personal reactions were better addressed by counselling and/or psychotherapeutic work, even if they had been activated by the work environment.

POSITIVE ASPECTS OF THE WORK

The emphasis within many studies has been on the negative aspects of work with sex offenders. However, positive aspects about such work have also been reported (Bird-Edmunds 1997; Farrenkopf 1992; Freeman-Longo 1997; Jackson et al. 1997; Leicht et al. in preparation; Rich 1997; Scheela 2001). Those positive aspects contributing to job and professional satisfaction have included a sense of mission through reducing the risk of future victims (Jackson et al. 1997; Leicht 2003), making a difference in people's lives (Freeman-Longo 1997; Jackson et al. 1997; Rich 1997), witnessing positive changes and psychological growth in sex offenders (Freeman-Longo 1997; Jackson et al. 1997; Leicht et al. in preparation; Scheela 2001) and in their families (Freeman-Longo 1997; Jackson et al. 1997), being party to the sex offender's increased development of empathy and compassion (Farrenkopf 1992) and contributing to the safety of the community (Scheela 2001). Two studies (Leicht et al. in preparation; Scheela 2001) reported that being able to work competently with such complex clients had increased therapists' sense of confidence and positive self-regard. In the study by Leicht (2003) the psychologists identified an added attractiveness in their work with sex offenders through the development of a specialisation and an associated improvement in career prospects.

Some of the psychologists in the study by Leicht *et al.* (in preparation) also acknowledged the experience of pleasure, fascination and voyeurism as part of that 'interest' and 'challenge', usually with a caveat of being mindful of the possible implications of those particular responses. The experience of fascination, attraction, titillation and voyeurism were also reported by therapists in the research of Ellerby (1997), Erooga (1994) and Weiss (1998). However, the descriptors 'challenging', 'absorbing' and 'interesting' were used by half the psychologists in the study by Leicht *et al.* (in preparation). Finally, the therapists surveyed by Scheela (2001) wanted to continue in that work because they viewed the work as providing an opportunity and challenge that stretched their knowledge and skills.

SUMMARY AND CONCLUSIONS

The provision of treatment to sex offenders is intensely demanding work for therapists but it can also be intensely rewarding. Studies have identified a number of elements within the provision of such treatment that are inherently stressful. These include the information and the people encountered in the process, issues of countertransference, vicarious traumatisation, burn-out, stigmatisation and the resolution of role-conflict. Studies suggest that a full range of coping strategies should be employed to increase therapists' resilience to the risk of psychological distress associated with the work. The support of both supervisory staff and professional peers has been identified as an extremely important factor in reducing such risks and contributing to effective self-care and the client–therapeutic interactions. Although beyond the scope of this chapter, issues related to effective therapist characteristics and issues of specialist training in preparation for working with sex offenders cannot be overlooked when considering the effect of working with this client group.

REFERENCES

Abel, G. (1983) 'Preventing Men from Becoming Rapists.' In G. S. Albee and H. Leitenberg (eds) *Promoting Sexual Responsibility and Preventing Sexual Problems.* Hanover, NH: University Press of New England.

Aubrey, M. and Dougher, M. J. (1990) 'Ethical issues in outpatient group therapy with sex offenders.' *Journal for Specialists in Group Work 15*, 2, 75–82.

Bengis, S. M. (1997) 'Personal and Interpersonal Issues for Staff Working with Sexually Abusive Youth.' In S. Bird-Edmunds (ed) *Impact: Working with Sexual Abusers*. Brandon, VT: Safer Society Press.

Bird-Edmunds, S. (1997) *Impact: Working with Sex Offenders*. Brandon, VT: Safer Society Press.

Crothers, D. (1995) 'Vicarious traumatization in the work with survivors of childhood trauma.' *Journal of Psychosocial Nursing 33*, 4, 9–13.

DeCarvalho Petry, S. S. (2005) 'The Impact on Male Therapists Treating Sex Offenders: A Phenomenological Study with a Focus on Gender, Race, and Ethnicity.' Doctorate dissertation submitted to Seton Hall University, New York.

Ellerby, L. (1997) 'Impact on Clinicians: Stressors and Providers of Sex-offender Treatment.' In S. Bird-Edmunds (ed) *Impact: Working with Sexual Abusers*. Brandon, VT: Safer Society Press.

Ennis, L. and Horne, S. (2003) 'Predicting psychological distress in sex offender therapists.' *Sexual Abuse: A Journal of Research and Treatment 15*, 2, 149–157.

Erooga, M. (1994) 'Where the Professional Meets the Personal.' In T. Morrison, M. Erooga and R. C. Beckett (eds) *Sexual Offending Against Children: Assessment and Treatment of Male Abusers*. London: Routledge.

Farrenkopf, T. (1992) 'What happens to therapists who work with sex offenders?' *Journal of Offender Rehabilitation 18*, 3–4, 217–223.

Freeman-Longo, R. E. (1997) 'A Personal and Professional Perspective on Burnout.' In S. Bird-Edmunds (ed) *Impact: Working with Sexual Abusers*. Brandon, VT: Safer Society Press.

Garrison, K. (1992) *Working with Sex Offenders: A Practice Guide*. Norwich: Social Work Monographs, University of East Anglia.

Gerber, P. N. (1995) 'Commentary on counter-transference in working with sex offenders: the issue of sexual attraction.' *Journal of Child Sexual Abuse 4*, 1, 117–120.

Giovannoni, J. (1997) 'Increasing Efficacy and Eliminating Burnout in Sex-offender Treatment.' In S. Bird-Edmunds (ed) *Impact: Working with Sexual Abusers*. Brandon, VT: Safer Society Press.

Glaser, B. (2003) 'Therapeutic jurisprudence: an ethical paradigm for therapists in sex offender treatment programs.' *Western Criminology Review 4*, 2, 143–154.

Hedge, B. (2002) 'The Impact of Sexual Assault on Health-care Workers.' In J. Petrak and B. Hedge (eds) *The Trauma of Sexual Assault: Treatment, Prevention, and Practice*. Chichester: John Wiley & Sons.

Jackson, K. E., Holzman, C. and Barnard, T. (1997) 'Working with Sex Offenders: The Impact on Practitioners.' In S. Bird-Edmunds (ed) *Impact: Working with Sexual Abusers*. Brandon, VT: Safer Society Press.

Kearns, B. (1995) 'Self-reflection in work with sex offenders: a process not just for therapists.' *Journal of Child Sexual Abuse 4*, 1, 107–110.

Lane, S. (1986) *Potential Emotional Hazards of Working with Sex Offenders*. Denver, CO: Interchange, Cooperative Newsletter to the Adolescent Perpetrator Network, Henry Kempe National Center for the Prevention and Treatment of Child Abuse and Neglect.

Lazarus, R. S. and Folkman, S. (1984) *Stress, Appraisal, and Coping*. New York, NY: Springer Publishing Company.

Lea, S., Auburn, T. and Kibblewhite, K. (1999) 'Working with sex offenders: the perceptions and experiences of professionals and paraprofessionals.' *International Journal of Offender Therapy and Comparative Criminology 43*, 1, 103–119.

Lee, R. M. (1993) *Doing Research on Sensitive Topics.* London: Sage.

Leicht, S. K. C. (2003) 'Working with Sex Offenders: A Qualitative Study of Clinical Psychologists' Perspectives and Experiences.' Doctorate dissertation submitted to Canterbury Christ Church University College, Kent.

Leicht, S. K. C., Holttum, S. and Sperlinger, D. (in preparation) 'Working with Sex Offenders: A Qualitative Study of Clinical Psychologists' Perspectives and Experiences.'

Lion, J. R. (1999) 'Countertransference in the Treatment of the Antisocial Patient.' In G. O. Gabbard (ed) *Countertransference Issues in Psychiatric Treatment.* Washington, DC: American Psychiatric Press Inc.

Maslach, C. and Jackson, S. E. (1982) 'Burnout in Health Professions: A Social Psychological Analysis.' In G. S. Sanders and J. Suls (eds) *Social Psychology of Health and Illness.* Hillsdale, NJ: Lawrence Erlbaum.

McCann, L. and Pearlman, L. A. (1990) 'Vicarious traumatization: a framework for understanding the psychological effects of working with victims.' *Journal of Traumatic Stress 3*, 1, 131–149.

Mitchell, C. and Melikian, K. (1995) 'The treatment of male sexual offenders: countertransference reactions.' *Journal of Child Sexual Abuse 4*, 1, 87–93.

Mothersole, G. (2000) 'Clinical supervision and forensic work.' *Journal of Sexual Aggression 5*, 1, 45–58.

Peaslee, D. M. (1995) 'Countertransference with specific client populations? A comment on the treatment of male sexual offenders.' *Journal of Child Sexual Abuse 4*, 1, 111–115.

Rich, K. D. (1997) 'Vicarious Traumatization: A Preliminary Study.' In S. Bird-Edmunds (ed) *Impact: Working with Sexual Abusers.* Brandon, VT: Safer Society Press.

Ryan, G. and Lane, S. (1997) 'The Impact of Sexual Abuse on the Interventionist.' In G. Ryan and S. Lane (eds) *Juvenile Sexual Offending: Causes, Consequences, and Correction.* San Francisco, CA: Jossey-Bass Publishers.

Scheela, R. A. (2001) 'Sex offender treatment: therapists' experiences and perceptions.' *Issues in Mental Health Nursing 22*, 749–767.

Steed, L. and Bicknell, J. (2001) 'Trauma and the therapist: the experience of therapists working with the perpetrators of sexual abuse.' *Australasian Journal of Disaster and Trauma Studies 5*, 1, Available at www.massey.ac.nz/~trauma/issues/2001-1/steed.htm, accessed on 19 March 2008.

Strasburger, L. H. (2001) 'The Treatment of Antisocial Syndromes: The Therapist's Feelings.' In M. J. Reid (ed) *The Mark of Cain: Psychoanalytic Insight and the Psychopath.* Hillsdale, NJ: Analytic Press, Inc.

Temple, N. (1996) 'Transference and Countertransference: General and Forensic Aspects.' In C. Cordess and M. Cox (eds) *Forensic Psychotherapy: Crime, Psychodynamics and the Offender Patient. Volume 1, Mainly Theory.* London: Jessica Kingsley Publishers.

Van Deusen, K. M. and Way, I. (2006) 'Vicarious trauma: an exploratory study of the impact of providing sexual abuse treatment on clinicians' trust and intimacy.' *Journal of Child Sexual Abuse 15*, 1, 69–85.

Weiss, J. M. (1998) 'Some reflections on countertransference in the treatment of criminals.' *Psychiatry 61*, 2, 172–177.

Weiss, D. S. and Marmar, C. R. (1995) 'The Impact of Events Scale – Revised.' In J. P. Wilson and T. M. Keane (eds) *Assessing Psychological Trauma and PTSD: A Practitioner's Handbook.* New York, NY: Guilford Press.

Winer, R. (2001) 'Evil in the mind of the therapist.' *Contemporary Psychoanalysis 37*, 4, 613–622.

List of Contributors

Andrew Aboud is a consultant forensic psychiatrist with Queensland's Forensic Mental Health Services. Previously at Broadmoor Hospital, he trained at St George's and then the Maudsley Hospital. Obtained a masters degree in Clinical Forensic Psychiatry and Psychology at the Institute of Psychiatry. Has worked as psychiatrist and group therapist with specialist sex offender services in south London.

Alison Beck is a consultant clinical and forensic psychologist close to the completion of training as a family therapist. She is Associate Director of Psychology and Psychological Therapies for the borough of Merton within South West London and St Georges Mental Health Trust. She is keen to develop systemic practice with people who have committed serious offences and their families in a range of settings.

Jackie Craissati is a consultant clinical and forensic psychologist, and Head of Forensic Psychology in south-east London. She has a special interest in the community assessment and treatment of high-risk sexual, violent and personality-disordered offenders, and has published widely in this area.

Sarah Galloway is a forensic community psychiatric nurse and lead nurse with the Sex Offender and Forensic Mental Health Services, Shaftesbury Clinic, London. She led the development and implementation of a psycho-educative group for partners of sex offenders. She is also attached to Kingston University as an honorary lecturer.

Tim Green is a chartered clinical psychologist with extensive experience of assessing and treating sex offenders with a wide range of offending behaviour and clinical presenting problems. He has presented at the National Organisation for the Treatment of Abusers conference and other forums on mental illness and sex offending.

Natalie Hogg is a chartered clinical psychologist working with the Sex Offender Service, Shaftesbury Clinic, where she is involved in assessing and treating sex offenders and their partners. She qualified from the University of Bristol and has completed further training in neuropsychology at the Institute of Psychiatry, King's College London.

Julia Houston is a consultant clinical and forensic psychologist at the Forensic Mental Health Services, Shaftesbury Clinic in London, where she is lead for psychology and psychological therapies and team leader of the Sex Offender Service. She has published previously in this area and is the author of *Making Sense with Offenders: Personal Constructs, Therapy and Change* (Wiley 1998).

Sharon Leicht is a consultant clinical and forensic psychologist at West London Mental Health NHS Trust Forensic Services. She has over 20 years' experience working in community, general and psychiatric hospitals, and in prison settings. She has developed and implemented sex offender treatment programmes in both Australia and England. She has extensive experience in the assessment and treatment of sex offenders, with and without mental health problems, and in working with other agencies to manage risk.

Sandra MacPhail is an independent approved forensic social worker. Previously she was the team manager of the Social Work Department, Shaftesbury Clinic, London. She was lead social worker with the Sex Offender Service and is a lecturer and tutor on the Diploma in Forensic Mental Health, St George's Hospital, University of London, UK.

Olumuyiwa Olumoroti worked with the Sex Offender Service at the Shaftesbury Clinic, London while training as a general psychiatrist. He completed additional forensic training at the Maudsley and now works as a consultant forensic psychiatrist in Croydon. His other interests include teaching, assessment and management of sex offenders, prison mental health and ethnic minority groups. He is married with three children.

Sharon Prince is a consultant clinical psychologist working as clinical lead within the Leeds Personality Disorder Clinical Network. The service was originally funded as one of Department of Health pilot sites in community specific personality-disordered services. Previously she worked for 10 years in a medium-secure service in south London, and her specialist interests include working with sex offenders on an individual and group basis, and developing a ward regime-based upon therapeutic community principles for individuals who had a diagnosis of personality disorder and/or mental illness.

Malcolm Scoales is a research assistant in the Division of Mental Health at St George's, University of London, as well as Honorary Assistant Psychologist in the Forensic Service at Springfield University Hospital. His research interests include motivation and personality disorder in sexual offenders, substance misuse, and risk assessment.

Adina Seupersad is a nursing team leader at the Shaftesbury Clinic, south-west London and St George's Mental Health Trust and Honorary Lecturer at Kingston University; also Module Leader for Pre-registration, Nursing in Forensic Settings. Special interest in Risk Assessment and Management and Practice Development.

Subject Index

'abstinence violation effect' 40, 181
access to services 103
actuarial models
  cross-cultural factors 103–4
  mental disorder and sexual offending
    75–6
'Acute 2000' 57–8
acute dynamic variables 76
addictions model, mental disorder and sexual
  offending 73
affect regulation 201
Africa 95–8
age 51
anti-libidinal hormonal medications 84–5
'apparently irrelevant decisions' 39
approach goals 35, 40
assessment
  cultural competency 103–4
  mental disorder and sexual offending
    81, 83, 85
  mentally ill offenders 17–18
  non-abusing parents 231–5, 237
  personality disorders 198–9
  Sex Offender Service (SOS) 134
assessment interview
  attitudes 164, 168–9
  barriers to treatment 164, 168–9
  confidentiality 159–60
  content 162–6
  current attitudes 168
  current functioning and trigger factors
    167–8
  denial and motivational interviewing
    166–7
  early life experience 162
  education history 163
  engagement, potential barriers 169
  forensic history 163
  head injury 163
  hobbies, interests and friends 163
  occupational history 163
  offending behaviour 164–6
  previous treatment 163
  psychiatric treatment 163
  psychological functioning 164
  psychosexual history and relationships
    163, 164
  questioning techniques 161–2
  self-harm 163
  self-image 163
  substance misuse 163
  suitability for treatment 169
  therapeutic style 160–2
attachment
  negative relationship with mother 55

problems 73
sexual abuse as a child 56–7
single status and short-term relationships
  55
attachment styles 30
'attachment-theoretical revision' of integrated
  theory 28
attachments 28, 30
Australia 111
'authentic intimacy' 249
avoidance goals 40
Axis I disorders 70, 144, 145
Axis II disorders 71, 144–5

behaviours, maladaptive 175
beliefs, underlying 30–2
Bichard Inquiry Report (2004) 115, 125
Bichard, Sir Richard 125
biological factors 28
biological theory 28
Bracton Clinic 131
Brian, case study 171–2, 190–2
British Crime Surveys 14
burn-out 271–2
buspirone 84

Canada 111
castration 84–5, 111
Challenge Project 131, 147
chemical castration 85, 111
child molesters
  empathy deficits 60
  recidivism rates 46, 51
  sexual abuse as a child 55–6
  visual imagery 54
child sexual abuse, variations in definition 94
childhood experiences 28–9
children as sexual beings (implicit theory) 31
children, commercial sexual exploitation 96
Chinese 96
civil preventative orders 114–15, 116–17
clinical approaches, risk assessment 62–3
clinical assessment
  assessment interview 159–69
  case study 171–2
  collateral information 158
  considerations for assessor 158
  context 153
  developing understanding of questions
    posed by referrer 156
  formulation of offending behaviour
    170–2
  informants 159
  process 155–9

psychometric personality assessment
  158–9
purpose 153–5
setting and context 156–7
steps 155–6
systemic issues 154–5
clinical model of legislation 111–12
coercive sex, and social norms 100
cognitive behavioural therapy (CBT) 177,
  178, 179, 180, 185–6, 187, 202–3
cognitive distortion model 180
cognitive distortions 30, 35
collaborative working 206
collective guilt 270
collectivism 93
community protection model of legislation
  110–11
comorbidity 17
compliance 62
confidentiality 122–4, 159, 186–7
confluence model (Malamuth) 38–9
conviction, stages of process 15
coping strategies 273–6
countertransference 266–8
court diversions 15–16
Crime and Disorder Act 1998 113
crime statistics 14
Criminal and Immigration Bill 2007 118
Criminal Justice Act 2003 114, 118, 155,
  159
Criminal Justice and Court Services Act 2000
  113–14, 118, 126
criminal justice service 131
Criminal Records Bureau (CRB) 125
critical risk management 121–2
cross-over 52–3
cultural competence 103–4, 106
culture 90–1
  and assessment 103–4
  definition 91
  disclosure of sexual assaults and re-
    sponses 94–5
  maternal responses to child abuse 98–9
  and rape 99–100
  and reporting of offences 102–3
  in sexual behaviour and coercion 93–4
  and treatment 104–5
cybernetic explanations 257–8
cyproterone acetate 84

'Dangerous Order' (Denmark) 111
dangerous world (implicit theory) 31, 32
Data Protection Act 1998 124
date rape, perceptions 101–2
denial 60–1, 166–7, 188–9

Department for Children, Schools and Families (DfCSF) 125
Department for Education and Skills (DfES) 125
developing countries 95–8
development, sexual 29–30
developmental experiences 28–9
developmental factors, mental disorder and sexual offending 73
deviant sexual interest 61
Diagnostic and Statistical Manual of Mental Disorders (DSM-IV) 69, 159, 196
disclosure 94–5, 123–4
disinhibition theories, mental disorder and sexual offending 74
Disqualification Order 117
dissonance 272
distal factors 76
distraction 182
Domestic Violence, Crime and Victims Act 2004 126
dopamine 75
'duty to co-operate' 114, 122–4
dynamic variables 56–62
    general self regulation 61–2
    intimacy deficits 59
    pro-offending attitudes 60–1
    sexual self-regulation 61
    social competencies 59

Education Act 2002 124
education, protection of children 124–5
emotional dysregulation 201–3
'emotional loneliness' 30
empathy deficits 60
entitlement (implicit theory) 31, 32
escalation 54
ethnicity 90–1
    and assessment 103–4
    data 92–3
    definition 91
    and treatment 104–5
European Convention on Human Rights 112
Exhibitionism *see* indecent exposure
'external control' 127

family backgrounds 28–9
family therapy *see* systemic therapy
fantasies 29–30, 35
female offenders 236
Foreign Travel Order 117
forensic mental health 131
forensic mental health service 131–2
formulation, of offending behaviour 170–2
four preconditions model (Finkelhor) 32–5, 180, 239
    blockage 33
    emotional congruence 33
    limitations 32, 34–5
    motivation 33
    overcoming external inhibitions 34
    overcoming inhibitions 33
    overcoming internal inhibitions 33–4
    overcoming resistance of the child 34–5
    sexual arousal 33

gender shame 270
general self regulation 61–2
Germany 111
goals, approach and avoidance 40, 182–3
gonadotrophin-releasing hormone (GnRH) agonists 84
'good lives' model 152, 174, 180, 182–3

grooming 34, 118
group treatment 178, 183–90

Hadood Ordinance 99
high risk situations 39–40
HIV 96
Home Office, Mental Health Unit 126
hospital detention 111
hospital orders 111–12
Hudson, B. 214
'human goods' 183

Impact of Events Scale – Revised 270–1
implicit theories 31, 199
incest, recidivism rates 51
indecent exposure 53–4
Independent Barring Board (IBB) 125
indeterminate sentencing 110–11, 112
Indians 96
individualism 93
information-sharing 122–4, 159
insight, offenders' 153
integrated theory 28, 30
    hypothetical cases 78–80
    mental disorder and sexual offending 76–8
    weather analogy 80–1, 83
'internal control' 127
International Statistical Classification of Diseases and Related Health Problems 69
internet, legislation against abuse 118
internet pornography 54–5
    legislation 118
    recidivism rates 46
interpersonal functioning 30
Interpersonal Reactivity Index 60
interpersonal skills 207–8
interprofessional working 213
intimacy deficits 59
intraprofessional working 213

Kansas v Hendricks (1997) 112
Kenya 96
key vulnerabilities 38
knowledge, theoretical 16

'lapse' stage 40
lapses 181
Latin America 100
learning, sexual 29–30
legislation
    England and Wales 112–16
    models 110–12
levels of risk management 120–2
List 99 124–5
lithium 84
Locus of Control Scale 59
luteinising hormone-releasing hormone (LHRH) agonists 84

maladaptive behaviours 175
Malays 96
male sex drive is uncontrollable (implicit theory) 31
Managing Sex Offenders in the Community 218
media coverage, sexual offending 109
medroxyprogesterone acetate (MPA) 84
'Megan's Law' 110–11
mental disorder 69–72
Mental Health Act 1983 112
Mental Health Act 2007 115–16
Mental Health Unit, Home Office 126

mental illness, prevalence 17, 69–71
mentally disordered offenders
    dearth of literature 175–6
    rates of report and conviction 15–16
    recidivism rates 46–7
meta-analytic reviews 177
Millon Multi-axial Clinical Inventory, 3rd edition (MCMI-III) 139, 144, 148, 159, 185
minimisation 159, 188, 274
misogyny 93, 94
models of legislation 110–12
mothers
    negative relationship with 55
    responses to child abuse 98–9
    vulnerability 127
motivation 206
motivational interviewing 167, 206
multi-agency public protection 113, 114, 118–20
multi-agency public protection panel 118–20, 122, 159, 212–13, 218
multi-agency risk management 120, 127
multi-agency working 189
    case study, Mr A 222–4, 226–7
    case study, Mr C. 219–22
    challenges 215–16
    communication 217
    definition 212–14
    definitions 213–14
    good practice 216–18
    individual qualities 218
    organisational culture 217
    power differentials 217
    rationale 214–15
    role ambiguity 224
    with sex offenders 218–19
    skill mix 218
    team task behaviours 216–17
multi-factor model (Wolf) 35–6
multidisciplinary working *see* multi-agency working

National Institute for Clinical Excellence (NICE) 192
National Offender Management Service 131
nature of harm (implicit theory) 31
Netherlands 111
neurobiological models 74–5
New Zealand 111
Nigeria 96
non-abusing parents
    assessment 231–5, 237
    case study, Mrs E. 242–4
    case study, Ms P. 244–5
    complexity of position 245
    in context of Sex Offender Service (SOS) 235–45
    engagement 241–2
    feelings and perceptions 236
    group evaluation 240–1
    lack of research 230
    as part of risk assessment 230
    plans for protecting children 234–5
    prognostic indicators 232–3
    psycho-educative group 238–40
    referrals to Sex Offender Service (SOS) 235–6
    risk management 240
    role in child protection 229–30
    sexual boundaries 240
    stereotyping of abusers 238–9
    support 245

non-abusing parent *cont.*
  stalking with children 239–40
  understanding abusive behaviour
      233–4, 239
non re-offenders 174
Notification Order 117

Obscene Publications Act 1964 118
offence analysis 165–6
offence patterns 14
offence process, theories of 39–42
offences within families, rates of report and
    conviction 15
offenders
  heterogeneity 27
  insight 153
  knowledge of victim 16
  sexual victimisation 29
offending against adults, theories of 38–9
offending against children, theories of 32–7
offending behaviour
  formulation 170–2
  functional analysis 164–6
Office for Standards in Education (OFSTED)
    125
ordinary risk management 120

Pakistan 99
paraphilias, mental illness 70
Parole Board 126
partnership working 133
pathways model (Ward and Siegert) 36–7,
    75, 148, 180
  antisocial cognitions 37
  deviant sexual scripts 37
  emotional dysregulation 37
  intimacy deficits 37
  multiple dysfunctional mechanisms
      36–7
patriarchy 93
peer group influences 106
penile plethysmograph (PPG) 81, 83
penile plethysmograph (PPG) studies 29
personality disorders
  adaptive functioning 198
  assessment 198–9
  challenges to therapists 205–8
  definitions 196–7
  developing working relationships
      205–8
  emotional dysregulation 201–3
  interpersonal dysfunction 197
  prevalence 17, 71–2, 195
  psychopathy 203–5
  representations of self 197
  and risk 56
  schemas 199–201
  and sexual offending 198–205
  treatment and public protection 208
'Phases of Impact' model 264
pornography 54–5
post traumatic stress disorder 268
PPG *see* penile plethysmograph (PPG)
practitioners
  burn-out 271–2
  coping strategies 273–6
  countertransference 266–8
  effects of work 263
  emotional responses 207, 212
  interpersonal skills 207–8
  'Phases of Impact' model 264
  positive aspects of work 276–7
  range of emotions 265
  'remodelling process' 264–5

safety precautions 269
stigmatisation 272–3
subjective experiences 263–5
supervision 275–6
support 275
vicarious traumatisation 268–71
predispositions 28
preventative detention 111
previous charges or convictions, sexual 51
previous convictions 51
prior non-contact offences
  indecent exposure 53–4
  pornography 54–5
  voyeurism 54
pro-offending attitudes 60–1
probation boards, victim consultation 126
probation officers, working with forensic
    mental health services 132, 133
'problem of immediate gratification' (PIG)
    40, 181
Protection of Children Act 1999 113, 125
psychometric personality assessment 158–9,
    185
psychopaths 56
psychopathy 203–5
Psychopathy Checklist – Revised (PCL-R)
    56, 104, 204
psychosexual profiles 72
psychotropic medications 83–4
public concern 14, 45
Public Safety and Emergency Preparedness
    Canada 50
publication, delays 175

Quadripartite model (Hall and Hirschmann)
    38

race, definition 91
randomised controlled trials (RCT) 176,
    177–8
rape
  cultural influences on reporting 102–3
  and culture 99–100
  Latin America 100
  Pakistan 99
  partners and ex-partners 16
  race, gender and class 101
  rates of report and conviction 14–15
  recidivism rates 46, 51
rape myths 100–1
Rape Myths Scale 60
'rape proclivity' 38–9
Rapid Risk Assessment of Sexual Offense
    Recidivism 104
rapists
  mental illness 70
  personality disorders 71
  visual imagery 54
recidivism 176–7
recidivism rates 46–7
reconviction 176–7
relapse prevention model 39–40, 179–83
relapses 181
religion 98–9, 105
'remodelling process' 264–5
reoffending 45
reporting of offences 14–15, 102–3
reports, critical 214
retrospective studies 14
risk
  known and unknown 14
  managing 120–2
  systemic issues 154–5
  types of 45

risk assessment
  actuarial approaches 47–9
  clinical approaches 62–3
  dynamic variables 56–62
  key steps 63–4
  levels of 120–2
  mental disorder and sexual offending 85
  professional judgement 47–8
  Sex Offender Service (SOS) 134
  static measures 49–50
  static variables 50–6
Risk for Sexual Violence Protocol (RSVP)
    58–9
risk management
  multi-agency 127
  non-abusing parents 240
  see also multi-agency public protection
Risk Management Authority (Scotland) 49
Risk Matrix 2000 49, 50
Risk Matrix 2000/S 50, 75
Risk Matrix 2000/V 50
Risk of Sexual Harm Order 116–17

*Safeguarding Children: An Evaluation of the
    Procedures for Checking Staff Appointed by
    Schools* 125
Safeguarding Vulnerable Groups Act 2006
    115, 125
safety precautions 269
'Sarah's Law' campaign 126–7
schemas 30–1, 199–201
schizophrenia 17, 69, 70
'seemingly irrelevant decisions' 39, 181
selective serotonin reuptake inhibitors (SSRIs)
    83–4
self-esteem 35
self-regulation model of offending 40–2
  Approach-automatic pathway 41
  Approach-explicit pathway 41
  Avoidant-active pathway 41
  Avoidant-passive pathway 41
serotonin 75, 83
Sex Offender Act 1997 112–13
Sex Offender Needs Assessment Rating
    (SONAR) 56–7, 76
Sex Offender Registration Act (USA) 110–11
Sex Offender Service (SOS) 13, 153, 175
  advice, consultation and liaison 135–6
  assessment 134
  case study 190–2
  composition of treatment groups 185–6
  considerations prior to treatment 184–5
  current provision 134–6
  demographic data 137–8
  formulation-based approach 189–90
  group rules 186–7
  history and development 132–4
  managing denial 188–9
  multi-agency working 189, 212
  multidisciplinary team 212
  offence data 138
  psychometric personality assessment
      185
  referrals 136–8
  research, teaching and continued profes-
      sional development 136
  Shaftesbury Clinic 183
  suitability for treatment 185
  therapeutic team 184, 185
  treatment 135
  treatment content 186–8
  working with non-abusing parents
      235–45

Sex Offender Service (SOS) research study
        139–49
    childhood experiences 141, 142
    comparison with other samples 147–9
    descriptive data 139
    mental health problems 143–4
    offence-related information 140–1
    personality functioning 144–6
    referrals 139
    research sample 139
    sexual development 141–3
Sex Offenders Register 120, 122
sexual abuse as a child 56–7
sexual assaults, influences on reporting
        102–3
Sexual Behaviour Unit, Newcastle 131
sexual development 29–30
sexual exploitation, of children 96
sexual learning 29–30
Sexual Offences Act 2003 114–15, 118,
        125–6, 127
Sexual Offences Prevention Order 116
Sexual Offences Review 109
sexual offences, statistics 122
sexual offending
    extent 14–16
    media coverage 109
    political agenda 109
sexual self-regulation 61
sexual victimisation, of offenders 29
Sexual Violence Risk – 20 (SVR-20) 58
single mothers, vulnerability 127
single status and short-term relationships 55
social competencies 59
social norms 100
societal reaction 272–3
societies, varying attitudes to sexual behaviour
        91–2
'Stable 2000' 57
stable dynamic variables 75–6
state factors 77
Static 99 49–50, 53, 75, 104
static variables
    age 51
    attachment 55–6
    clinical relevance 50–6
    personality disorder: psychopathy 56
    previous charges or convictions, sexual
        51
    previous convictions 51
    prior non-contact offences 53–6
    victim variables 52–3
    violence 51–2
statistics 122
STEP battery 185
stereotyping 103
stigmatisation, of practitioners 272–3
street children 97
structural family therapy 249
supervision, for practitioners 275–6
support, for practitioners 275
surgical castration 84–5, 111
Switzerland 111
systemic therapy
    aim of therapy 250–1
    case study, Julian 254–5
    case study, Yolande 259
    change, potential for 258
    changing patterns of relating 251–2
    circularity 257–8
    client-led therapy 254
    difference 260–1
    evidence base 248–9
    experimental treatments 250–4

feedback loop 253, 257–8
    listening 256
    literature 249
    making meaning 255–6
    outcome predictors 253–4
    relationships as key 250
    responsibility for the crime 250–1
    responsibility of therapist 258–9
    self-reflexivity 256–7
    therapist's experience and skills 255
    transgenerational patterns 259

Tanzania 97
'TBS Order' (Netherlands) 111
team working
    approaches 215–16
    specific task behaviours 216–17
teams, definitions 213
testosterone 75
theoretical knowledge 16
theories
    biological 28
    disinhibition 74
    implicit 31
    integrated 28, 30
    offence process 39–42
    offending against adults 38–9
    offending against children 32–7
therapeutic model of legislation 111–12
therapists see practitioners
trans-theoretical model of motivation 167
treatment
    collaborative working 206
    content 186–8
    as dynamic 178–9
    effectiveness of models 177–80
    ethnicity and culture 104–5
    evaluation 175
    evidence base 248–9
    formulation-based approach 189–90
    group 178
    medical 177
    mental disorder and sexual offending
        83–5, 86
    multi-agency working 189
    preparatory programmes 188–9
    prior considerations 184–5
    psychopathy 204–5
    and public protection 208
    relapse prevention model 179–83
    Sex Offender Service (SOS) 135
    studies of effectiveness 176–7
    suitability for 185
    theoretical models 180–3
tricyclic anti-depressants 84
triggering events 77

uncontrollable world (implicit theory) 31
underlying beliefs 30–2
USA
    human rights 112
    Sex Offender Registration Act 110–11

vicarious traumatisation 268–71
victim
    culture, and perception of abuse 92
    gender 52
    knowledge of offender 16
    relationship to offender 52
victim impact 45
victim liaison officers 126
victim variables 52–3
victimisation, perceptions of 102–3
victims, legislation 125–6

violence 51–2, 72
Violent and Sex Offenders Register 120
voyeurism 54, 277
vulnerability factors 77

weather analogy, for integrated theory 80–1,
        83
West Africa 96
women are sex objects (implicit theory) 31
women are unknowable (implicit theory) 31
women, rates of offending 16

Young Schema Questionnaire 201

Zimbabwe 96–7

Author Index

Abel, G. 30, 53–4, 147, 148, 268, 271
Adshead, G. 207
Ahlmeyer, S. 17, 148
Alaggia, R. 90, 98–9
Alda, A. 256
Alexander, M. 46, 180
Allen, J. 14
Allnutt, S. 17, 69
American Psychiatric Association 69, 85, 159, 196
Anderson, D. 160, 161
Araji, S. 74
Armstrong, A. 96
Asdigian, N. 258
Ashworth, C.D. 101, 102, 103
Aubrey, M. 272
Auburn, T. 264, 272

Bachman, R. 102
Baines, C. 15
Baker, A. 14
Baker, M. 147
Barbaree, H.E. 28, 29, 30, 36, 204
Bard, L.A. 54, 55
Barnard, T. 264
Bateman, A.W. 207
Bates, A. 176
Bateson, G. 260, 261
Baum, F. 214
Beck, A.T. 199
Beck, S. 59
Becker, J.V. 177
Beckett, R. 60, 154, 161, 166, 178, 184
Beech, A.R. 28, 30, 32, 41, 50, 56, 59, 60, 76–8, 80–1, 148, 176, 198, 206
Bellack, J.P. 216
Bengis, S.M. 263, 266, 268, 270
Bennice, J.A. 92
Bentovim, A. 233, 238, 241
Berner, W. 71, 84
Bichard Inquiry Report (2004) 115, 125
Bickley, J. 41
Bicknell, J. 270–1
Bilby, C. 177
Binder, R.L. 103
Bird-Edmunds, S. 269, 270, 271–2, 276
Black, D.W. 147
Blackburn, R. 203
Blackshaw, L. 46
Boer, D. 58
Bolen, R.M. 234
Boulet, J. 148
Bradford, J.M. 83, 148
Briggs, D. 47
Briken, P. 84

Bristol Royal Informary Inquiry 214
Brooker, C. 215
Brooks-Gordon, B. 177
Brown, G. 201
Brown, L.M. 199
Brown, S. 16, 112
Browne, K. 28, 30, 50, 54, 55, 59, 73, 148
Burgess, P. 69
Burt, M. 60
Burton, S. 137, 236
Bussiere, M. 46, 47–8, 60, 61, 73, 76, 202
Butler-Sloss, E. 14
Butler, T. 17, 69

Calder, M. 19, 238
Calkins, S.D. 201
Cann, J. 53, 148
Cantor, N. 198
Carnes, P. 73
Carr, A. 157, 160, 170
Carter, D.L. 29
Cellini, H.R. 74
Chan, C.A. 218
Chayet, E.F. 102
Chesterman, P. 17, 18, 47, 70, 72, 81, 147
Christopher, D. 29
Clarke, C. 214
Cochrane, R.E. 148
Cohen, M.L. 74
Coid, J. 203
Connelly, C. 110, 111, 112
Cook, G. 214
Cooke, D.J. 104
Coon, H.M. 93
Cormier, C. 204
Cowburn, M. 103
Craig, L.A. 50
Craissati, J. 15, 17–18, 28, 29, 53, 54, 55, 56, 60, 70, 73, 131, 147, 148, 166, 185, 189, 230, 232–3, 243
Crighton, D. 248
Crothers, D. 268
Curtin, F. 69, 71

Data Protection Act 1998 124
Davies, C. 47
Dawson, C.R. 217
DeCarvelho Petry, S.S. 264, 265
Denov, M.S. 19, 236
Department for Education and Skills (DfES) 113, 124, 125
Department of Health 115–16, 214
DiClemente, R.J. 95, 167
Dillon, D. 249
Dougher, M.J. 272

D'Silva, K. 204
Duggan, C. 204
Duncan, B.L. 253
Duncan, S. 14
Dunsieth, N. 149

Earle, R.H. 249
Eaton, L. 216
Eke, A. 19, 46
Ellerby, L. 266, 268, 269, 270, 271, 272, 275, 277
Elliott, M. 54, 148
Emmons, R.A. 40
Ennis, L. 275–6
Epstein, J. 101
Erooga, M. 178, 266, 269, 270, 271, 277
Estrich, S. 100

Falshaw, L. 15, 176
Farmer, E. 234
Farrell, M. 213
Farrenkopf, T. 264, 265, 266, 268, 269, 270, 272, 273, 275, 276
Fazel, S. 147
Feist, A. 15
Feldman-Summers, S. 101, 102, 103
Fernandez, Y. 160, 161, 188
Field, G. 85
Finkelhor, D. 16, 32–5, 36, 74, 180, 239, 258
Firestone, P. 53, 69, 72
Fisher, D. 30, 34, 53, 59, 60, 131, 148, 174
Fitzgerald, L.F. 100
Foley, L. 101
Folkman, S. 273
Forth, A. 56
Foster, H. 70
Frederick, R.I. 148
Freeman, A. 199
Freeman-Longo, R.E. 263, 268, 269, 270, 271, 272, 273, 276
Freeman, M. 213, 215
Fretz, A. 90
Freund, K. 84
Friendship, C. 53, 148, 176
Furby, L. 46

Gacono, C. 204
Garrison, A. 270
Gerber, P.N. 266
Gerrish, K. 214
Getman, K. 101
Gibbons, K. 214, 218
Giovannoni, J. 263, 273, 274
Gizzarelli, R. 199

Glaser, B. 271
Glasser, M. 53
Goodman, R.E. 28
Gordon, H. 83
Gorzalka, B.B. 95
Government of Pakistan 99
Gozna, L. 53, 148
Gradante, J. 234
Grisso, T. 148
Grubin, D. 17, 50, 53, 55, 74–5, 83, 84, 85, 131, 148, 176

Hadi, S. 99
Haffejee, I.E. 96
Hall, G.C.N. 36, 38, 74, 94, 95
Hall, K. 41
Hamilton-Giachritsis, C. 206
Hanks, H. 16, 19, 137, 236
Hanson, K. 46, 47–8, 49–50, 51, 52, 53, 56, 58, 60, 61, 73, 75, 76, 104, 177, 198, 199, 202
Hardy, B. 216
Hare, R.D. 56, 203
Harris, A. 52, 56, 60, 61, 75, 198, 202
Harris, G.T. 47, 56, 178, 204
Hart, S. 49, 58–9
Heavey, C.L. 38–9, 199
Hedge, B. 268, 275
Heinemann, G. 213
Heise, L. 100
Hemming, M. 218
Heras, P. 105
Higginbotham, E.B. 101
Hill, A. 84
Hillbrand, M. 70
Hinshelwood, R.D. 205
Hirschmann, R. 36, 38, 74
Hirt, M. 70
HM Inspectorate of Constabularies 127, 218
HM Inspectorate of Probation 127, 218
Hodes, P. 18, 70
Holland, K. 218
Holttum, S. 264
Holzman, C. 264
Home Office 16, 109, 112, 113, 114, 115, 118, 122, 123, 125, 126, 127, 155, 159
Hood, R. 176
Hooper, C.A. 234
Horne, S. 275–6
Houston, J. 29, 92, 131, 139, 147, 148
Howard, D. 47
Howitt, D. 54
Hubble, M.A. 253
Hudson, B. 217
Hudson, S. 35, 73, 202
Huq, Z. 217

Irvine, R. 214

Jackson, K.E. 264, 266, 268, 269, 270, 272, 273, 275, 276
Jackson, S.E. 271
Jahangir, A. 99
Jecmen, D. 249
Jilani, I. 99
Jones, B.R. 217
Jones, M. 217

Kafka, M.P. 70, 83
Kallerberg, A. 214
Kaplan, M.S. 85
Kearns, B. 266, 268, 271
Keen, S. 55

Keenan, T. 31, 168, 199
Keene, J. 215
Kelly, L. 137, 236
Kemmelmeier, M. 93
Kemshall, H. 109, 121–2
Kennington, R. 131
Kenworthy, T. 248
Kershaw, C. 14
Kibblewhite, K. 264, 272
Kidd, R.F. 102
Kilcoyne, J. 54, 148
Kingston, D. 41
Kirsch, L.G. 177
Klosko, J.S. 199
Kosson, D.S. 104
Kroner, D. 56
Krueger, R.B. 85
Kudrati, M. 97–8

Lalor, K. 96
Lalumiere, M.L. 29
Lamb, L.J. 234
Lambert, M.J. 253
Lane, S. 266, 267, 268, 269, 272
Langenbaum, S. 101
Långström, N. 104
Langton, C. 204
Laws, D.R. 179, 189
Lazarus, R.S. 273
Le Gris, J. 217
Le Vine, R. 96
Le Vine, S. 96
Lea, S. 264, 272, 273, 274
Leathard, A. 213
Lee, R.M. 272
Lehne, G. 149
Leicht, S.K.C. 264, 265, 268, 269, 270, 271, 272, 273, 274, 276, 277
Leonard, R.A. 29
Lewis, P. 19, 47
Lindsay, W.R. 19
Linehan, M.M. 201
Linz, D. 38–9, 199
Lion, J.R. 266
Livesley, W.J. 197, 198, 201, 206
Long, C.A. 42, 174
Lonsway, K.A. 100
Lösel, F. 177, 178, 248
Lusignan, R. 202
Ly, L. 47

MacCullough, M.J. 52
Mackay, L. 217
Madsen, L. 17, 148
Malamuth, N.M. 38–9, 72, 94, 199
Maletzy, B.M. 85
Mann, R. 167, 176, 180, 199, 200, 201, 206
Marlatt, G.A. 39–40, 73, 180–2
Marmar, C.R. 270–1
Marques, J.K. 180
Marshall, M 213
Marshall, W.L. 16, 28, 29, 30, 36, 59, 73, 160, 161, 178, 180, 188, 195, 201, 202, 204–5, 206
Martin, T.N. 217
Martinson, R. 175
Maslach, C. 271
Matlin, M. 100
Matravers, A. 212
Maturana, H. 251, 258
Maynard, C. 90
McCallin, A. 213
McCann, L. 268

McCarthy, L. 204
McClurg, G. 15, 28, 29, 54, 55, 73, 131, 147
McElroy, S.L. 68, 69, 70, 71
McKibben, A. 202
Melikian, K. 266, 267, 273, 274, 275
Meloy, R. 204
Menzies-Lyth, I. 207
Meston, C.M. 95
Meursing, K. 96, 97
Michie, C. 104
Miller, C. 213, 215
Miller, S.D. 253
Miller, W.R. 167, 206
Millon, T. 139, 144, 159, 185
Ministry of Justice 118
Mitchell, C. 266, 267, 273, 274, 275
Moody, J. 214
Moore, K. 100
Morgan, S. 218
Morrison, T. 178
Morton-Bourgon, K. 46, 48, 49, 58
Mothersole, G. 266, 267, 276
Motiuk, L. 195
Moulden, H.M. 188
Mullen, P. 69
Murray, G. 47
Myhill, A. 14

Nakhle Tamraz, D. 230, 234
Nathan, P. 19
NHS London 214
Nicholas, S. 14
Niveau, G. 69, 71
Norris, J. 103
North East Thames and South East Thames Regional Health Authority 214
Norton, K. 205
Nowicki, S. 59

Office for Standards in Education (OFSTED) 125
Ogles, B.M. 253
Oliver, C.J. 147
Olver, M.E. 147
O'Neil, E.H. 216
O'Reilly, G. 19, 157, 160
Overholser, C. 59
Owen, M. 234
Owens, D. 216
Oyserman, D. 93

Parsons, S. 17, 148
Pawlak, A. 148
Payne, M. 215, 216, 217, 218
Peacock, E. 204
Pearlman, L.A. 268
Peaslee, D.M. 275
Pellegrin, A. 231
Perkins, D. 131
Pethybridge, J. 216
Phillips, S.L. 70
Pietroni, P. 213
Pithers, W.D. 39, 73
Polaschek, D.L.L. 28, 31, 168
Polkinthorne, J. 218
Ponton, L.E. 95
Porporino, F. 195
Prendergast, W.E. 204
Prentky, R.A. 28, 70, 74, 175, 177
Prochaska, D.L.L. 167
Proulx, J. 72, 202
Putz, B.E. 217

Quinsey, V.L. 29, 47, 53

Rajani, R. 97–8
Rao, K. 95
Raymond, N.C. 68, 70, 71
Regan, L. 137, 236
Reid, W.D. 204
Resick, P.A. 92
Rice, M.E. 47, 56, 178, 204
Rich, K.D. 264, 268, 269, 270, 272, 273,
    275, 276
Roberge, L. 94
Rollnick, S. 167, 206
Rosen, I. 61
Rosenberg, R. 71
Rosler, A. 85
Ross, N. 213, 215
Rouleau, J.L. 147, 148
Royal College of Psychiatrists 123
Russell, D. 95
Ryan, G. 267

Sahota, K. 17, 18, 46–7, 70, 72, 81, 147
Salekin, R.T. 204
Sanday, P.R. 93
Saradjian, J. 16, 19, 137, 236
Schechter, M.D. 94
Scheela, R.A. 264–5, 266, 268, 269, 270,
    271, 272, 273, 274, 275, 276, 277
Schmucker, M. 177, 178, 248
Schneider, B. 71
Schwartz, B.K. 74
Scmitt, M. 213
Scoales, M.W. 29, 92, 139, 147, 148
Seghorn, T.K. 74
Seidman, B. 30
Selvini, M.P. 260
Seto, M. 19, 46, 178–9
Shingler, J. 180, 199, 200, 201, 206
Shinn, L.J. 217
Siegert, R.J. 36–7, 75, 148, 180, 198
Simon, L.M.J. 177
Smallbone, S.W. 28
Smith, A.D. 70
Smith, G. 231, 232, 235, 236, 243, 249
Soothill, K. 14
Southill, K. 217
Sperlinger, D. 264
Stanley, C.R. 19
Steed, L. 270–1
Stewart, C.A. 152, 174, 182–3
Stinnett, R.D. 70
Strasburger, L.H. 207, 266
Stuart, M. 15
Sturup, G.K. 85
Sue, S. 94

Taylor, P.J. 70
Templar, D.I. 92
Temple, N. 267
Templeman, T.L. 70
Teten, A.L. 94
Tewksbury, R. 110
Thompson, D. 217
Thomson, P. 131
Thornton, D. 36, 38, 46, 49–50, 53, 56, 59,
    60, 75, 104
Thylefors, B. 217
Toubia, N. 100
Towl, G. 248
Trapnell, P.D. 95
Turrell, A. 216
Tyrer, P. 207

Van Deusen, K.M. 275
Van Eyk, H. 214
Varela, F. 251, 258
Varelas, N. 101
Vivian-Byrne, S.E. 249

Wagner, W.G. 231
Walker, A. 14
Wallace, C. 69
Ward, T. 19, 28, 31, 32, 34, 35, 36–7, 38,
    39, 40–2, 59, 73, 75, 76–8, 80–1,
    148, 152, 165, 168, 174, 179, 180,
    182–3, 189, 198, 199, 202
Way, I. 275
Webb, C. 217
Webb, L. 55
Weeks, R. 55
Wegner, D.M. 40
Weinrott, M. 46
Weishaar, M.E. 199
Weiss, J.M. 263, 266, 267, 277
Weiss, D.S. 270–1
Wells, H. 177
West, J. 92
White, P. 85, 248
White, T. 147
Whyte, L. 215
Widom, C. 55
Wiederman, M.W. 90
Williamson, S. 110, 111, 112
Winer, R. 267, 274
Wingate, S. 50, 55
Wistow, G. 216
Witztum, E. 85
Wolf, S.C. 16, 35–6, 180
Wong, D. 95
Wong, S.C.P. 147
World Health Organisation (WHO) 69
Wragg, J. 131
Wriggens, J. 101
Wyatt, G.E. 101, 102

Xuefang, L. 215

Yates, P.M. 41, 42, 174, 179
Young, J.E. 30, 199, 200, 201

Zgoba, K.M. 177